Paranapanema
Londrina
Tibagi
SÃO PAULO
SÃO PAULO
BR 153
BR 376
PARQUE ESTADUAL DE GUARTELÁ
Tibagi
Castro
NÁ
BR 116
Ponta Grossa
PARQUE ESTADUAL CAMPINHOS
Tunas do Paraná
ntópolis
BR 153
PARQUE ESTADUAL VILA VELHA
Guaraqueçaba
PARQUE NACIONAL DE SUPERAGÜI
BR 277
CURITIBA
Antonina
Superagüi
São José dos Pinhais
Paranaguá
Ilha do Mel
Pontal do Sul
Lapa
Matinhos
BR 476
Guaratuba
itória
Joinville
São Francisco do Sul
Porto União
BR 101
Jaraguá do Sul
BR 116
Blumenau
Itajaí
Treze Tílias
SC 453
Balneário Camboriú
Brusque
BR 470
Bombinhas
Porto Belo
A CATARINA
PARQUE ESTADUAL DA SERRA DO TABULEIRO
Gov. Celso Ramos
Lages
Canoas
FLORIANÓPOLIS
BR 116
PARQUE NACIONAL DE SÃO JOAQUIM
Garopaba
São Joaquim
BR 101
Vacaria
PARQUE NACIONAL DA SERRA GERAL
Urussanga
Laguna
Criciúma
Cambará do Sul
Araranguá
Oceano Atlântico
N
O
L
S
s do Sul
PARQUE NACIONAL DE APARADOS DA SERRA
Canela
ramado
Torres
ãos
Três Coroas
Sapiranga
PORTO ALEGRE
HORIZONTE
GEOGRÁFICO
Guaíba
BR 101
dos Patos
0
66
122 km
Mostardas
River
State Capital
City
State Boundary
Park
Paved Road
Dirty Track
Airport
PARQUE NACIONAL DA LAGOA DOS PATOS

Philips Guides

THE SOUTH BRAZIL

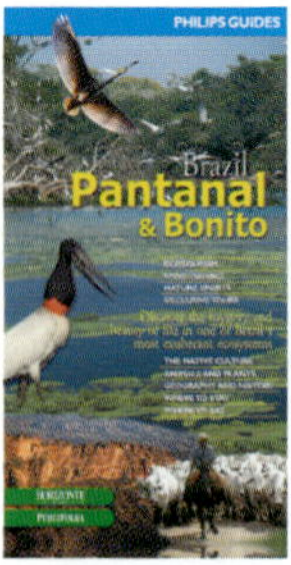

Philips Guides
PANTANAL
& BONITO

Philips Guides
NATIONAL
PARKS

Philips Guides
THE AMAZON

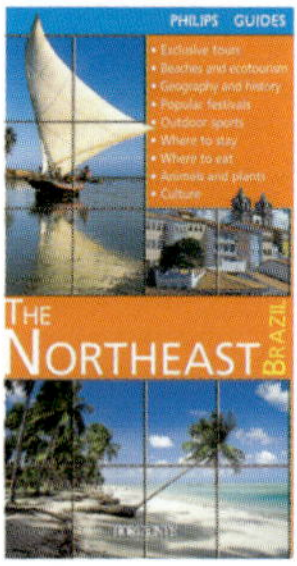

Philips Guides
THE NORTHEAST

Philips Guides of
Brazilian Ecological Tourism Series

These guides are part of the Philips Brasilis Project whose aim is to promote Brazilian culture and art, as well as its historical and natural heritage

www.philips.com.br

THE SOUTH BRAZIL

HORIZONTE
GEOGRÁFICO

HORIZONTE
GEOGRÁFICO

General Director: Peter Milko

Philips Guides

THE SOUTH BRAZIL

Editor-in-chief: Peter Milko
Managing editor: Martha San Juan França
Art Director: Marco Cançado

Editors: Fabrício Brasiliense e Marilena Rocha
Senior Writers: Flávia Pegorin, Maria Celeste Corrêa, Rosângela Rezende, Verônica Dantas
Copy editor: Kátia P. Pereira
Translation into English: Kátia P. Pereira and Alison Kau Entrkin de Souza
Page Layout: Ana Cristina Silveira, Evandro Moura, Gilda Lima
Photography Editor: Elisa Rojas
Associate Contributors: Cacá Riva, Christian Knepper, Christiane Ceneviva, Davi Santos Jr, Eduardo Tavares, Egberto Nogueira, Heitor Reali, Iolita Cunha, João Correia Filho, José Roberto Ciolini, Leonardo Papini, Marcos Amend, Mauro Goulart, Monica Canejo, Nani Gois, Nelson Kon, Paulo Flores, Renato Grimm, Rogério Monteiro, Victor Andrade, Zig Koch (photography);
Hiroe Sasaki (illustrations); Vera Grandisky Lerner (maps), Leonardo Bussadori (cover design); Regina Rossi Alvarez (Image Bank)
Administrative Manager: Mauro de Melo Jucá
Distribution: José Augusto Pires de Abreu
Customer Service: Marcos Fernandes
Graphic Production: Mauro de Melo Jucá

Horizonte Geográfico
Av. Arruda Botelho, 684 – 5º. andar
CEP 05466-000, São Paulo – SP – Brasil
Tel: (11) 3022-5599 Fax: (11) 3022-3751
E-mail: horizonte@horizontegeografico.com.br
Site: www.horizontegeografico.com.br

All information in this guide was obtained by April 2003. We recommend users to always check schedules, prices and other useful data. The Publisher cannot be held responsible for possible losses due to changes in information.

Horizonte Geográfico would like to thank you for sending data to help us update the information and services included in this publication.
Please send us information by mail, fax or e-mail: horizonte@horizontegeografico.com.br.
To keep updated and get further information, visit our site
www.horizontegeografico.com.br

Philips Guides Series of Brazilian Ecological Tourism
Published in June 2003 by Horizonte Geográfico

Summary

DEAR READER,

Exploring the southern region with its bucolic scenery made up of hills, waterfalls, beaches and tropical forests is a real pleasure. Hills are countless from Paraná to Rio Grande do Sul, their names changing several times, but always showing the beauty of the jagged landscape, still covered in many places with the verdant Atlantic Forest. In Serra da Graciosa and Marumbi, the spectacular mountains extend to very near the coastline, where Paranaguá bay is the great holder of the beautiful landscapes of the coastal region of Paraná State. In Rio Grande do Sul, the Serra Geral hills present an irregular relief with gorges and canyons impressing all those who visit them. In Santa Catarina, the island and capital of Florianópolis is an attraction both for its beaches as well as for its historical heritage: fortresses and cave paintings remind us of the many generations that have already existed in this region.

The people formed since colonial times, mixing Portuguese and Spanish people, confronted in the conquest of the New World, was highly influenced by the territories of the River Plate basin. Many past confrontations such as the Paraguayan war, the Farroupilha Revolution and other skirmishes created the borders as we know them today, conveying especially to the *Gaúchos* with their traditions of the pampas.

The European immigrant groups arriving in the South over the last 200 years provided their own characteristics to many cities they have founded. Regarding either the German colony of Blumenau, the Austrian colony of Treze Tílias, the Italian colony of Serra Gaúcha or the Azoreans of Santa Catarina, southern Brazil acquired its own features and the eminently Old World flavor with festivities and traditions that take us back in time and space.

The adequate transport network and the relatively close attractions make of this region an excellent choice for road trips. In spite of the winter (April to September) being considered high season, with possible frosts and even the greatly welcomed snow on the hills of Rio Grande do Sul and Santa Catarina, summer is really wonderful to explore the coastline and go trekking in the backlands, with nice temperatures.

From penguins to whales, caves and islands, folkloric festivities and centenary traditions, your stay in the southern region will be full of attractions, which our team has thoroughly researched in each place and now introduces for you to choose from this Guide. Enjoy!

Peter Milko
Chief Editor

How to use this guide

To help you plan the trip, this guide offers useful information about how to reach each place, its festivities, main highlights, and an identification of the Southern animals and plants at the end. The contents are divided in four parts: the first offers general aspects of the region, the second includes the main cities in the States of Paraná, Santa Catarina e Rio Grande do Sul, the third shows the services (hotels, restaurants, etc) and the forth the characteristic flora and fauna.

Discovering the South, Ecological Scenery and The man in the South

In these chapters, there is a lot of information referring to the region, tips on how to prepare your trip, the best time of the year to know each place, the festivities, along with cultural, historical and geographical aspects of the South

Tours

Here you will find information on the varying human and geographical aspects of each State.

The main highlights with their full addresses and descriptions of how to enjoy them

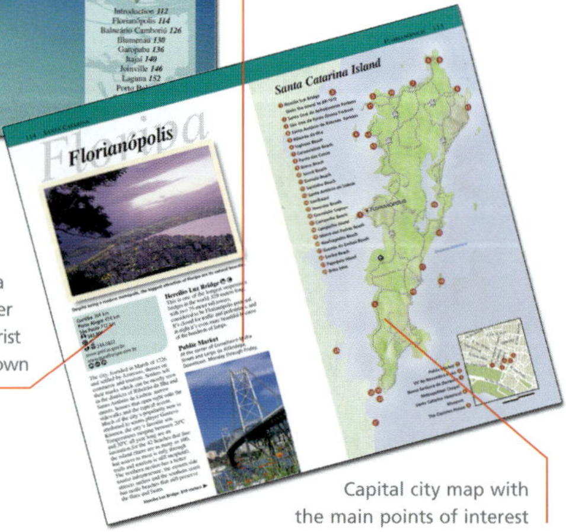

The colored table shows distances (in kilometers) to the main cities; number of inhabitants; area code and phone number of the main tourist information bureau in town

Capital city map with the main points of interest

Each chapter has its own color, identified by the superior edge

We have also included the item 'Surroundings', where we list nearby places of interest worth visiting and specific boxes with historical and cultural information

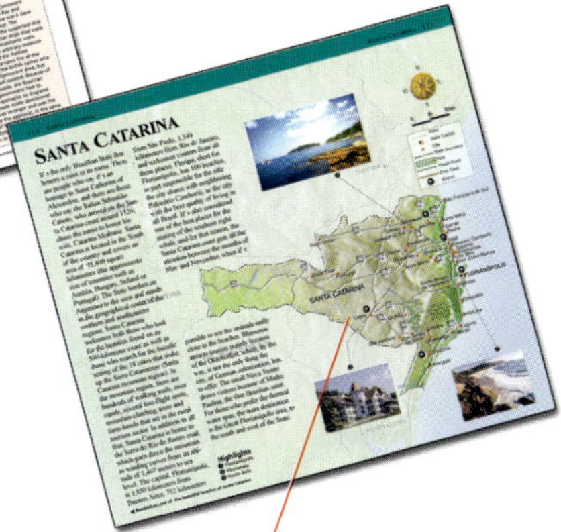

The 'star' indicates the best places in each city. Other symbols, explained at the end, show some important aspects of each attractions

Services

Here there is a list of the main support services for tourists. It begins with the capital of the state and follows the alphabetical order of the cities, including the sorroundings. Options on lodging, dining and useful phone numbers; airports, bus stations, travel agencies, banks, hospitals, and places to shop. We also give suggestions of books.

The illustrated maps show the State's main attractions; the most important rivers, parks and preservation areas; the most relevant paved roads and dirt roads and the towns included in the corresponding chapter

Fauna and Flora

In this chapter there are illustrations of some animals and plants of the South Region, with descriptions, habits and curiosities

Index:

- The guide has a table of contents including page numbers on the first page of each chapter. At the end there is an index of all the cities.

DISCOVERING THE SOUTH

WHAT TO SEE IN THE SOUTH

The southern region, once known as "a cowboy´s paradise," still favors rural life

The South thrives on a territory of contrasts, molded by geography and enriched by the strong presence of immigrants, mainly Europeans. This guide helps you discover the best there is in the area. The South encompasses the States of Paraná, Santa Catarina and Rio Grande do Sul and it´s the smallest region in Brazil, covering an area of 577,214 square kilometers, corresponding to 6.75% of the territory. There are a little over 25 million inhabitants, which represents 15% of the Brazilian population. Demographic density is 43.49 inhabitants per square meter and around 81% of the inhabitants live in urban areas. The fertile soil produces expressive crops, mainly wheat, soy, rice, corn, beans, onions, tobacco and apples, among others. Livestock, poultry raising and pig raising are also important sectors of the economy, besides an expanding industrial production, lower only than in the Southeast. The South has the second highest Internal Net Revenue in the country, answering for 17% of the total.

In winter, snow isn´t so rare

◀ The Paranaguá-Curitiba railroad, in Paraná

COLD AND SNOW

In one of the extremes are the prairies and the mountainous regions that give the South its characteristics, among them the cold weather. It´s also where pine trees reign supreme, with around 1,500 botanical species. It´s a land where the taste of *pinhão*, the edible pine seed, predominates, and it´s used to feed both the forest animals and men. In harsh winter mornings, frost covers the vegetation, and sometimes it even snows. Then, not only the landscape is different. For many people, snow is almost

Migrants keep their European traditions

synonymous with holiday: people go out on the streets to photograph or film the scenery, families get together, children make snowmen and tourists are drawn by the spectacle. In a prairie region – 908 meters above sea level – stands Curitiba, the city known worldwide for the urban solutions that have been developed along decades. Its urban planning is, at once, a model and a design label, comprising all the districts in town, encompassing transportation, with its tube-like bus stops and bi-articulate buses to tourist spots such as Ópera de Arame, a metallic-and-glass-structure theater house, a good-humored copy of Paris Opera. Great altitudes also produced some of the most fascinating Brazilian landscapes formed by canyons, from the Guartelá, in Paraná, to the impressive walls of Itaimbezinho, Fortaleza, Malacara and Monte Negro, on the border of Santa Catarina and Rio Grande do Sul. It´s a beautiful stone world and includes the Second Plateau of Paraná, with rock formations in Vila Velha, Furnas and Buraco do Padre. The region became known, in the past, as "the cowboys´ paradise," because of the prairie region, which was the ideal setting for cowboys to rest along their journey.

ETHNIC BLEND

Cowboys laid the foundations for the historic towns of today. In the 18th century, they stopped in places that had been chosen months earlier to rest on their way from Viamão, in Rio Grande do Sul, to Sorocaba, in São Paulo, taking mules and goods, thus boosting the trading business in the region. In Paraná, the cities of Castro, Tibagi and Lapa tell of this saga, which lasted over 200 years. Lured by the cold climate and the promise of land to plant, thousands of Germans, Italians, Polish, Ucranians, Swiss, Japanese and many other foreigners came to the

TRADITIONAL FESTIVALS AND EVENTS

Event	Place	When
Pomerana Feast	Pomerode (SC)	January
The Shrimp Feast	Imbituba (SC)	January
Summer Festival	Imbituba (SC)	January
Procession of Our Lady of the Navigator	Porto Alegre (RS)	February 2nd
Feast of Our Lady of the Navigator	Gov. Celso Ramos (SC)	February
The Grape Festival	Caxias do Sul (RS)	February or March
"Mariscada"	Penha (SC)	February (until Carnival)
Curitiba's Theater Festival	Curitiba (PR)	March
Crioulo Horse Nat. Rodeo	Praia Grande (SC)	March
Italian Colonial Festival	Garibaldi (RS)	March/April
Ballooning Festival	Torres (RS)	April/May
Theater Festival	Londrina (PR)	April and June
The Holy Ghost Feast	Gov. Celso Ramos (SC)	May
The Holy Ghost Feast	Penha (SC)	May (during Pentecost)
Our Lady of Caravaggio Feast	Farroupilha (RS)	May
The Mullet Festival	Balneário de Barra do Sul (SC)	June
The Mullet Festival	Barra da Lagoa in Florianópolis (SC)	June and July
The Pine Seed Festival	Lages (SC)	June
The Farmers Feast	Itajaí, (SC)	July
Joinville Dance Festival	Joinville (SC)	July
"Carneiro no Buraco" National Feast	Campo Mourão (PR)	July
Film Festival	Gramado (RS)	August
St. Francis of the 3rd Order Feast	Curitiba (PR)	September
The Farroupilha Week	Porto Alegre and other cities (RS)	September
Music Festival	Porto Alegre (RS)	from September till November
"Marejada" (Portuguese and Fish Festival)	Itajaí (SC)	October
The Apple National Feast	São Joaquim (SC)	October
"Oktoberfest" (The Draft Beer Festival)	Blumenau (SC)	October
National and International Draft Beer Feast (Fenachopp)	Joinville (SC)	October
"Fenarreco"	Brusque (SC)	October
Christmas Lights	Gramado (RS)	from November till January
Christmas Dreams	Canela (RS)	from November till January
"Boi-de-Mamão" Festival	Sambaqui (SC)	from December till February

◀ **Curitiba: parks galore**

The rivers that criss-cross the canyons, like in Urubici, invite visitors to go rafting

South between the 18th and 20th centuries. This ethnic blending brought both development and traditions from the other side of the Atlantic, and, above all, created a culture that feeds on cultural diversity. And the *chimarrão* is as linked to the cold climate as the immigration waves that hit the South at the time. *Chimarrão* (matte tea passed from hand to hand in a gourd and drunk with a metal straw) is the favorite drink of those who live in the plateau and in the pampas region. Tourists who go to the rural area are attracted by the locals´ firm and musical accent, the traditional cuisine and the typical dances.
Another favorite for those who like to drink is the wine made by the descendants of Italian immigrants. And the chocolate, wool and leather items, colonial coffee lunches and the soothing capelletti soup all combine to draw hordes of tourists to the Serra Gaúcha cities. For adventure buffs, extreme sports can be found all over, such as rafting, mountain climbing, trekkings, hang-gliding or paragliding.

TROPICAL ECOSYSTEMS

As the altitude gets lower, the plateau and its firm vegetation give in to tropical ecosystems, adorned by lush forests. In Paraná, you can see the last Brazilian preserves of the Stationary Forest. The Iguaçu National Park is home to the largest continuous portion of this biome. And in the heart of the park are the Iguaçu Falls, one of the most fascinating natural spectacles in Brazil, placing Foz do Iguaçu as one of the most important tourist destinations in the country. In the surroundings is the Itaipu Hydroelectric Plant, the second

Italians brought the wine culture

Coastal highlights, like Ilha do Mel ►

largest in the world, a development that is at once grandiose, bold and technologically advanced.

Going down Paraná to the east, till you reach Rio Grande do Sul, the Rainforest emerges as home of one of the most impressive biodiversities on the planet, housing 15% of all known living species. One of the most well-preserved sections is in the region of Guaraqueçaba, on the northern coast of Paraná, where the beauty of its vegetation, the delicate landscapes and the impressive diversity of animal life make the place one of the best destinations for ecotourists from all over the world.

The southern coast offers the comfort of beach inns. They are beautiful places, mainly in Santa Catarina, where inlets, bays and open-sea beaches are carefully set in the landscape, forming a perfect combination with the dunes. Many of those beaches with cold and crystal-clear waters have perfect waves for surfers and body boarding aficionados. This is also where people speak in a quick and musical way, an accent inherited from the Portuguese settlers, who also brought the art of embroidery (*bilro* and *crivo*) and some typical dances (*pau-de-fita* and *boi-de-mamão*).

Missões, National Landmark for All Humanity

QUALITY OF LIVING

Due to the Portuguese need to guide boats and defend the Brazilian coast from the Spanish, several lighthouses and fortresses were built, and, up to now, chunks and bits of Brazilian history can be found at these sites. The way of living of the first settlers left its mark on the Rupestrian inscriptions, archaeological sites and primitive sculptures found on the beaches. A little of all this can be felt in Florianópolis, capital of Santa Catarina, which boasts high rates of quality of living and also very beautiful landscapes. To boot, the city is highly regarded as a gastronomic paradise, and its restaurants include a wide range of fish and shrimp dishes.

In Porto Alegre, capital of Rio Grande do Sul, however, the gastronomic feast includes a lot of barbecue and all of its accompaniments, besides a varied international cuisine. The city is proud of its traditions and culture and honors its artists and intellectuals, promoting constant discussions about its roots and tendencies, in all realms of art and knowledge. Besides all this, Porto Alegre surprises visitors who go on walking tours along the well-preserved Historic Downtown or those who go boat riding in the Guaíba River, from where you can see an unforgettable sunset. To round off the itinerary made by nature and completed by man, it´s a real must to see the vastness of the Rio Grande do Sul prairies, lined with small and continuous hills and where the Minuano wind blows hard on the skin. That´s where you can find traces that tell a little of the beginnings of the Jesuit Missions, whole communities that were abandoned by the kings of Spain and Portugal and then killed by the trailblazers who slaved the Indians and stole their cattle and crops. A bit of this history can be found in the São Miguel Ruins, declared a World Heritage Site for All Humanity by UNESCO. Welcome to the South!

Barbecue, 'Gaúcho' style

HOW TO GET READY

In Brazil, almost anywhere in the country, you do not have to worry about the weather. It usually rains a lot more during certain months than in others, but the temperature is high all year round. However, in the South region it is quite different. Here from June till September the winter is cold, windy and very rainy. Temperature rarely gets to freezing point, and when it does, it turns into quite an event on TV news. The coldest region is Rio Grande do Sul's inland, the country's southernmost region. However, it occasionally snows on the Santa Catarina's central plateau. In summer, from October till March, it´s very hot. Moreover, sometimes it is hotter than in some historically hot regions, like in the Northeast. During vacations, Santa Catarina beaches are crammed with Brazilians and people from neighboring countries, as Argentines and Uruguayans.

BEST SEASON

Because of the distinct seasons, the trip to the South region may be different depending on the time of the year. The best months to go to the Serra Gaúcha are June, July and August, when the cold weather invites you to go to parks and enjoy the landscape. Summer is perfect for waterfall showers in the Sierra. The wineries are a must in February and March, when the grapevines are bursting with fruit and you can watch the grape harvest. If you are looking forward to visiting the beautiful scenery of Aparados da Serra, you should travel from May to August, when the landscapes are clearer and the roads are not impracticable because of the rain. The best time to visit Foz do Iguaçu is in the summer, when the waterfalls have the greatest water volume and, therefore, they are more impressive. The same applies to the beaches, which are an irresistible attraction from October to March (if you want to have an unforgettable experience, remember that the best time to see the whales on the Santa Catarina shores is from March to November). However, during other seasons, the weather is very cold and coastal cities become almost empty. On the other hand, hotels and restaurants are cheaper but tourists may find many are closed at this time of year.

During summer, beaches are crowded, but during the low season, many restaurants and hotels close

Woolen clothing and thick coats are necessary to protect oneself from the cold

FACILITIES

More than any other place in Brazil, the South has the best travel facilities. Every capital has its tourist information center, complete with maps and brochures. These centers are open during business hours. The highways are better than in other regions, and airport services and bus lines are good enough. You can even travel by train or by boat in certain places. If you travel by car and want to go to neighboring countries, as Paraguay, Uruguay and Argentina, you must have the car's property certificate and your driving license, ID card or passport. In the State capital cities the constant flow of visitors makes exchange bureaus easy to find. But if you are far from a large center, plan how much you intend to spend in the period. In the chapter Services, we indicate the appropriate places to exchange money in each place. Credit cards are easily accepted in the State capitals but rarely in the smaller towns and villages. In nearly all the cities there are branches or cash machines of Banco do Brasil. In addition to the fabulous scenery, the South region is famous for its typical cuisine. Prepare yourself for a real treat. And we are not talking just about the traditional *churrasco* or German food. You can eat *barreado,* a dish cooked with different kinds of meat, in Morretes; sausages and bread from the Ukranian cuisine in Prudentópolis; teals stuffed with cabbage in Brusque, desserts in Pelotas, Italian food in Santa Felicidade (a neighborhood in Curitiba), fish and seafood in Florianópolis.

WHAT TO TAKE

A last warning: If you come to the South in the summer, do not forget to bring your bathing suits, even if you only go inland, to make the best of the waterfalls. The heat and little or no shade to hide call for sunblock.
If you plan to visit the Lagoa do Peixe Park and the Taim Ecological Station it's important to have your binoculars to observe the animals, insect repellent and comfortable shoes. You'll need woolen clothing and heavy coats to protect yourself from the cold winter anywhere in the region. Prepared for the trip, visitors are sure to find excitement for all tastes and have an unforgettable stay in the South.

ECOLOGICAL SCENERY

THE SHAPING OF THE RELIEF

Vila Velha rocks, in Paraná, extend over land which had been submerged under the sea

The Brazilian territory is known to be formed by ancient geological structures, some of which are older than the current configuration. This took place several hundred million years ago. However, the contours of the current landscape are quite more recent. They result from the transformations suffered by the original material, which were caused by the enormous spilling of lava, rocks eroded by torrential rains, strong winds and all sort of climate inclemencies that took place a few million years ago, and which are still remodeling the land.

CHANGES

Such a configuration resulted in the most varied scenery, formed by plateaus and tablelands, canyons and depressions. Sedimentary soils partially covered by volcanic lava (basalt) and abundant marine fossils show that, subsequently to the Pre-Cambrian, that is, seven hundred to six hundred and fifty million years ago, the South and Southeast were submerged under a primitive sea. The sandy and basaltic lands in Vila Velha, Paraná, for example, so interesting because of the shapes of the eroded rocks, were covered by the sea in the past. That primitive sea was gradually silted up and the water pressure consolidated the continental platform, as we know it today.

VOLCANIC ACTIVITIES

Nearly two hundred million years ago, the landscape changed again as a result of the intense volcanic activity that caused the basalt to spill over an area of 1.2 million square kilometers. It was the origin of the Guarani aquifer system, a gigantic spring of fresh water covered by a basalt layer of up to 1,700 meters in depth (read Water treasure). The sandy soils that remain from such period may be seen in locations, such as the region of Lages, in the Santa Catarina Plateau. All of the land was then transformed into a large desert, larger than the Sahara, which the geologists named Botucatu. This desert covered the whole area where the states of São Paulo and Minas Gerais extend today, in addition to certain areas of Uruguay, Argentina, and Paraguay. In a subsequent period, another alteration of gigant proportions took

◀ The shifting of the land originated canyons and mountains in the South

place. The immense continent comprising the areas which would later turn into America and Africa started to 'crack', and the sea was invaded by this crack, giving rise to the new continents. These movements resulted in the formation of new faults, which in turn originated the Aparados da Serra, in Rio Grande do Sul. Plate tectonics would still give rise, nearly twenty- three and a half million years ago, to the enormous mountain ranges that we know today as the Alps, the Andes and the Himalayas.

MOUNTAINS AND PLATEAUS

During more than two hundred thousand years, the relief in the south of the continent was gradually sculpted by Nature and by the strength of the sea advancing and retreating. During the glacial periods, the sea retreated. The shifting ice blocks resulted in erosion and sedimentary depositions. Such continental sedimentary deposits extended over the last seven million years, providing the definite shape that the southern coast presents today. Further crust shifting resulted in the formation of the southern mountains and the plateau region. Mountains, canyons, slopes, depressions, and rock fissures appeared. In a region greatly favored by the abundant rivers, brooks and lakes, water began to delineate its path, forming rapids, spilling into waterfalls, and outlining the undulating scenery.

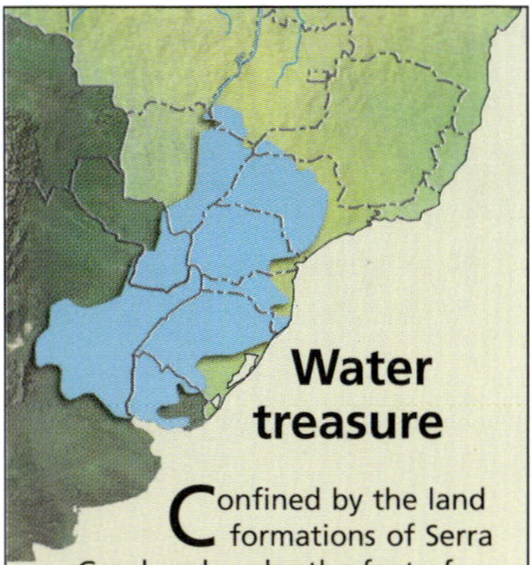

Water treasure

Confined by the land formations of Serra Geral and under the feet of Brazilians, Argentines, Uruguayans, and Paraguayans, the natural reservoir of Guarani is the largest aquifer system in the world. It is a gigantic fresh water spring extending over 1.2 million square kilometers, whose formation started nearly two hundred million years ago. Composed of small amounts of clay and mostly sand, and with 90% of the area covered by a basalt layer of up to 1,700 meters, it is of the highest quality. Research has shown that the reservoir may provide water for 150 million people yearly, but the extraction is minimal. At certain locations, the water table comes up to the surface. However, it is generally necessary for wells to be perforated to an average depth of 10 meters to reach it.

THE KINGDOM OF PARANÁ PINES

This is the symbolic tree of the State of Paraná. According to the Guarani people, Curitiba was the place of the Paraná pines (*Araucaria angustifolia*), though there are few of those trees remaining in the region at present. The forest was originally distributed over the high lands of the plateaus and the mountains of southern Brazil, the States of Rio Grande do Sul, Santa Catarina, Paraná, and São Paulo. A small portion of these forests permeated into Rio de Janeiro and Minas Gerais. It is the least tropical formation in Brazil since it may only exist on fertile soil but with moderate to low temperatures during the winter. It is believed that, during the glacial periods, the temperatures in the South were lower and favored the expansion of those forests.

"BLACK FOREST"

Until early twentieth century, the Southern landscapes were dominated by the interlaced crowns of the Paraná pines that were 50 meters tall. The dark green shade of the Paraná pine leaves provided the forest with its name, 'black forest'. However, the forest does not only have that tree species, also called *pinheiro-do-paraná* or *pinheiro-brasileiro*. It shelters nearly 1,500 types of plants, among which over 400 species are woody. We should mention the *yerba mate* (*Ilex paraguariensis*), the *imbuya* (*Ocotea porosa*), the *pinheiro-bravo* (*Podocarpus lambertii*), and the different species of cinnamon.

Pine nuts are highly appreciated by birds

ROUNDED CROWN

The Brazilian tree catches the attention due to its round and erect trunk, crowned with limbs that form a rounded crown like an umbrella. Each tree may be up to 50 meters tall, with a trunk of up to 2.5 meters in diameter and live for nearly 300 years. The leaves are hard, pointed, and perennial, directly fastened to the trunks.

Two characteristics should be highlighted in the Paraná pine forests. In the first place, the production of pine nuts, which is highly appreciated in national cuisine; and in the second place, the fact that their seeds are dispersed by a beautiful bird whose song is unmistakable due to its shrillness: the azure jay (*Cyanocorax caeruleus*). In spite of its beauty, the azure jay is predatory and eats eggs and smaller birds' nestling. It remains aloof and rarely lands on the ground. It may 'plant' the pine nuts by chance, if the seeds get lost during its flight.

Other birds are attracted to these forests. Over 250 species have already been identified, which equals to nearly 15% of all the autochthonous birds of Brazil. Among them, the striolated tit-spinetail (*Leptasthenura striolata*) draws attention, an autochthonous bird that feeds on the larvae of a butterfly that harms the Paraná pine reproduction organs. The nests are built among the branches of the tree and are mistaken by

◀ In Aparados, in Rio Grande do Sul, phenomenal changes

◄ **Azure Jay: song related to the forest**

pinecones. For being very small and remaining near the treetop, it is very difficult to come in sight of it.

THE AGOUTI

Besides the birds, the vegetal diversity attracts a great variety of animals, such as the eastern cougar or puma (*Felis concolor*) and jaguar (*Panthera Onca*), the Brazilian tapir (*Tapirus terrestris*), the brown howler monkey (*Alouatta fusca*), small rodents, bats, reptiles and numerous invertebrates. The agouti (*Dasyprocta agouti*), a medium-sized rodent, appreciates pine nuts so much that it follows groups of brown howler monkeys and birds that travel among the treetops, opening pinecones to take out the seeds. Within this process, many seeds fall to the ground. Its highly developed hearing helps the animal to identify when mature pinecones fall from the trees. When it eats his fill, the agouti buries the rest of the seeds and demarcates the location. As a result, part of those seeds germinates.

DESTRUCTION

Different factors contributed to tumble the autochthonous forests of Southern Brazil: the gradual occupation of the territory with the construction of new cities, the expansion of agricultural borders and the activities related to cattle breeding. However, the revenue obtained with the exploitation of wood bears an enormous responsibility in their destruction. From 1915 to 1960, Brazil exported 11 million tons of wood, equal to 18.5 million cubic meters of forest. Most of it came from the Paraná pine forest. In addition to the pine, other magnificent trees were chopped down such as the *imbuya*, the cedar, the *ipê-amarelo* (*Tabebuia alba*), the *canjerana* (*Cabralea canjerana*) and diverse cinnamon species. The soft light wood, taken from compact areas, was used even as firewood and coal for domestic and industrial uses. However, it was also used to build houses, for carpentry, finishes, planks, furniture, ceilings and floors, matches, toys, toothpicks, vessels and domestic utensils, in addiction to the

The agouti eats the pine seeds

manufacture of paper and cardboard. Its resin was employed in the chemical industry.

THE END OF WOOD

The price of such copiousness and easiness to extract was paid not long afterwards. From the original forest area, equal to 457 times the size of Curitiba town, barely fragments remain today that, as a whole, add up to seven times the size of Curitiba. The destruction of the forest also resulted in soil depletion, erosion, climatic changes, and the dramatic alteration of the hydric system in the Southern Region. Even the industry suffered because of this destruction. During the 70's, the companies were still extracting wood from this area. Afterwards, they had to begin importing it from other states.

The pine tree is up to 40 meters tall ►

ATLANTIC FOREST

The variety of species on the Superagüi Island, one of the refuges within the Atlantic Forest

During the sixteenth century, when European colonizers arrived in the American Continent, the coastal forests named "Atlantic Rainforest" by the Portuguese, extended along the entire Brazilian seashore, side by side with the mountain ranges of the Northeast to Rio Grande do Sul. This is not so any more. Throughout history, the forest was devastated by agricultural progress, city growth, and industrialization. A significant portion of such total area may be found in the South of Brazil, mainly between the Serra do Mar mountains and Ilha do Mel (see section on Paraná). However, it is in the north coast of the region, where the Paraná territory meets with the Lagamar refuge of São Paulo, that the forest manifests itself with grandeur. There, a place composed of hills and flatlands covered with thick vegetation, sandbanks, mangle and fine-grain sandy beaches, a wide range of birds live, such as the red-throated piping guan (*Pipile nattereri*), the Brazilian tanager (*Ramphocelus bresilius*), parrots, in addition to mammals, reptiles, fish and shellfish. It is one of the largest lake-estuary areas in the world, where the mangrove swamp acts as nurseries of several species.

The remaining thick forest in Paraná ▶

The difficult access and the geographical isolation helped in saving this intact refuge in the Atlantic Forest. It also ensured a significant portion of the area to be environmentally protected and, therefore, only open to researchers.

EXUBERANCE

The humidity distribution mechanism of the Antarctic Pole mass accounts for the exuberance and diversity of the forest. The winds that carry humidity are obstructed along the seashore, unloading a great volume of water in this region. As a result, there is a thick

forest formation, with tall trees and covered trunks, where a wide range of plant species prevail such as *ipês*, purple glory (*Tibouchina granulosa*), cedars, palm trees, cinnamon, and trumpet trees. The Atlantic Forest is famous because it has the greatest diversity per hectare among tropical forests in the world.

COPIOUS FAUNA

Like the exuberant vegetation, fauna is most impressive in this region. Most of the endangered Brazilian animal species come from the Atlantic Forest, such as the black-faced lion tamarin (*Leontopithecus caissara*), the Neotropical otter (*Lontra longicaudis*), the jaguar, the giant armadillo, and the small blue macaw. Visitors of certain sections in the Salto Morato reserve and the Superagüi National Park, in Paraná, come upon the great egret (*Casmerodius albus*) with other animals which are hard to come into sight with, such as the tropical pewee, the Geoffroy's cat (*Oncifelis geoffroyi*), and the agouti (*Agouti paca*). This region is also inhabited by the jaguars, the ocelots (*Leopardus pardalis*) and the collared anteater (*Tamandua tetradactyla*). Among the local endangered species, the black-faced lion tamarin (*Leontopithecus caissara*), and the red-browed, red-topped or red-crowned Amazon parrot (*Amazona rhodocorytha*) call the attention. Discovered in 1990 in the island of Superagüi, the black-faced lion tamarin only inhabits the North coast of Paraná. A little smaller than a squirrel, it feeds

on insects, flower nectar and small fruits. It finds its shelter on the treetops, lives in small groups, and emits squeaks to communicate with the other members of the group. The deforestation and the

A typical bird threatened with extinction

illegal hunting are the two largest threats for the survival of this species.

THE THREATENED PARROT

The red-crowned Amazon parrot inhabits the coasts of the States of São Paulo, Paraná, and Santa Catarina. This bird faces the same enemies as the monkey, that is to say, deforestation and smugglers who steal their newly born nestling from the nests, including the eggs. A proof of the destruction that the Atlantic Forest endures is recorded in the names of two cities of Paraná coast. Guaratuba means 'many *guarás*' in Tupi-Guarani. And Guaraqueçaba means 'place where the *guarás* live.' These town names belong to locations which, centuries ago, were full of birds with lively red feathers, twisted beaks and up to 58 cm tall. These birds lived in flocks and fed on crabs, insects, and snails. However, their feathers attracted first the attention of the native people, who used them to embellish their clothing. Later, the *guarás* were hunted down by colonizers until they became extinct in the South.

THE INTERIOR FOREST

Within the waterfall park there remains a sample of the forest

Almost on the border with Argentina lies the Iguaçu National Park, an 1,8 km^2 reserve of autochthonous forest that comprises the transition between the mixed Atlantic Forest and the so-called seasonal forest, or as the specialists call it, the tropical and subtropical rainforest of hinterland plateaus. Such forest originally covered the entire Paraná plateau, spreading over the fertile red lands and the sandy soils. Precisely because it covers the most developed and densely populated regions, and is associated with soils that are fertile and desirable to expand the agricultural frontiers, it became one of the most devastated biomes in the Southern Region.

THE WEATHER ISSUE

This type of biome is subject to the influence of cold and hot weather, dry winters and rainy summers. The cold and a decrease in the water available in the ground, coupled with other environmental features, result in most of the tree species in this forest to lose their leaves during winter, thereby decreasing water consumption and reducing the growth cycle of plants. The forest area of Iguaçu National Park, has been preserved only because this region comprises one of the most spectacular natural landscapes in the world: the Iguaçu Falls. The Park has three main vegetation formations: the Paraná pine forest, at altitudes of over 600 meters, where the weather is colder; the seasonal forest, at a height of 400 to 500 meters, and the gallery forest, located on the margins of the rivers and subject to periodical floods. Imposing because of its biodiversity, the forest has magnificent tree species such as the rosewood, the fig (*Ficus enormis*), *pau-marfim* (*Balfourodendron riedelianum*), the *palmito-doce* (*Euterpe edulis*), the *cabreúva* (*Leguminosae-Papilionoideae*) and several cinnamon species. Orchids and bromeliads are quite abundant in all of the surroundings. Among the various animal species are the crab-eating foxes (*Cerdocyon thous*), the agoutis, the capybaras (*Hydrochoerus hydrochaeris*), the wild pigs, the dears, the armadillos, the coatimundi (*Nasua nasua*), the otters, the ocelots and the jaguars, in addition to hundreds of butterflies, crabs and fish. Also, there are 288 bird species classified in the region, such as toucans, trushes, hawks, herrons, house wrens,

Copious butterflies in the Iguaçu National Park ▶

Swallows on the waterfall walls

Neotropical cormorants (*Phalacrocorax brasilianus*), and the parrot. Some of these birds are endangered species, such as the crimson-crested woodpecker and the solitary tinamou (*Tinamus solitarius*). There are also curious species, such as the sooty swift, which finds shelter next to the rocky walls of the falls, with water running along its back.

THE ENCHANTMENT OF WATERS

The region was initially inhabited by Guarani people. The first European who visited the falls was the Spanish captain Nunez Cabeza de Vaca, in 1542. He had crossed the Brazilian territory from the region of Florianópolis, followed by 240 indigenous people, heading toward Paraguay. In the early twentieth century, the falls were already acclaimed on account of its natural beauty, attracting many travelers such as the aviator Santos Dumont, who visited the place in 1916. Captivated by what he saw, the Brazilian inventor of the airplane turned to be one of the greatest champions of the preservation of this place. Thus, in 1939, the area surrounding the falls was declared of public use, and escaped from the devastation already taking place in the west of Paraná. At present, out of the 1,853 square kilometers of the park, only 5% is open to the public. The rest is considered as land restricted to scientific exploration and research.

WORLD HERITAGE

Since 1986, Iguaçu National Park has earned the status of Natural World Heritage by Unesco. The river giving birth to the falls crosses an astonishing distance from the source to the mouth. It starts in Curitiba, crosses Paraná state from east to west, and goes across two plateaus, over 1,320 kilometers. In the region of Foz do Iguaçu, the river runs calm and shallow on a bed spreading over a width of four kilometers. Near the falls, the bed is narrower, the speed of the current increases and the waters spill, violently and dangerously, into 282 falls, resulting in a boisterous scene that charms millions of visitors every year. Further ahead, the Iguaçu river flow increases, becomes deeper and narrower, with a bed of only 100 meters, forming rapids. Within the same region, there is another large South Brazilian river that remains untouched, the Floriano river. From its source to the mouth, this river is within the boundaries of the Iguaçu National Park. This scenery is also dazzling: the river with its rapids runs side by side with the thick forest very near its margins. It encompasses the same variety of animals as the park. That is why it becomes necessary to protect it.

FLAT LANDS

The Campos Gerais, in the Paraná plateau, were used for agricultural purposes

A great part of the South of Brazil consists of grasslands, also known as savannas and steppes. Although this name is related to the low lands, they may be found at heights of over one thousand meters. The grasslands extend over an area of 210,000 square kilometers, across the State of Rio Grande do Sul and over the borders with Uruguay and Argentina. The land is generally flat, barely undulated, and extremely fertile. It is almost completely covered by grass and grass-like vegetation, as *capim caninha* (*Andropon lateralis*), lemongrass (*Cymbopogon citratus*), red threeawn (*Aristida longiseta*), *grama-jesuíta* (*Axonopus fisifolius*) etc. However, it may also be interrupted by gallery forests (those growing along the rivers) and pastures, where there is cattle breeding. If there are trees present, such as the *urunday* (*Astronium balansae*), the earpod tree (*Enterolobium contortisiliquum*), the *aroeira-cinzenta* (*Schinus lentiscifolius*), the *guajayvi* (*Patagonula americana*) among others, these are scattered. At times, it may also present *capões* (isolated woods in an open field), with higher concentration.

CATTLE BREEDING

Most of the grasslands, especially in Rio Grande do Sul, are used to breed cattle and sheep. In the past, it was the perfect place for cattle escaping from the Jesuit missions of Paraguay to breed, originating the cattle breeding vocation in southern regions.

UNDULATING LANDSCAPES

When the grasslands are not used for cattle ranches, they are inhabited by different species of felines, deer, snakes, amphibians, lizards, and rodents, such as the agoutis and capybaras. They are also the habitat of dozens of bird species, such as hawks, owls, swallows, and humming birds, besides sanderlings (*Calidris alba*),

The sanderling (*Calidris alba*) lives in flat lands

guan, and white-naped jays (*Cyanocorax cyanopogon*). Covered by grass, the undulating landscapes of Campos Gerais, on the Paraná plateau, are rare today due to the automated agriculture advancing over the smooth relief areas. In the depressions of these grasslands, where there are water springs and the soil favors the growth of larger vegetation, there are usually *capões* of Paraná pines. The word *capão* is indigenous and means 'round forest'. The *capões* are of an almost circular shape. Some of them have hundreds or even thousands of Paraná pines, composing a landscape that has become harder to be found in the South Region.

The threatened maned wolf

THE MANED WOLF

The gradual invasion of agriculture and cattle breeding in the grasslands threatens the survival of the autochthonous fauna: especially, the maned wolf (*Chrysocyon brachyurus*), which is the largest canine in Latin America, measuring up to 1.30 meters long and 80 centimeters tall. Aloof and reserved, the maned wolf may occupy a territory ranging from 20 to 30 square kilometers. The reddish brown fur on his body contrasts with the black fur of its legs. The food, consisting of small rodents, birds, fish, wild fruits, roots, and stems, is increasingly scarce.

Down along the coast of Rio Grande do Sul, the landscape is represented by marshlands, that is, flooded biomes, with thick vegetation of junco, *gravatás* (purple bromeliad) and water hyacinth that turn to be a perfect habitat for a great variety of animals such as herrons, teals, deer, jaguars, ocelots and capybaras. The Taim marshland in Rio Grande do Sul is an example of that sort of sandy flatland very important due to the richness of the soil. Absurd attempts to drain it for agricultural purposes were definitely abandoned in 1979, when the area became an environmental station and, therefore, a protected area.

Amidst the Paraná grasslands, there may be *capões*, or clusters of Paraná pine trees

BIRD NURSERY

Ground vegetation and plenty of water in the area of Lagoa do Peixe

The sea tide and ebb over the last 200,000 years has created along the southern Brazilian seashore a low sandy and saline surface, covered with ground plants and small bushes, that are attractive because of the string of lagoons. The sandbank affected by the sea extends over an area of up to 25 kilometers from the seashore and along the coast of Rio Grande for more than 620 kilometers. There is so much water that many of those lagoons are quite visible even in satellite photographs from very high altitudes.

There are 61 lagoons, among which three stand out: the Mangueira lagoon, with an area of 802 square kilometers; the Mirim lagoon, with an area of 3,520 square kilometers; and the Dos Patos lagoon, with an area of 9,280 square kilometers, which is still being formed due to the large sedimentation coming from the estuary of the Guaíba river, where the city of Porto Alegre is located.

VEGETATION

These lagoons are located in very vast flatlands, and many of them are surrounded by high dunes formed by the wind. The scarce and ground vegetation extends all along the beach, with species such as *espartina* (*Spartina ciliata*), *macela-graúda* (*Senecio crassiflorus*) and paspalum grass. Near the dunes, there are species such as Brazilian pennywort (*Hydrocotyle leucocephala*), alemangrass (*Echinochloa polystachya*), and sprawling signalgrass (*Panicum reptans*). Meanwhile, in the humid places of the dune slopes, there are

Dunes on the beach at Guaraqueçaba ▶

Flamingoes may be seen in Taim

capões of bushes such as *capororoca-vermelha* (*Rapanea umbellata*), *ombu* (*Phytolacca dioica*), *bugreiro* (*Lithraea brasiliensis*), and *embira* (*Daphnopsis recemosa*). On the flat and dry areas, the grassland vegetation is thriving, where the southern sandspur (*Cenchrus echinatus*), the *capim-membeca* (*Andropogon leuchostachyus*) stand out. Juncos, sprawling signalgrass, cattail (*Typha domingensis*), and pickerel weed (*Pontederia lanceolata*) grow in the marshlands. Finally, the scrubs have small forests of *vacunzeiro* (*Allophylus edulis*), *murta* (*Blepharocalux salicifolius*), and *figueira-do-mato* (*Gaylussaca brasiliensis*).

LAGOA DO PEIXE

The sandbanks are visited by hundreds of birds, many of which are migratory, where they find a place to rest and eat their fills to face their long trips. This is what happens in the Lagoa do Peixe National Park, that comprises part of the Rio Grande do Sul towns of São José do Norte, Tavares and Mostardas. Its brackish water, abundant with plankton, crustaceans, and fish, is a source of nourishment. There are 182 bird species, 26 of which are migratory birds from the Northern Hemisphere and five from the Southern Hemisphere. Flamingoes arrive from Chile and Argentina. The red knot (*Calidris canutus*) comes from the north. The park also shelters mammals such as the capybara and other animals such as the broad-snouted caiman (*Caiman latirostris*). Such a wide range of bird species is also present in the Taim Marshland. Its role is to ensure the survival of the neighboring biomes: usually, lagoons. Whenever there is a drought, the marshland provides water for the lagoons; whenever there is an overflow, it stores it. The marshlands have large amounts of organic material resulting from the decomposition of junco and grass. At the bottom of the food chain are the algae that still act as a biological filter, just like large water treatment plants. They serve as food for mollusks that are eaten by fish, which in turn are eaten by birds and certain rodents. Among the several species of birds that are closely related with the sandbanks are the red knots, the terns, the swallows.

THE SOUTHERNERS

THE EARLY DAYS

The first inhabitants had shell ornaments and instruments made of polished rock

The first traces of the human occupation of Brazil point to approximately 12,000 years ago, with the discovery of the archeological site of Lagoa Santa in the state of Minas Gerais. But it is not known how long it took for the first inhabitants to reach the country's three southernmost states. On the coast, however, the first *sambaqui*-dwelling communities date back 7,500 years (read below). It is now a densely populated region, with extensive areas dedicated to agriculture and mining, in addition to roads and dams.

MANY TRACES

Many archeological sites were destroyed for this reason, hindering

The history told by the *sambaquis*

This is the name of the prehistoric sites formed by the accumulation of land, river and sea shells. The hunters and collectors that first came to the Santa Catarina coast used to eat mollusks and fishes. After that, these sites were used as dwellings, cemeteries, lookouts and meeting places. Inside the *sambaquis* vestiges of fireplaces, cutting, grinding and sawing instruments were found, in addition to mammal remains and fish, reptile and whalebones. Human bones were also found along with their belongings. There are many traces of *sambaquis* along the entire south coast. The State of Santa Catarina have the highest sambaquis in the world, spread along the coast. They are hundreds of meters long by 25 meters high and are approximately 5,000 years old. Specialists believe that they took hundreds of years to form.

Piles of shells are ancient vestiges ▶

◀ The Gaúcho, typical inhabitant of the South

The division of the continent

Before Brazil was officially discovered, the Portuguese and the Spaniards had already carved it up. The Treaty of Tordesillas was signed by both countries on 7 June 1494, with the approval of Pope Alexander VI. As a result of this division, the coastal land to the right of the imaginary line of the Tordesillas meridian belonged to Portugal. And the land to the left of Tordesillas was Spanish domain. In the south, Portuguese possession was limited to the coastal region of the states of Paraná and Santa Catarina, ending at the town of Laguna, where there is now a monument to this division. According to the treaty, all of Rio Grande do Sul belonged to Spain.

research and making it impossible to arrive at more precise scientific conclusions. It is known, however, that some of the populations that lived in the *sambaquis,* aproximately 1,500 years ago, already produced axes of polished rock, ornaments made with shells, instruments made with bones and zoolites or small animal sculptures in rock. Some of their most likely migration routes are also known.
When the first Europeans arrived in what is now Brazil more than 500 years ago, the southern region was inhabited by natives belonging to two distinct lines: the Tupi and Macro-jê tribes. There were thousands of natives scattered throughout the three southernmost states, from different tribes with different languages and dialects.

THE GUARANI

The Tupi belonged to the Tupi-Guarani family and lived in hotter areas. In addition to the coast, they also lived in the vicinity of the seasonal forest, in the areas of the Floresta Estacional in the west of the state of Paraná, in the outskirts of the city of Curitiba, and in several locations in the state of Rio Grande do Sul. They fished, hunted, navigated along rivers, produced hammocks to sleep in and had sophisticated farming and pottery techniques. The Tupi-Guarani were more willing to establish contact with the colonizers, influencing their customs and enriching the vocabulary of the Portuguese language. They gave names to animals (*jacaré*, *jabuti*), trees (*pitanga*), fruits (*araçá*), rivers (*Iguaçu*, *Jacuí*, *Ivaí*), landforms (*Itaimbezinho Canyon*), cities (*Curitiba*, *Urubici*) and even the state of Paraná.

THE *COROADOS* AND *BOTOCUDOS*

Tupi-Guarani tribes collaborated with the Portuguese colonizers at different stages in the history of Brazil. They showed Portuguese and São Paulo miners the best places to mine for gold in the Paranaguá region (Paraná) in the 16th century. They helped the whites to cross the natural barriers between the coast and the Paraná highlands. The people from the Macro-Jê group, on the other hand, were reluctant to have contact with whites, inhabited the coldest regions, especially the highlands and mountain ranges. Belonging to the Jê linguistic family, and called Caingangues, they were nicknamed *Coroados* (crown wearers) because of the way in which the men cut their hair. They collected pine seeds and fruits. They carried out rudimentary farming activities, as well as fishing and hunting. They lived mostly in the states of Paraná, Santa Catarina and Rio Grande do Sul. The region was still home to tribes of Xóclengues or Xocrens, also of the Jê family, called *Botocudos* because of the *botoque* or lip plug they wore in their lower lips.

THE MISSIONARY SETTLEMENTS

Before the arrival of the colonizers, the South of Brazil was the land of the Jesuit Missions

Throughout the 17th and 18th century, the Guarani Indians that lived in what is now the northeast of Argentina, southeast of Paraguay and northeast of Rio Grande do Sul, were only nominally under the domain of Portugal or Spain. In practice, they were ruled by the Company of Jesus, the powerful Jesuit order. The first self-sufficient indigenous settlement around a Jesuit mission was built in 1610. They created a society without precedents. The Jesuits wished to catechize the indigenous communities, providing them with knowledge about economy, the arts and science. And the Guarani peoples, in addition to accepting the Christian faith, taught the priests what they knew about plants, farming techniques, the climate, and their way of life.

THE SETTLEMENTS

The whites and Indians then formed the 30 settlements of the Jesuit missions: seven in Rio Grande do Sul, 12 in Paraná and the others scattered about near the frontiers of Argentina and Paraguay (read Rio Grande do Sul). There were 150,000 natives, and they formed centers of some importance, planting Yerba-mate, wheat, corn, manioc, cotton, fruit and legumes. Efficient techniques for cattle raising were developed. The natives elected their peers to positions of political representation.

IDEAL SOCIETY

Catholicism became the official religion of the missionary society. The children learned to read and write in Spanish and Guarani. Girls also learned to spin, weave and cook. Children sang religious songs, while young Indians and adults produced musical instruments with extreme precision - violins, harps, bassoons, drums and guitars.

The missionary settlers learned innumerous professions (from blacksmiths to carpenters), but they were truly outstanding in architecture and sculpture: they erected buildings and churches, decorated with wooden and stone representations of angels and saints that were reminiscent of baroque art. They lived in harmonious and prosperous communities for approximately 150 years. Traces of these communities can still be seen in the ruins of the missions that remain in the South of Brazil, as well as in Argentina and Paraguay.

EXPULSION

In the beginning, King Phillip II of Spain, who ruled over Portugal and Spain from 1580 to 1640, was supportive of the Jesuits' catechizing activities. When Portugal became independent again, Spain wanted the missions to guarantee their domination in South America. In this era, the missionary settlements were already struggling against the first settlers, who ended up taking more than 20,000 native prisoners and destroying many settlements.
As the missionary organization prospered, however, relations between the Jesuit order and the Iberian monarchies deteriorated. The Portuguese and Spanish kings were making administrative reforms and in 1750 signed the Treaty of Madrid, redefining their territories. The agreement established that the natives had to abandon the missions and move to areas of Spanish domain, leaving behind flocks, plantations and properties that now belonged to Portugal. The seven missionary settlements were left to the Portuguese, who, in return, handed over the colony of Sacramento to Spain.

RESISTENCE

Priests and natives rebelled against the decision. The Guaranítica War began in 1754, leaving thousands of casualties and culminating in the destruction of the missionary communities two years later. In 1761, the Treaty of El Pardo annulled the Treaty of Madrid and allowed the surviving natives to return to the seven missionary settlements. However, the Jesuits were expelled from the region in 1768.
Meanwhile, the Caingangue resisted the occupation of their land until the 19th century. Protected by the Brazilian pine forests, they were not troubled by the first settlers passing through the South of Brazil in the 16th century. In the 17th century, the few remaining communities that the whites managed to locate – always guided by the Tupi-Guaranis, arch enemies of the *Coroados* – did not allow themselves to be dominated. The military expeditions created for mineral prospecting purposes and to evaluate the possibility of establishing settlements were also repelled by the *Coroados*.

OCCUPATION

There were 11 official expeditions beginning in 1768 in the state of Paraná alone. The Indians carried out a series of attacks, retarding the occupation of the Guarapuava region by more than 40 years. The gradually increasing occupation of the land in the south by German and Italian immigrants, from the 19th century, also caused the *Coroados* to react. The first villages were established in the 19th century, but the successive confrontations quickly caused a loss of unity and cultural roots. Many of their descendants, almost all of whom live in official indigenous areas, still fight to keep their culture alive.
The first organized group of settlers arrived in Rio Grande do Sul in 1740. Coming from the Azores, they were supported by the Portuguese government, which wanted them to settle in the vast area previously occupied by the missions. But the many difficulties they encountered caused them to settle in the area that is now the city of Porto Alegre.

Indigenous communities still live in the South

Guarani mate

The *gaúchos*, as people from Rio Grande do Sul are called, made mate a symbol of their land and people. The people of Paraná claim their land to be the birthplace of Yerba-mate. Both are fully justified. Yerba-mate (*Ilex paraguariensis*) was scientifically described in 1822 by the French naturalist Auguste de Saint-Hilaire, using a sample collected around the city of Curitiba. As it is a plant that always grows near pine forests, and Paraná had the largest forests of this type, it was natural that it also had the largest quantity of this plant.

But the tradition of drinking this tea is still much more strongly rooted among the *gaúchos*. The true discoverers of this drink, however, were the Guarani people, who already had this habit long before the discovery of Brazil. Called *caa-i*, which means flavorsome herb, they drank the infusion constantly from gourds with straws made of bamboo with a base of woven fibers, which stopped the chopped leaves from being sucked up with the liquid.

The drink was adopted by the Spanish conquerors, who acquired the habit of the Guairá natives, in the west of Paraná. In spite of the revitalizing and curative properties it was claimed to have, the Catholic Church condemned it because the natives attributed it magical powers. People were imprisoned and fined, and bales of Yerba-mate were even burned in public. All of it was in vain. The habit took root even further and was adopted by the people of Uruguay, Argentina, Paraguay, Chile, Peru and the South of Brazil.

During the era of the missions, in around 1660, the first Yerba-mate plantation was planted and cultivated using farming techniques in the settlement of São Xavier, making the system of production more dynamic. Historical records show that the product was so valuable that it was even used as a form of currency. In addition to being a drink, it was used for medicinal purposes and as a means of disguising the taste of the dirty water in some regions. Because of Yerba-mate, thousands of natives were enslaved by the Spanish, who forced them to work in the native plantations in the forests, carrying 60-kilo bales. Many died of malnutrition and bad treatment. In the missions, however, the systematized production prospered and became a big business.

With the expulsion of the missionaries in 1768, Paraguay took over the production of Yerba-mate, until it went to war in the second half of the 19th century. Also in this period, the economy of Paraná was based on the production and exportation of Yerba-mate.

In the painting by Debret, the history of the teams of drovers

THE PATH OF THE DROVERS

The missions disintegrated, but left a legacy that was the base of the Rio Grande do Sul economy for a long time: the large herds of cattle and horses, raised running loose through the prairies. These herds attracted the Portuguese colonizers, who began to settle in the region in a more systematic manner. Around the 18th century, the discovery of gold mines in the state of Minas Gerais created a demand for the cattle of the region and consolidated the occupation of the territory.
The first connection between the town of Viamão (Rio Grande do Sul) and Sorocaba (São Paulo) was recorded in 1712. But it was in 1731 that the first complete journey along the path of the drovers took place, marking the exact trajectory of an economic movement that survived for more than 200 years. Born of the need to supply the region of Minas Gerais, droving began to forge paths through the uninhabited interior of Brazil during the era of gold and precious stone mining. Teams of horsemen conducted mules, cattle and merchandise through the backlands with the skill, courage and resistance to face journeys.After decades of supporting mining, the drovers were also fundamental in the success of the sugar cane and coffee eras. In a country without roads, almost no trains and few ports, the incessant movement of the drovers was important to the Brazilian economy.

URBAN CENTERS

With the passing of time, the drovers' places of rest became urban centers, making occupation easier (see Lapa and Castro in Paraná). And Rio Grande do Sul, constantly involved in territorial and political battles, became an important supply center, integrated with the rest of the country. The drovers saw wars and revolutions, the Portuguese crown filling its coffers with the wealth generated by their work, the transformation of the Empire into a Republic, and the birth of many towns.

◀ **The habit of drinking *chimarrão* spread through Rio Grande do Sul**

A HISTORY OF SEVERAL WARS

The mixing of peoples gave rise to a roving population, whose daily meal was barbecue

The *gaúcho* came into being in the hard, solitary life of the pampas. At the beginning of the colonial period, due to the Tordesillas Treaty, Rio Grande do Sul belonged to the Spanish. Portuguese presence was restricted to certain stretches of the coast and, almost 200 years later, the region of Porto Alegre. From the 16th century to the beginning of the 18th century, Rio Grande do Sul was the birthplace of a roving, free people, a mixture of Spanish conquerors, Portuguese adventurers, people from São Paulo that roamed the territory in search of natives who inhabited the region.
In addition to the Guaranis, there were also the Charrua and Minuano tribes, originally from Uruguay, who crossed Rio Grande do Sul on their migration routes. *Gaúchos* became a resistant, hardy people, accustomed to the vast plains, the cutting cold of the winds from the southwest, the struggle to tame the wild cattle and constant skirmishes over land. Riding horses, using knives and daggers, droving cattle, slaughtering animals, working with leather and producing beef jerky were useful skills when most of this human contingency worked as laborers on large cattle farms.

PIT FIRE

As they inhabited land in constant turmoil, the *gaúchos* also became accustomed to combat and were always ready to take up arms to defend their frontiers. Their daily meal was barbecue prepared over a "pit fire", where meat was placed on wooden skewers and roasted over a brazier in the ground. Their loud, clear, frank and open way of speaking, mixing indigenous and Spanish expressions – was retained through the centuries. In the same

The battle of Farrapos: the uprising against taxes ▶

manner, they conserved their traditional attire, called *pilcha*, composed of wide, loose trousers, a *chiripá* (a rectangle of cloth, generally of red wool, which was passed between the legs and attached to the waist), linen shirt (for festive occasions), boots with spurs, a hat with a chin strap and a handkerchief tied around their neck, and a poncho. The most deeply entrenched of all their habits has also survived time: the *amargo* ("bitter") – the fond nickname given by *gaúchos* to *chimarrão*, their faithful companion.

DIFFICULT TIMES

Hardship, internal conflicts and many wars marked the history of the people in this region. Times were difficult between one revolution and another, until finally peace was established in the 20th century. There were many battles to conquer new lands by order of the Portuguese crown. And uncountable fights to preserve the integrity of Brazilian geography. Then there were struggles against the Empire and its taxes, for republican, abolitionist and parliamentary ideals. And the struggle for land that shed the blood of thousands of Caboclos, who fought the government in Contestado. Following is the history of the wars that had such a great influence on the lives of the people in this region.

THE CISPLATINA WAR (1825-1828)

In 1821 Brazil annexed the eastern strip (now Uruguay) to its territory, calling it the Cisplatina Province. Located at the entrance of the Plate River estuary, the area was economically valuable as it provided control of navigation and commerce in the region. Four years later, with the support of Argentina, Uruguayan troops lead by Antonio Lavalleja and Fructuoso Rivera surrounded the city of Montevideo and declared the independence of Uruguay. The Brazilian troops sent by King Pedro I were defeated in 1827, in the battle of Passo do Rosário. The following year, England intermediated in the negotiations that led Brazil and Argentina to recognize Uruguay's independence.

THE FARROUPILHA REVOLUTION (1835-1845)

Also known as the Farrapos War, the longest Brazilian civil war was sparked off by the *gaúcho* cattle ranchers who saw their wealth dwindling as the result of two actions by the Empire: the charging of high taxes on the beef jerky produced in Rio Grande do Sul and the importation of the same product from Uruguay. Led by colonel Bento Gonçalves da Silva, the revolution was soon joined by abolitionists and

sympathizers with the republican cause. Promoted to general, Bento Gonçalves was taken prisoner. Even locked in a cell, he was elected president of the Republic of Rio Grande, proclaimed by general Antonio de Souza Netto, another revolutionary leader. After escaping from prison in Salvador, Bento Gonçalves reassumed control of the revolution, which gained the support of Italian Giuseppe Garibaldi (read Santa Catarina) in 1837.
The revolt arrived in Santa Catarina, which also declared its independence and founded the Juliana Republic. It was in this town in Santa Catarina that Garibaldi met Ana Maria de Jesus Ribeiro, who, at the age of 18, left her husband in order to follow him. She participated in countless battles and was respected for her courage and spirit of leadership, going down in history in both Brazil and Italy as Anita Garibaldi (ten years after the Farrapos War, after four children and pregnant with her fifth, she died of typhoid, fighting alongside Garibaldi to free Italy). Without money or supplies, in addition to heavy losses and desertions, the leaders of the revolution ended up divided. Bento Gonçalves renounced his presidency and Davi Canabarro accepted a peace agreement with Luís Alves de Lima e Silva, who was outstanding in the Paraguayan War (the Duke of Caxias).

THE PARAGUAYAN WAR (1865-1870)

The desire to possess the strategic Plate River region caused the outbreak of the biggest war in South America, involving Brazil, Paraguay, Argentina and Uruguay. By order of the Paraguayan President Francisco Solano López, in December 1864, the Brazilian province of Mato Grosso was invaded. Paraguay soon managed to open new fronts, invading as far as Rio Grande do Sul. In 1865, with the signing of the Triple Alliance, Brazilians, Argentineans and Uruguayans began to undermine the Paraguayan resistance. The counter-offensive was commanded by Argentinean General Bartolomeu Mitre, who invaded Paraguay in 1866. In the following years, Brazilian Manuel Luiz Osório and Luís Alves de Lima e Silva, the Duke of Caxias, led a succession of victorious battles. Asuncion, the capital of Paraguay, was taken in 1869 and Solano López was killed the following year. Two thirds of the population of Paraguay were among over 50,000 casualties of war. At the end of the conflict, the black people ont the victorious side refused to remain slaves, giving momentum to the abolitionist movement.

THE FEDERALISTA REVOLUTION (1893-1895)

The political interests of rival *gaúcho* leaders led to the Federalist

Attack on the island of Cabrita during the Paraguayan War: impulse for the abolition of slavery

Pica-paus: support for the government

Revolution. On the one side were those representing the Federalist Party, made up of Party, old members of the *Partido Liberal do Império* and led by Gaspar Silveira Martins and General João Nunes da Silva Tavares. Called *Maragatos*, they had the support of the navy. Pro-parlamentarists, they wanted the Constituition to be reformed to stop Júlio de Castilhos remaining in power. On the other side were the members of the *Partido Republicano Rio-grandense*, commanded by Castilhos. Called *Pica-paus*, they wanted to maintain their domains. In 1893, a year of election, the rival factions began a bloody civil war. President Floriano Peixoto turned down a request for federal intervention made by the *Maragatos*, and declared support for the *Pica-paus*. In retaliation, the *Maragatos* also advanced on Santa Catarina and Paraná, taking the city of Curitiba. In an episode known as Cerco da Lapa (read Paraná), the local population fought off attacks by the *Maragatos* for almost a month. In 1895, under the government of President Prudente de Moraes, a peace treaty was signed: Júlio de Castilhos was maintained in power and the federalist rebels were granted amnesty by the Brazilian National Congress.

THE CONTESTADO WAR (1913-1916)

A violent social conflict marked the western region of Santa Catarina, on the Paraná border, disputed at the time by the two Brazilian states. The revolt was born in 1906, when the Brazilian government struck and agreement with North American businessman Percival Farquhar, who had just taken over the Companhia Estrada de Ferro São Paulo-Rio Grande. In exchange for the construction of stretches of railroad, Farquhar was authorized to colonize and use the lands along the railway, with exclusive rights over 15 kilometers on each side of the railway. The lands to the west of the state, however, were inhabited by Caboclos. In 1912, the "monk" José Maria, preacher and medicine man, attracted many of them to a place called Taquaruçu. They were expelled from there by hired assassins working for Colonel Francisco de Albuquerque and installed themselves at Vila do Irani, in the center of the Contestado region. There were new fights until the death of the "monk" and the commander of the Paraná police force. In the following years, belief in the return of the "monk" spread throughout the region, increasing the number of followers in places such as Taquaruçu, Caraguatá and Timbó. The community leaders released a monarchist manifesto and announced a "holy war" against the coronels, the land companies and the state and federal authorities. Approximately 12,000 civilians fought the military troops for three years. The Contestado War ended in 1916 with the downfall of the Caboclo population. At least 10,000 civilians were killed, in addition to one thousand soldiers and military officers. Lumber stepped up its operations and went down in history as the largest lumber dealer in Latin America, chopping more than 15 million pine trees. At the end of that year, the Paraná and Santa Catarina governments signed a border agreement.

Contestado: trenches against the Caboclos

THE EUROPEAN PRESENCE

The Azoreans who arrived in Florianópolis kept their architecture and traditions alive

The arrival of different European nationalities to the South of Brazil was one of the factors which most influenced the cultural and economic profile of the region strongly focused on farming, manufacturing, exports, commerce and, more recently, tourism. The Portuguese colonizers were the first to settle in the region and took distinct paths: some sought easy wealth, others were involved in projects that aimed to ensure possession of the lands of the New World for the Portuguese crown.

PARANÁ

The Portuguese presence was already felt on the coast of Paraná by around 1549. Coming from Cananéia in the state of São Paulo, adventurers came in search of gold. Ten years later, Luso-Brazilian miners founded the village that would later be transformed in Paranaguá, the first population center in Paraná. It was also the Portuguese, *Paulistas* from São Paulo, and mestizos that climbed the mountains to found, in 1639, the first town in the Paraná highlands, which was later to become Curitiba. In Santa Catarina, the coast was inhabited by Carijó natives at the time of the discovery.

SANTA CATARINA

It was in 1726 that the pioneer Fernão Dias Velho founded the town of Nossa Senhora do Desterro (now the city of

Lacemakers: on the coast of Santa Catarina

Bumba-meu-boi: traditional festival

Florianópolis), promoting the slavery of the indigenous communities, or indeed their very extermination. The Portuguese identity began to form in 1748 with the arrival in Desterro of more than 5,000 Azoreans. Finding similarities in the scalloped bays, the Portuguese continued with their cultural traditions (today, they continue their lace-making activities, in the *pau-de-fita* and *bumba-meu-boi* legends and dances), their colonial rows of houses and the economy based on fishing. This influence spread to other coastal towns such as Itajaí, São Francisco do Sul and Laguna.

RIO GRANDE DO SUL

In Rio Grande do Sul, sixty Azorean couples founded the village of Nossa Senhora do Porto dos Casais (now the city of Porto Alegre) in 1752. The creation of the port, on the margins of the Guaíba River, was fundamental in the economic development of the state. The Spaniards left their strongest mark in Rio Grande do Sul, in a territory that once belonged to Spain under the Tordesillas Treaty. There, the lands with imprecise frontiers, the proximity to the Plate River communities, the physical isolation from the rest of the country and the contact with the Spaniards through war and commerce, meant that the population would speak Spanish for a long time, assimilating terms and words which became part of *gaúcho* regionalisms. The language and customs were also disseminated by the missionary communities, with dozens of thousands natives speaking Spanish as well as Guarani.

GERMAN HERITAGE

Other foreigners only began to arrive in the South in the 19th century. The need to occupy the territory and to develop a workforce to carry out economic activities gave rise to the process of attracting immigrants, who, for their part, were interested in leaving behind Europe, devastated by unemployment and war. The first to arrive in the region were the Germans. In Paraná, in 1829, there was already

Typical dances are reminiscent of the European immigration in the three southern states

a German colony in the municipality of Rio Negro. Many of these immigrants moved to Curitiba. They also settled in Itajaí Valley, in Santa Catarina, giving origin to cities such as Joinville, Blumenau and Pomerode. In Rio Grande do Sul, the German influence spread from Porto Alegre, to Guaíba, Novo Hamburgo and climbed the mountains to consolidate its presence in cities such as Gramado, Canela and Nova Petrópolis. This process of occupation underwent a solid cultural influence, maintaining the language, folklore and cuisine. The economic activities, first centered around agricultural production, led to the growing industrialization of the region.

THE ITALIANS

The Italian immigrants also arrived in the South in the 19th century. From Curitiba, extending to several municipalities in the interior of Paraná, to towns in the mountains of Rio Grande do Sul, such as Caxias do Sul, Garibaldi and Bento Gonçalves, they also retained their customs and traditions – craftwork in wicker and straw – as well as their tasty cuisine that turns over millions of dollars a year in places such as the Curitiba district of Santa Felicidade. The cold and mountain altitudes provided the ideal conditions for the extensive vineyards that, until today, produce some of the best wines in the country. The farming communities also made wheat plantations and other cereals prosper. Their entrepreneuring spirit also propelled industrialization, generating important centers in the mechanical, furniture and metallurgical industries. Their passion for political action led the Italians to organize unions, cooperatives and immigrant protection associations. In the municipality of Palmeira in Paraná, they founded the colony of Santa Cecília, the first anarchist community in Brazil.

The present of immigrants from Poland and Ukraine was greater in Paraná, where there are now approximately 800,000 Polish descendents and 350,000 Ukrainian descendents. These communities have influenced the speech of the region, cultural manifestations, architecture and the type of economy. Other foreigners settled in smaller numbers in the South, nevertheless forming colonies that are very significant until today. This is the case of the Austrians who gave Treze Tílias in Santa Catarina its identity, the Japanese who, together with the *Paulistas* and *Gaúchos*, helped colonize the north of Paraná, in addition to the Swiss, Belgians, Israelites and Arabs who are scattered through the region, composing a complex human mosaic.

Italian immigrants began wine-producing activities in the mountains of Rio Grande do Sul

Communities of Polish origin maintain their traditions in the interior of Paraná

The recent colonization

The occupation of Paraná did not occur in a homogeneous manner. Between the conquering of the coastal region and the occupation of the north of Paraná, there was a gap of almost 400 years, with three very distinct phases. The first Luso-Brazilians arrived in the Paraná coast in 1549, in search of gold. Little more than a decade later, Paranaguá became a village and later the first town founded in the South of Brazil. Mining activities also attracted a contingency of adventurers up the mountainside, bringing about the founding of Curitiba in 1693, well before Florianópolis (1726) and Porto Alegre (1752). Human presence in the area of the drovers' route, between Viamão (Rio Grande do Sul) and Sorocaba (São Paulo), transformed travelers' inns into towns and areas of cattle raising and farming from early 18th century. This process took place in a balanced manner in the three southernmost states. Until the beginning of the 20th century, however, the western, southwestern and northern regions of Paraná were still little inhabited. The actions of colonizing companies, the coffee and lumber eras attracted many people. Families from Rio Grande do Sul and Santa Catarina, especially German, Italian or Polish immigrants or descendents began to live in the west and southwest of Paraná. The northern region was occupied by people from São Paulo, Minas Gerais, the northern states of Brazil, Japanese immigrants and the descendents of European immigrants. All this population helped to found cities that are much more recent, such as Londrina, in 1934, and Maringá, in 1947.

Homage to Ukrainians in Curitiba

GLOSSARY

The musical accent and the use of the second person singular (*tu*) are what is most heard on the streets of the South. In Paraná, what calls attention is how Curitiba local residents accentuate the words. The following are expressions and words that can be heard when you travel to any of the three southern States. After each word or expression, we give an indication of the State it most often occurs.

Agüentar o tirão (RS) – same as "agüentar o tranco," meaning take the responsibility. Tirão refers both to the task and the responsibility.

Algariado: (RS) – a confused person, like a teenager who doesn´t know where to put the hands or what to do with all the energy he´s got.

Arrombassi, Layla! (SC) – an expression referring to great achievements. It can be used as either an accomplishment or threat.

Atucanado (RS) – worried, upset, overburden.

Ba (RS) – oftentimes spelled Bah, it can mean both approval and disapproval. It´s been said to be a shortened form of the word *barbaridade* (barbarity, but meaning overwhelm). Used as an emphatic expression to something said or done, meaning "you´re right."

Bagual (RS) – something very good. The usage started on farms, since bagual means an untamed horse.

Barbaridade (RS) – A generic exclamation used to either approve or disapprove a situation. It´s pronounced with a strong accent in the first syllable.

Bergamota (RS) – the fruit called tangerine in the rest of the country.

Boi-de-mamão (SC) – a popular festival in Santa Catarina, similar to Maranhão´s Bumba-meu-boi.

Cacetinho (RS) – a small loaf of bread, for hot-dogs.

Carcá (SC) – leave, beat it.

Chamar na chincha (RS) – call someone´s attention, make clear what his responsibility is.

Charque (RS) – salted beef meat, sun-dried in layers.

Chimia (RS) – from the German word *schmier* (lubricating oil), a kind of jam with fruit to spread on the bread.

Chineque (PR) – it´s a sweet bun, that is, filled with eclair.

Como é que pode, né? (SC) – expression used to demonstrate admiration, unbelief or irony.

Cuque (PR) – a kind of cake, with flour and sugar topping

Cusco (RS) – a synonym for dog, but used almost as an insult.

Dê-le que te dê-le (RS): expression to describe all the effort put into a task (as the Spanish expression *dale que dale*).

Deu pra ti (RS): expression meaning Enough! No more of that!

Eito (RS) – length of time. If someone takes a long time to arrive, they say "it took him an *eito*."

Em cima do laço (RS) – at the right time, on the spot.

Encarangar (RS) – the body´s reaction, when it´s too cold.

Engruvinhado (SC) – being quiet in a corner, from cold.

Enxaimel (RS, SC, PR) – logs that, put together, form the structure of a house. This building technique was brought by the Germans.

És um monstro! (SC) – a compliment meaning "You´re the best!"

Fazer charqueada (RS) – to buy goods.

Fiasquento (RS) – someone who´s afraid of everything.

Gaitada (RS) – a loud laugh.

Gringo (SC e PR) – how any foreigner is called. In Rio Grande do Sul, the word refers only to Americans and English.

Guisado (RS) – can be used to designate either ground or chopped meat (which in Santa Catarina is called *boi ralado*) or the dish made with it.

Istrová (SC) – get in the way, complicate (comes from "*estorvo*").

Laço (RS) – a synonym for a real or figurative spanking. When a soccer team loses, it´s said it "had a *laço*."

Mandrião (SC) – lazy, a bum.

Mané (SC) – a local resident of the Santa Catarina backlands, naive.

Maria-Congueira (SC) – a children´s play, similar to hide-and-seek.

Me admira de ti! (SC) – expression used to say that the person is surprising, in a bad sense.

Mimosa (PR) – tangerine

Mofas cá pomba na balaia! (SC) – expression used to say that someone will get tired of waiting, will not get what he wants.

Não istrova! (SC) – don´t get in the way, don´t bother me!

Necas de pitibiriba (SC) – never.

Negrinho (RS) – how the Gaúcho calls a kind of chocolate sweet, called *brigadeiro* in the rest of the country.

Ó-lhó-lhó! (SC) – an admiration expression.

Pechada (RS) – a car crash or when two friends bump into each other, literally.

Pêssanka (PR) – a Ukranian word, designating the delicately painted Easter eggs.

Piá (SC and RS) – a child.

Pila (RS) – currency in Porto Alegre, meaning Real. It´s always, one pila, a thousand pila etc.

Pilchado (RS) – all dressed up.

Polaco (PR): expression used to designate anyone who has very light skin.

Prenda (RS) – a young woman.

Quedê-le? (RS) – where is it?

Rancho (RS) – "Make *rancho*" means buy groceries. *Rancho* can also mean "in excess," such as in "a *rancho* of laundry."

Si qués qués, si num qués diz! (SC) – if you want something, say it right away. Used to rush things.

Tchê (RS) – a general calling.

Tchê de Deus (RS) – Good Lord!

Torrada (RS) – two slices of loaf bread filled with ham and cheese, grilled. In the rest of the country it´s called *misto quente*.

Tri (RS) – an adverb to express a lot of something. It´s said to have originated at the World Soccer Championship in Mexico, when Brazil was three-time champion.

Trilho de renda (SC) – a kind of model, a drawing done in cardboard and later put on cushions so that embroiderers can follow the pattern.

Vai deitar (or vai dormir), Vinagre! (SC) – expression used to say that someone is disturbing, that it´s better if he or she leaves.

Viamão (RS) – a driver who doesn´t obey traffic laws.

PARANÁ

PARANÁ

The State of Paraná borders on the State of São Paulo to the north and northeast; on the Atlantic Ocean to the east, on the State of Santa Catarina to the south, on Argentina to the southwest, on Paraguay to the west and on the State of Mato Grosso do Sul to the northwest. The capital, Curitiba, is 408 kilometers from São Paulo and 304 kilometers from Florianópolis, in Santa Catarina. Structural problems that afflict large metropolises are not an issue in Curitiba. The city is home to state-of-the-art industries such as car makers, but still has one of the highest levels of quality of living in the country. The State is known worldwide for the waterfalls in Foz do Iguaçu and the rock formations in Vila Velha, but the State has other little-known spots, like the waterfalls region in Prudentópolis, impeccably well-preserved houses in the city of Lapa, the wild nature of the Superagüi National Park and all the region in secluded Guaraqueçaba. Ilha do Mel is still a favorite with the young crowd and the Guartelá State Park houses the sixth longest canyon in the world (32 kilometers), and is regarded as one of the most beautiful in Brazil. Taking a train from Curitiba to Paranaguá is a must for those who wish to see one of the most well-preserved sections of the Rainforest in the south of the country. Morretes is a stopover in the middle of the trip and the best place to taste *barreado*, a typical dish of the region. The ethnic variety is an attraction in

itself. Thanks to waves of Ucranian, Polish, German, Japanese, Arab and Italian immigrants, just to mention some, Paraná is admirably diversified, be it in architecture, culinary or the way the people behave.

◀ **Araucária is the symbol of Paraná State**

Highlights
❶ Curitiba
❷ Foz do Iguaçu
❸ Ilha do Mel
N
O
L
S
0
50
100 km
River
State Capital
City
State Boundary
Park
Paved Road
Dirty Track
Railroad
Airport
Paranapanema
Londrina
BR 369
Tibagi
BR 153
BR 376
Tibagi
PARQUE ESTADUAL DE GUARTELÁ
PR 340
Castro
BR 151
PARQUE ESTADUAL CAMPINHOS
Tunas do Paraná
BR 476
Reserva Natural Salto Morato
PARQUE NACIONAL DE SUPERAGÜI
Guaraqueçaba
Ilha do Superagüi
PR 440
Antonina
Graciosa
Morretes
Paranaguá
Ilha do Mel
Pontal do Sul
Matinhos
Guaratuba
BR 376
CURITIBA
S. J. dos Pinhais
Lapa
BR 476
Ponta Grossa
rudentópolis
BR 373
PARQUE ESTADUAL VILA VELHA
BR 277
União da Vitória
BR 153
SÃO PAUL
BR 116
SANTA CATARINA
POLIS

Curitiba

The ecological capital of Paraná has 18 million square meters of green areas

Foz do Iguaçu 639 km
Florianópolis 304 km
Porto Alegre 711 km
1,586,898
41
352-8000
viaje.curitiba.pr.gov.br

The city became known in the rest of Brazil for its innovative urban solutions. The transportation system is one of the most efficient in the country. The tube-like bus stops became a trademark of Curitiba: the ticket is bought before boarding, which makes everything faster, and the passenger can change buses as many times as he wishes along the way. There are also many lanes exclusively for buses spread along most of the neighborhoods, so traffic flows easily. The city gained ecological capital status because of its 18 million square meters of green areas (circa 54 square meters per inhabitant, more than triple of what is recommended by the World Health Organization). There are groves, squares and parks with great entertainment areas. The different nationalities that peopled the city are honored in the typical architecture of buildings and monuments of many squares. This can be observed in the round shapes of a Ucranian church, colorful ornaments bending from the front of Polish houses, typical eaves of Japanese roofs, mosaics of an Arab mosque or the upright poles used in the framework of typical German houses. Such ethnic diversity is also present in culinary, making the city a gastronomic center par excellence. The Brazilian colonial heritage is present in historic downtown, with buildings that are reminders of the time when cowboys roamed the region. Summer is mild, with an average temperature of 22º C (the city is almost 1,000 meters above sea level). Winter, on the other hand, is harsh, with an average temperature of around 10º C and frosting is pretty common. Even in summer it´s advisable to pack a coat. Locals are used to such season moods, and usually joke about the "onion effect" — you dress in layers in the morning and take it all off along the day. Curitiba has one of the best social indicators in the country: illiteracy is almost null, child mortality is half the Brazilian average and 42% of the families belong to classes A and B (the national average is 22%). The suggested itinerary in the guide is divided by regions in the city. Follow the

The land of pine seeds

The name of the city derived from the Indian Tupi-Guarani language, and means "a lot of pine tree seeds." The pine tree produces an edible seed known as "pinhão," the symbol of Paraná, and the tree is easy to spot: it has a very tall trunk and a large crown resembling a wine glass. Currently, only 2% of the original forest area remains. The city was founded because of the many economic cycles that happened in the South. The gold cycle was the first, in 1649, attracting miners from the Southeast. In 1693 the settlement gained village status, was named Nossa Senhora da Luz dos Pinhais, but was forgotten for many years, during the period it belonged to the São Paulo Province. It was only in the 18th century, with the cowboys´ cycle, that the village began to prosper, when, in order to take mules, cattle and food to the Southeast, cowboys stopped there on their way from Rio Grande do Sul to São Paulo. It was then that the State was emancipated and Curitiba became the capital of Paraná. Next came the timber and matte cycle. From mid-18th century on, European immigrants started to arrive and gave the city a multi-ethnic character, still visible today.

N.S. da Luz dos Pinhais: the first name

map. Attractions along the **Linha Turismo** (Tourism Line), an efficient bus that travels along the most interesting places in town, are marked by 🚌.

★ Historic Sector

A good starting point for a tour is Tiradentes Plaza, to see the **Basílica Menor de Nossa Senhora da Luz Cathedral**, built in 1893 in neo-Gothic style. To the left, take José Bonifácio Street to the hectic Travessa Nestor de Castro. At this point, check out artist **Poty Lazzarotto´s panels**, depicting the old street market fairs and the modern buildings, a landmark of the city. Cross Nestor de Castro Street through an underground passageway, and enter the heart of historic

Riding buses

An easy way to get to know Curitiba is to take the Linha Turismo (Tourist Line), a bus that takes visitors to 22 tourist spots and leaves every half-hour. All you have to do is buy a boarding pass that allows you to board once and re-board 3 times anywhere in town. A good option for the first day: Jardim Botânico, Ópera de Arame, Tanguá Park and Torre Mercês; choose other four attractions for the second day. Buses leave from downtown Curitiba, at Tiradentes Plaza, Tuesday through Sunday, from 9 am to 5:30 pm. The bus takes just over two hours to complete the itinerary, but tickets allow passegers to get off at the stops and rejoin the trip.

Buses leave every half-hour

The main attractions

1. XV de Novembro Street
2. Avenida Palace
3. Boca Maldita
4. Tiradentes Plaza
5. Basílica Cathedral
6. Guaíra Theater
7. UFPR (University)
8. Former Paraná Museum
9. Garcez Building
10. Largo da Ordem
11. Casa Romário Martins
12. Rosário and Presbyterian churches
13. Relógio das Flores
14. 24-Hour Street
15. Paiol Theater
16. Botanical Garden
17. Passeio Público
18. Novo Museu
19. Bosque do Papa
20. German Grove
21. Unilivre
22. Ópera de Arame
23. Tanguá Park
24. Tingüi Park
25. Santa Felicidade
26. Barigüi Park
27. Mercês Panoramic Tower
28. Shopping Estação/ Estação Natureza
29. Shopping Müller
30. Shopping Cristal Plaza
31. Shopping Novo Batel

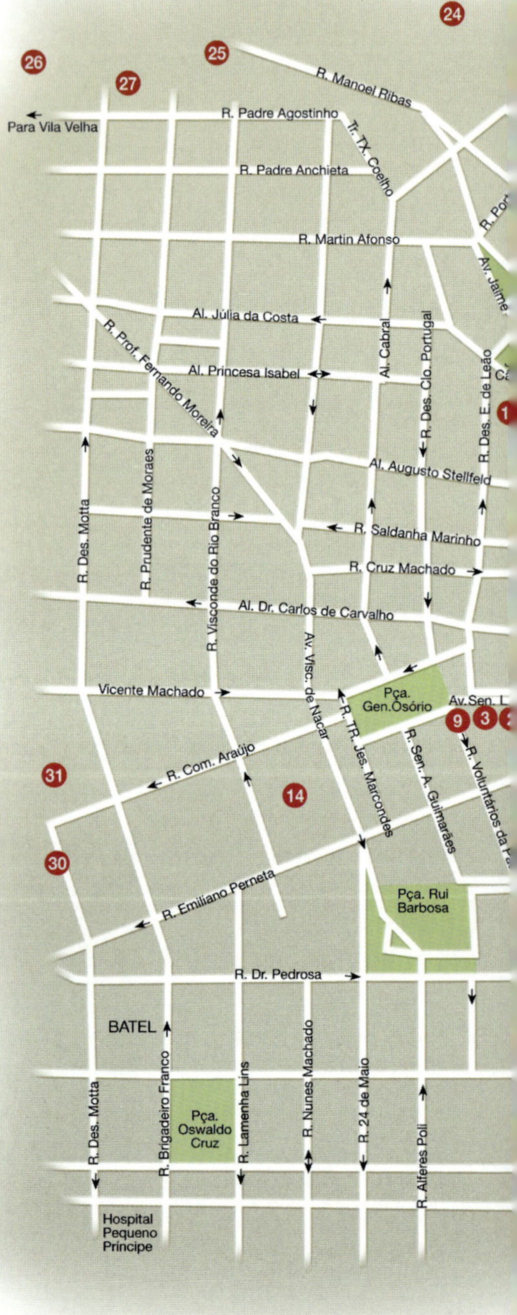

of Curitiba

Para Pilarzinho
Para Palácio do Iguaçu
R. João Manuel
R. Inácio Lustosa
R. Barão de Antonina
R. Sen. Xavier da Silva
R. Mal Hermes
R. Com. Fonseca
R. da Glória
GLÓRIA
R. Maria Clara
Alm. Barroso
R. Trajano Reis
R. Duque de Caxias
R. Mateus L
Av. Candido de Abreu
Av. João Gualberto
R. Pe. Antônio
Pça. Garibaldi
R. Paula Gomes
Pça. 19 de Dezembro
R. Heitor Stocler de França
R. Luiz Leão
R. Pres. Carlos Cavalcanti
Passeio
Av. Agostinho Leão Júnior
Largo da Ordem
R. São Francisco
Círculo Militar
R. General Carneiro
R. Pe. Camargo
R. Ubaldino do Amaral
R. 13 de Maio
Pça. Tiradentes
R. Cons. Araújo
R. Cândido Lopez
R. Pres. Faria
R. Amintas de Barros
Pça. Santos Andrade
ALTA DA XV
R. XV de Novembro
Pça. Zacarias
R. Mal. Deodoro
CENTRO
R. José Loureiro
R. Benjamin Constant
Pça. Carlos Gomes
R. Pedro Ivo
R. Com. Macedo
R. Francisco Torres
R. Dr. Favre
R. Mariano Torres
R. André de Barros
R. Nilo Cairo
Al. Mal. Floriano Peixoto
R. Lourenço Pinto
R. Barão do Rio Branco
R. Travessa da Lapa
R. João Negrão
R. Conselheiro Laurido
R. Tibagi
R. da Paz
Av. Visc. de Guarapuava
Pça. Eufrásio Corrêa
Av. 7 de Setembro
Av. Afonso Camargo
Av. Silva Jardim
Para Aeroporto e BR 376
1
4
5
6
7
8
10
11
15
16
17
18
19
20
21
22
23
28
29

Basílica Menor de Nossa Senhora da Luz Cathedral: built in 1893 in neo-Gothic style

downtown: the **Largo da Ordem**. There are important buildings such as **Casa Vermelha** (red house), dating from 1891, that sells books; **Casa Romário Martins** (dating from the 18th century and standing today as the only construction reminiscent of Portuguese-Brazilian architecture in the city), today a site for exhibitions; and **Igreja da Ordem**, the oldest church in town (1737), next to the **Sacred Art Museum**. Right in the middle of the square, a drinking fountain for animals is what was left from the time that cowboys and farmers stopped there. Nearby, facing each other, are the **Rosário Church** and a **Presbyterian Church**, and also **Solar do Rosário**, a small gallery that houses an antique shop, bookstore, an art school and a pleasant café. A few meters ahead, at the Garibaldi Plaza, see the **Relógio das Flores** (flower clock), 8 mm in diameter, surrounded by old houses turned into bars, stores and antique shops. A little farther up stand the **São Francisco Ruins**, with the remains of a church that was never finished. Going back to the old drinking fountain, just down from the Presbyterian Church, is the **City Memorial**, where exhibitions, theater plays and musicals are held. The area is especially colorful on Sunday mornings, with the traditional **art fair**.

15 de Novembro Street

It´s the main commercial street in the city and the first in Brazil to become a pedestrianized zone. Start by the **Guaíra Theater**, and cross **Santos Andrade Plaza** to the building that houses the **Universidade Federal do Paraná**, with its neoclassical lines. Inside it, the **Musa** (art museum) opens Monday through Friday, from 9 am to 6 pm and Saturday, from 9 am to 1 pm. No cars can go beyond this point. 15 de Novembro Street, more popularly known as Rua das Flores (flower street), has many buildings dating from the end of the 19th century and beginning of the 20th century. Most of the façades were restored and some stores have true relics, such as the old "**Louvre**, o Rei das Sedas," one of the most traditional stores at the time (today Lojas Marisa), with its 1913 art nouveau façade. Inside the store, see the magnificent French glass window behind the staircase. A little farther ahead, at the corner, check the Portuguese tiles of this 1883 building where the **Itaú Bank** is today. From Barão do Rio Branco Street, go to **Generoso Marques Plaza**. It has some of the most beautiful constructions in downtown Curitiba. A highlight is the sumptuous art nouveau building of the old **Paranaense Museum**. Back to 15 de Novembro, find a streetcar. If it´s a Saturday morning, you´ll see lots of children drawing and painting on paper spread all over the ground (see Kids barricade). At the corner, behind it, is

Kids barricade

In 1971, Curitiba was the first city in Brazil to have an all-exclusive pedestrian street. However, at the time, local store owners weren´t fond of the idea, because their clients wouldn´t be able to park their cars right in front of the stores anymore, like they used to. The Mayor heard about the discontentment and decided to implement the new system over a weekend, to prevent a legal attachment. Store owners tried to organize a motorcade in front of the street, in retaliation, but, to their surprise, when they got there throngs of small children from public schools in the neighborhood were drawing and painting on paper spread all over the ground, right in front of the stores. No one dared take them away, and the pedestrian street remained. It has become a tradition, and up to now, every Saturday morning you can see lots of children on 15 de Novembro Street drawing, painting and having a lot of fun.

Saturday is play day

the **Palácio Avenida**, today HSBC Bank, which was once one of the most luxurious theater houses in Latin America. In December, the building is decorated for Christmas and every night a choir sings from the windows to a crowd out in front. Opposite the building, there´s a small street where cars are allowed, and which is known as "the smallest avenue in the world," officially called Luís Xavier Street. Exactly at this point, you´ll come across the **Boca Maldita** (evil mouth), an institution in town. "See no evil, hear no evil, say no evil" is the motto of this free forum, created in 1957 and formed only by men, who are said to have been responsible for ousting governor Haroldo Leon Peres, in the 1970´s. Stop by **Café da Boca** and watch the old folks reunited in small gatherings. A little farther ahead, before Osório Plaza, is the 8-floor **Garcez Building**, built in 1929 (the first "skyscraper" in Curitiba). The most interesting thing about it are its art deco architecture and the details of its trims, fences and railings, with stylized piñons (edible pine seeds), according to the Paraná architectural movement in vogue at the time. (Read more in Novo Museu)

Sacred Art Museum in the historic sector

24-hour Street

Between Visconde de Nácar and Visconde do Rio Branco streets, downtown.
225-1732

Built in 1991, in order to revitalize downtown, making it a safe place any time of day or night, with all kinds of services. Today, not all the stores are open 24 hours, but there´s always a bar open in the middle of the night. Main services include newsstands, art shops, cafés, bars, tourist information center, free Internet access, ATM and a police unit.

★ Paiol Theater

Chile Street, Prado Velho.
322-1525

An old gun powder storehouse dating

from 1906 was rebuilt and made into an arena theater in 1971. It represented, for a long time, a nucleus of cultural resistance in the city. The entrance walls display pictures of the grand opening (Vinícius de Moraes, Toquinho, Marília Medalha and Trio Mocotó were present) and of more recent presentations. There are also posters with shows by artists Nara Leão, João Gilberto, Elis Regina, Dorival Caymmi and many others. The theater´s circular shape, like in Roman constructions, offers perfect acoustics.

★ Botanical Garden

Engenheiro Ostoja Roguski Street, Jardim Botânico.
☎ 362-1800
Open daily, from 6:00 am to 8:00 pm
This large garden is Curitiba´s postcard, resembling its traditional French counterparts, bearing well-trimmed bushes and trees. In the many footpaths that crisscross the garden, you´ll see peach trees and pine trees. There´s a good jogging trail around the garden. The hot house, emulating the English crystal palaces, is the most photographed construction in town – on weekends, brides line up before it. At sunset, the view is even more stunning. Near the hot house there´s a museum that houses an herbarium where flora species from all over the world are studied.

Passeio Público

Luiz Leão Street, Downtown.
Open Tuesday through Sunday, from 6:00 am to 7:00 pm
It used to be an important meeting place of the elite in the decades right after its construction, in 1886. Today it houses a mini-zoo with several kinds of birds, snakes and fish. The main gate is a copy of one that existed at the Dog Graveyard, in Paris.

Bosque João Paulo II

Wellington Oliveira Vianna Street,

Curitiba´s vampire

Trevisan: privacy

Seen and heard by few. Dalton Trevisan, an important Brazilian writer who was born in Paraná, makes it a point to avoid contact with the media, and thus was nicknamed Curitiba´s Vampire. In fact, that´s the title of one of his books that tells the story of a lonely and unhappy young man from Curitiba, who goes out at night in search of pleasure. Trevisan´s characteristic is the short, telegraph-like text, and he builds his stories around themes such as social conventions, aristocracy and traditionalism. He lives in Curitiba, but is not an enthusiast of its modernisms; he says in one of his texts: "Man, what happened to my town/in the other one no houses no cars/no people/oh Lord no boring people," and, in the end: "Curitiba is just a whistle made by sticking two fingers in the mouth/ Curitiba was and is not anymore."

Centro Cívico. 350-8375
Open daily, from 6:00 am to 8:00 pm
The park houses the Polish Immigration Memorial and is known as The Pope´s Grove, in honor of the Pope, who visited the city a year before its opening. It´s formed by seven typical Polish houses, with a stage for presentations. The houses were built with logs that fit perfectly into one another, without the use of nails or any other resources and were originally assembled in a Polish colony near the city and later transported to the park.

★ Novo Museu

Marechal Hermes Street, 999, Centro Cívico. 254-6633 – www.novomuseu.org. Open Tuesday through Sunday, from 1:00 to 6:30 pm
It´s the newest and most daring construction in town. The museum was opened in December 2002, and bears the unique architectural style of its creator, architect Oscar Niemeyer. A giant suspended "eye" is the most visible spot of the building, with an illuminated roof. Behind the "eye" stands the Castelo Branco Building, also an exhibition space, and also designed by Niemeyer. Originally, the project was intended to be the government headquarters of an African country. As negotiations failed, Paraná State bought the project and, for many years, the building was home to several State agencies. The museum´s collection displays many important works by Paraná´s local artists and some foreign artists, as well, such as Alfredo Andersen, Theodoro de Bona, Guido Viaro, Miguel Bakun, Erbo Stenzel, João Turim, Frederico Lange de Morretes and Poty Lazzarotto. Some were the founders of a movement known as "paranismo," searching to praise a national cultural identity. Outside of the museum there are sculpture exhibitions.

Bosque e Memorial Alemão

Niccolo Paganini Street, Jardim Schaffer. 338-6835
Open daily from 6:00 am to 8:00 pm
The park has the coziest green area in town. At one of the entrances, there´s a replica of an old Presbyterian church, with neo-Gothic elements. Inside it is the Bach Oratorium, a concert hall that seats 150 people. Nearby, there´s a bridge that leads to an observatory, which affords a fine view over the city and the Serra do Mar in the background. Then go down a semicircular stair to a gravel trail. The trail will particularly appeal to children, because there are signs telling the story of **Hansel and Gretel**. There´s also the **Witch´s Cabin**, a library with children´s books (open daily from 9 am to 5 pm). On weekends, storybook characters tell stories during Story Time (11 am and 4 pm). At the other entrance, there´s a typical German building.

★ Universidade Livre do Meio Ambiente

Victor Benato Street, Pilarzinho 254-5548 – www.unilivre.org.br
Open daily, from 8 am to 6 pm
Built in an area where there used to be a

◀ The hot house: English style

stone quarry, today the Unilivre University is a study center for the environment and ecology. At the opening, in 1992, oceanographer Jacques Cousteau was present. At the entrance, a catwalk over the water and surrounded by native forest takes visitors to the wooden headquarters, with a ramp leading to a 25-meter observatory. In one of the rooms, check an interactive exhibition with panels, multi-media and light beams inspired by the book *Invisible Cities*, by Italian author Italo Calvino. From Monday through Friday, from 9 am to 12 noon and 2 pm to 5 pm; Saturday, Sunday and holidays, from 10 am to 12 noon and 2 pm to 5 pm.

★ Ópera de Arame

João Gava Street, Pilarzinho
354-2662. Open Tuesday through Sunday, from 8:30 am to 10:00 pm

One of the most famous sights in the city, it is used as a theater, seating 1,648 people. It was built in the hole of an old stone quarry, with a tube-like iron structure and walls made of temperate glass and fiberglass, like the old Paris Opera. From there you can see **Paulo Leminski stone quarry**, currently a giant open-air amphitheater.

★ Tanguá Park

Dr. Bemben Street, Pilarzinho

Built on the site of a stone quarry. It has several entrances and two very well-defined areas. From a plateau, on the edge of the stone quarry, flows a cascade from where an immense green area and a lake can be seen. An excavated tunnel in the rocks leads visitors to an observatory. There´s a bicycle track, a jogging trail, sports courts and snack bars.

Estação Natureza

Located at Shopping Estação,
232-8091. Tue-Fri, from 2 pm to 5:30 pm; Saturday and Sunday, from 3 pm to 6:30 pm

The Amazon Forest or the flora and fauna from Pantanal (swamplands) and from other regions can be seen in detail in this space created by Fundação O Boticário, in 1999, to awaken the population to the need to preserve nature. Besides giving the impression

◀ **Novo Museu: unique style of Niemeyer**

you´re on a trip across the country, the place has interactive games and other activities related to the environment.

Tingüi Park

Access through Fredolin Wolf Street, São João ☎ 336-8467 Open Tuesday through Sunday, from 2:30 pm to 6 pm. Memorial (Tuesday through Sunday, from 9 am to 6 pm) and art shops.

The park was designed to honor the Indians that inhabited the city, but the main attraction is the Ucranian Memorial, represented by a replica of an Orthodox church with its circular shape. Built with logs, it has a 21-meter high dome. In its interior, pictures and embroidery tell the history of immigration and culture and also the ancient art of the *pêssanki* – eggs painted in millimetrical perfection (learn more about Ucranian immigration in Prudentópolis).

Santa Felicidade

This is the gastronomic neighborhood. Curitiba boasts scores of traditional restaurants, and much of its fame is due to the Santa Felicidade district. It started in 1878 with the arrival of the Italians from the regions of Veneto and Trentino who didn´t adapt to the heat of the coast. The neighborhood was named after a lady, called Felicidade, who lived there and donated land to recently-arrived immigrants. At the time, wine production was extensive in the region, and currently, Festa da Uva (Grape Festival) gathers many descendants of these first immigrants. Check out the traditional **Vinicola Durigan** (vinhosdurigan.com.br), on Manoel Ribas Avenue, belonging to an Italian family who came to the district in 1845. But it is gastronomy that plays a major role in the area, having **Madalosso** as its exponent, considered to be the world´s second largest restaurant, for over 4,000 people. On an as-much-as-you-can-eat basis, there´s a lot of chicken, Italian porridge, risottos, radicci, mayonnaise salad and several types of pasta.

The first restaurant to open in the region was Cascatinha. Other eating places in the neighborhood serve barbecue, seafood and French food.

24-hour street: bars are always open

São Lourenço Park: lake, jogging trails, paddleboats and footpaths

Barigüi Park

Take BR-277, heading towards Ponta Grossa or Candido Hartmann Avenue, Bigorrilho. 335-2112

It´s the locals´ favorite venue, and also the largest park, boasting long jogging trails, bicycle tracks, a theme park, sports courts, paddleboats and footpaths that crisscross a dense forest. Don´t be surprised if, in the middle of the lake, you see an alligator, taken there as a baby. Round the tour off with a sweet drink, called "leite de jacaré" (alligator milk), at the bar near the chimney of an old factory, inside the park. In front of the park there´s an Automobile Museum.

★ Mercês Panoramic Tower

R. Prof. Lycio Grein de Castro Vellozo, 191, Mercês. 352-4021.Open Tuesday through Friday, from 12:30 pm to 8:30 pm; Saturday and Sunday, from 10:30 am to 8:30 pm.

The 109-meter-high telephone tower affords a fine view over the city and the immense green area that surrounds it, and you realize why Curitiba is regarded as the ecological capital of Brazil. There´s a panel by Poty Lazzarotto that tells the history of the city and of the telephone system in the State.

SURROUNDINGS

★ Curitiba – Paranaguá railway

Rodoferroviária. Av. Pres. Affonso Camargo, 330, 323-4007, serraverdeexpress.com.Br

Daily, from December to Carnaval and in July. From Thursday through Sunday, from April to June and August to November.

It´s one of the most recommended outings. The train travels along one of the best-preserved regions of the Rainforest in the South. Built between 1880 and 1885, the construction covers 110 kilometers of trails, has 13 hand-chiseled tunnels, 30 metallic bridges – one of them, the 113-kilometer **São João**, is 58 meters high.

Along the way, don´t miss the **Ipiranga Reservoir**, the **Véu de Noiva Falls**, the **Cadeado Sanctuary** and the **Carvalho Viaduct**. The train makes a stop at Marumbi, for those

The Jesuits´ Cave is the largest in Campinhos

The train runs along one of the best-preserved areas of the Rainforest in the South

who wish to go mountain climbing. On weekends and holidays, there´s a more comfortable car, called Litorina, that stops along the way (learn more about it in Morretes, Paranaguá and Ilha do Mel).

Campinhos State Park

63 kilometers from Curitiba. Take BR-476, Estrada da Ribeira, Distrito de Tunas do Paraná. Visits are allowed with local guides. Tuesdays through Sundays, from 8:00 am to 5:00 pm.

For cave buffs, Campinhos is the right place to go. It covers an area of 2 square kilometers, and has a calcarean cave complex called Conjunto dos Jesuítas (Jesuits Complex). On the whole, there are four caves: **Gruta das Fadas** (Fairy Cave), **Portal Encantado** (Enchanted Gate), **Abismo das Fadas** (Fairy Abyss) and the **Gruta dos Jesuítas** (Jesuits´ Cave), the largest. The trail has parts through the Rainforest and a large variety of trees, several kinds of flowers and ferns.

TIPS

- Batel is the neighborhood where nightlife sparks in Curitiba, with bars, restaurants and trendy nightclubs.
- It´s easy to drive around town, because streets have lots of traffic signs. Signs with attractions are painted brown.
- If you are in Curitiba, try and take the train and go down Serra da Graciosa to Paranaguá and from there take a boat to Ilha do Mel; or make a stopover in Morretes to eat *barreado* and from there go back through the winding Graciosa Road. Adventurers should go up the Marumbi Complex (more information in the chapters Morretes, Mel Island and Paranaguá).

Castro

The Guartelá Canyon: Castro's main attraction is 32 kilometers long

Curitiba 150 km
Tibagi 62 km
Ponta Grossa 45 km
63,546
42
castrotur.com.br

Located in a prairie region, Castro is intrinsically linked to the cowboys´route. The city boasts a small but rather well-preserved architectural heritage. Most of the constructions, near Matriz de Sant´Ana Church, were built by slaves and bear either a colonial style or a mixture of various styles. Near the city, Castrolanda district is a Dutch colony and stands as one of the most prosperous agricultural co-ops in the South, which can be observed by the extensive plantations that dot the landscape. Nearby, the Guartelá Canyon and the city of Tibagi are two spots worth visiting.

★ Tropeiro Museum

11 Getúlio Vargas Plaza, historic downtown. Tuesday through Sunday, from 9 am to 11:30 am.

In the stucco house, an important collection of cowboys´time are among the most comprehensive in the country. There are theme halls that display attire, artifacts, furniture and tools used by the cowboys. Among the many items, there are precision scales, used to trade goods. In the room Witness of an Era, a

The origin of the cowboys´ routes

It was the beginning of the 18th century and the country had its eyes set on the wealthy gold mines and precious metals mines recently found in the Minas Gerais region. Access to the mines was difficult and miners had problems taking their goods across the country because of the trails, which were very bad. The solution found by them was to bring from Rio Grande do Sul thousands of mules that were out in the open fields. The trading route started at the city of Viamão (Rio Grande do Sul) and headed to the Sorocaba trade market (São Paulo), a commercial center for mules and also the main link with the South. Thus was born one of the most important movements that united Rio Grande do Sul to the rest of Brazil, making colonization possible. Castro, in Paraná, played a very important role in this route, since the Iapó River usually flooded, forcing cowboys to stop along the way. As the region was rich in pastures, it was also the place where the cattle was able to rest and gain weight to resume the long and tiring journey.

A museum tells the story of the trading route

Debret painting and chains are reminders of slave work, very much used by the cowboys. Religion is represented by sacred images and standards found in churches.

SURROUNDINGS

Castrolanda

Access through Coronel Olegário de Macedo Street, km 15.
castrolanda.com.br

When World War II came to an end, whole communities of affected countries decided to try their luck in Brazil. In 1951, with the help of Paraná State, a community from Holland settled in the region in order to develop agriculture. Today, Castrolanda, the city that emerged from this initiative, is one of the most well-succeeded co-ops in the agricultural sector in the South. For the visitor, the sights include long roads having corn, potato and wheat plantations, but also a Dutch windmill that houses the **Immigration Memorial** (Friday through Sunday and holidays, from 2 pm to 6 pm, 234-1231). It´s 37 meters high and its vanes span 26 meters. Nearby, be sure to visit the **Casa do Imigrante** (Fridays, from 2 pm to 5 pm), a replica of a typical farmhouse in Holland.

◀ **Immigration Memorial: a Dutch windmill**

Capão Alto Farm

Access through Castrolanda, km 17.
Tuesday through Friday, from 1 pm to 6 pm; Saturday, Sunday and holidays, from 8 am to 6 pm.

The ample and empty rooms of this farmhouse take visitors on a time travel. To a time well before its construction, in the beginning of the 18th century, when the region was just a resting place for cowboys, on the banks of the Iapó River, a time when the itinerary was defined by the course of the rivers. The Capão Alto farm was first ruled by Carmelite priests and later was also under slave domain for 100 years. In 1877 a colonel took possession of the land and had a sumptuous manor house built, almost exclusively with mud and wood, resembling coffee barons´ homes of the time. Frequent guests included all the aristocracy from Castro, who enjoyed the very complete library, boasting over 6,000 titles. The porcelain wash basins were brought from Portugal, but today the only thing that still remains in the house is the Nossa Senhora do Carmo altar, as well as the walls and the good memories of a wealthy era.

The trail at the Guartelá Park goes along waterfalls and natural pools

Salto do Rio Cotia

Castro-Tibagi Road, PR-340, km 20 and another 7 kilometers on a secondary road. Information on rappel, ☎ 232-2091.

The waterfall is formed by three 52-meter-high falls. The Cotia River is an affluent of the Iapó River, and very much sought-for by rappel aficionados.

★ Guartelá State Park

Castro-Tibagi Road, PR-340, km 40. Wednesday through Sunday, from 8:00 am to 5:00 pm.

Located between the cities of Castro and Tibagi, the almost 8 km² Guartelá Park is home to a 32-kilometer spetacular canyon, with walls reaching up to 200 meters high. It´s the sixth longest canyon in the world and it´s surrounded by a unique ecosystem: there are ferns typical of the Rainforest and marshes and trees that resemble the ones found in the bush country. The park is also home to rare species of birds, in addition to swallows and some falcon species. Before adventuring yourself into the region, you should go to the Visitors Center to fill out a form and get more information from guides. Cars are not allowed from this point on and all you have to do is follow the signs. The trail follows the Pedregulho stream along most of the way. A classical stopover for a good

Guarda-te lá!

There are several versions about the origin of the name Guartelá. The most accepted version tells that a man from Tibagi (a neighboring city) knew that the Kaingangue Indians would take the city. He then alerted his neighbors with the sentence: "Guarda-te lá, que eu aqui bem fico" (Watch out, stay there, I'll be here!) Thus the name Guartelá was born. The ones who sustain that this is the origin even point to the place where this conversation would have taken place: in the woods, on the right bank of the Tibagi River, today known as Capão da Benfica.

swim at this point is at the **large holes** that form as you go down, with lots of water everywhere. After you have had enough, go back to the trail and find an observatory, from where you can see two huge mountain ranges having the Iapó River at both sides. Go back a little, cross a bridge and follow a trail to the 200-meter-high **Ponte de Pedra Waterfalls**. The waterfall was named Ponte de Pedra (Rock Bridge) because of the natural bridge that formed on the rock where the coming and going of the water made a hole. Then the hole formed a natural passageway and the water started flowing underneath it. The park is a paradise for those who enjoy long hikes, and some of them can take up to three days. But for those long ones, it´s mandatory to take an autorized guide along. It is not advisable to go by yourself. Allow a whole day to go to the cave, where there are over 2,000-year-old rupestrian paintings.

Tibagi

62 kilometers from Castro, PR-340

The city of Tibagi is almost hidden at the end of a 60-kilometer road full of potholes. As you can´t drive at over 40 kilometers an hour, you can enjoy all the beauty the place has to offer: cultivated stretches of land interspersed among deep valleys and winding hills, nestled in a variegated verdant setting.
The small city of Tibagi consists of just a square, a church, a diamond museum, a restaurant and a hotel, and nothing else is needed. There´s also a river, two blocks down the square, where a stairway leads to the water. The sunset seen from the river is worth paying for, but it´s free and very few people know about it. One of the pastimes of local inhabitants is to number the natural treasures the region has to offer. Minerals were found and taken away in the 19th century. One of the diamonds found there is said to be in the crown of the English Queen, and the museum in front of the square tells that story. A few kilometers from the city there are two well-known waterfalls (**Salto Santa Rosa and Salto Puxa-Nervos)** and at least 10 others hidden in the surroundings (which you can visit with the help of a local inhabitant or guide). The place is very calm, but there are some extreme sports too: you can go rafting on the Tibagi River, rappelling on the Salto Santa Rosa or on a wall on São Damásio Farm, located right behind the Guartelá Canyon.

A museum tells the story of the diamonds

TIPS

• Near the city of Castro, there are around 20 farms that date back to cowboys´ time. The only one officially open to visitation is the Capão Alto Farm.
For more information on others that are private homes but also open to visitors who call beforehand, call the Tourism Department (☎ 232-7269).

Foz do Iguaçu

The Iguaçu Falls are formed by 275 falls that reach up to 70 meters high

Curitiba 639 km
Castro 582 km
Cascavel 141 km
258,368
45
fozdoiguaçu.pr.gov.br

The Iguaçu Falls are considered to be one of the greatest natural beauties in the world. The falls are formed by 275 falls that reach up to 70 meters high. The "big water," or Iguaçu in Tupi language, started to form around 200 million years ago, with the separation of South America and Africa. This rupture caused several geological changes in the American continent, with one of the greatest consequences being the successive basaltic spreads, which began around 110 million years ago. The several layers of lava can still be observed in the falls. This land was exposed to the erosion of rivers, thus forming the Iguaçu falls. Situated in the heart of the Prata River Basin, comprising the Paraná, Paraguay and Uruguay rivers, the Iguaçu National Park is one of the most important protected areas in the region, together with the Iguazú National Park, in Argentina. In 1986, the park was declared a Natural Landmark for all Humanity by UNESCO. The place is nicer in Spring, from October to December, when trees bloom and the temperature is around 23 ºC. The volume of the water in the Falls is larger, reaching 6,500 m³ per second. In Summer, excessive heat is intertwined by quick rainfalls. Today, the place boasts a model infrastructure, with tourist buses and cars parked outside of the park. Everyone is invited to board an exclusive bus with an acrylic roof that affords a beautiful view of the whole park. A recorded tape gives instructions on all the attractions of the three stops.
Other interesting attractions nearby include the Parque das Aves (Birds Park) and the Itaipu Hydroelectric Plant. As it is in a border region, visit also the Iguazú National Park, on the Argentine side, and Ciudad del Este, where small merchants go in search of cheaper electronic products.

Visitors Center, the beginning of the trip ▶

The volume of the water reaches 6.500 m³ per second ▶▶

★ Cataratas do Iguaçu

Rodovia das Cataratas, km 16 ☎ 529-8383, www.cataratasdoiguacu.com.br. Daily, from 8 am to 5 pm; Monday, from 1 pm.

The falls are on the border of Brazil and Argentina. The bus leaves the Visitors Center and stops in the beginning of the trail leading to the falls. Watch the coatis, at ease with the human presence (note that it´s forbidden to feed the animals), and the impressive number of butterflies. Through a 1.2-kilometer catwalk, the waterfalls, slowly revealing themselves, cause awe and admiration. This is true mainly when the catwalk advances into the river and the visitor is face to face with a water whirlpool. Be prepared to get wet. This section is known as Garganta do Diabo (Devil´s throat). From here, you´ll have to go up the stairs or catch an elevator to reach **Porto Canoas**, with a restaurant, bar, bathrooms, a theme store and a large grassland area to rest near the river. At the park entrance, it´s possible to hire a scenic helicopter flight over the falls. ☎ 529-7474, www.helisul.com).

★ Macuco Safari

☎ 523-6475, www.macucosafari.com.br. Leaving every 10 minutes, tours take 1h45 and the boat seats 25 people. Admission: for children under 6, free; for children from 7 to 12, half

Old fame

The first inhabitants to the region were the Guarani Indians. And the first European to arrive at the waterfalls was Spanish captain Nuñez Cabeza de Vaca, in 1542. He named it Santa Maria Waterfalls. In the years that followed, the Jesuitic missions came to the region. But later, with the arrival of the São Paulo trailblazers, the missions were attacked and the Indians were killed.In 1888, the west of Paraná received a more intense migratory wave, which was responsible for the extraction of wood and matte production in the region. At that time, the waterfalls were already famed for their natural beauty, luring many illustrious visitors, such as aviator Santos Dumont, who visited the region in 1916. It was then that proposals were made in order to establish a conservation unit there. At the time, the international tendency was to create conservationist areas, and Brazil followed suit, by creating the Iguaçu National Park in 1939. Up until the 1940s, the region had very few inhabitants, thus preserving the ecosystem. The Iguaçu was the first Brazilian national park to have services outsourced.

the ticket fare. Open daily, from 8 am to 5 pm; Monday, from 1 pm to 5 pm.

This is the first stop for the buses leaving the Visitors Center. There, visitors will board an electric vehicle through native jungle. The route is accompanied by guides who show the several flora species, such as the palmetto, the queenpalm, the fig tree, the cinnamon tree, bromeliads and orchids. From a given spot on, you have to go on foot through an easy footpath in the middle of the jungle. It goes through a small 25-meter-high fall, the Salto do Macuco, before reaching a deck from where boats take visitors to the base of the main falls. This is a stunning view of the falls. Be prepared to get wet when the boat gets near them.

Parque das Aves

Located 500 meters from the falls. 529-7474, www.parquedas aves.com.br. Open daily, from 8:30 am to 5:30 pm.

In this park, most of the bird species are not confined, unlike in most zoos. Birds fly freely and aren´t afraid of people. In all, there are 170 square meters of native forest that are home to some 900 tropical birds from 150 species from several continents. There are species from the Pantanal as herons, wood rails, European teals and agouaras. It´s possible to see cardinal birds, toucans, canaries, mockingbirds, cockatoos, parrots, ostriches and many other birds. At the end of the trail, you´ll come across a butterfly cage, with at least 30 species of butterflies.

SURROUNDINGS

Itaipu

Located 12 kilometers from Foz downtown. Access through Tancredo Neves Avenue, km 6. 520-5252

Open Monday through Saturday, from 8:00 am to 3:30 pm

This is one of the largest hydroelectric plants in the world and comprises a dam 8 kilometers long by 167 meters high. There are three visits to choose from: the tourist, the special and the technical one. The simplest is the first. All you have to do is get there at the right time (8 am, 9 am, 10 am, 2 pm, 3 pm or 3:30 pm) and join a group. Visits take an hour and a half and they include a documentary on the construction of

Itaipu is one of the largest hydroeletric plants in the world

Boats take 25 visitors at each time past Salto do Macuco, to the base of the waterfalls

the hydroelectric, a visit to the outside area of the plant and you can still see the open floodgates of the Main Spillway. The special visit requires an appointed time (☎ 520-6985), and the groups are of up to 12 people. It takes visitors to the interior of the dam, to the computer rooms, the turbines and the cliffs. It takes 2 hours. The technical visit, for engineers and researchers, includes the same route of the special visit, plus the axis of the main turbine, and takes 2 and a half hours.

Iguazú National Park (Argentina)

Buses leave Victoria Aguirre Ave., in Puerto Iguazú, towards the park. Open daily, from 9:00 am to 6:00 pm

In Argentina, the Parque Nacional del Iguazú borders on the Brazilian park. On the left bank of the Iguaçu River, the so-called "mata missionera" – the equivalent to the Rainfall – has a rich flora and fauna. In the park, there are trails and catwalks – the biggest being 3 kilometers long. On this side of the falls, it´s possible to have a view over the falls and get close to the Garganta do Diabo Falls.

TIPS

- Take a raincoat or rent one at the entrance if you don´t want to get wet on the catwalks or on the boat.
- If you wish to go shopping in Ciudad del Este, in Paraguay, it´s advisable to take a regular bus, because there are many robberies in the area.
- In Puerto Iguazú, near the customs building, there s a free shop with tax-free products and a little farther ahead, a casino. There are many stores that sell leather jackets downtown.

Birds such as the toucan are seen at the park

Guaraqueçaba

Superagüi National Park: Guaraqueçaba is the starting point

Superagüi 50 minutes (boat)
Paranaguá 3 h (boat)
41
482-1262

Guaraqueçaba is the starting point to get to know one of the most isolated regions of the well-preserved Rainforest in the South of the country. There are so many spots of green area that the region has many different conservation units created to protect its beauties: an APA (Permanent Protection Area), an RPPN (Private Natural Landmark Region) and even a national park, the Superagüi.
Bordering on São Paulo, the region is part of the Lake Estuary Complex of Iguape-Cananéia-Paranaguá, or just Lagamar. The meeting of the waters of the rivers and the sea forms

beautiful lagoon among islands and mangroves. The forest of the region is preserved today, but was very much exploited in the past. It´s a great option for those who like hikes, waterfalls, natural pools and a lot of wild nature.
Take BR-277 towards Paranaguá and follow the signs to Morretes and Antonina. Before reaching Antonina, take PR-440 and, upon arriving at Cacatu, it´s another 80 kilometers that takes 3 hours because the road is in bad condition. From Paranaguá, there are boats that cover the distance in the same amount of time, with a stopover at Ilha das Peças (☎ 482-1262). Having a Tupi origin, the name of the city means "guará land," a red bird that was abundantly found in the region, but became almost extinct because of hunters. Practically isolated, the city seems to have stopped in time, in spite of having had its heyday with the abundant production of fish and banana, in the beginning of the 20th century. Today Guaraqueçaba is home to the most well-preserved region of the Rainforest in the State of Paraná. To have a good idea of the majestic green area that surrounds it, look for the **Bom Jesus dos Perdões** Church as soon as you get to this small town. Behind the church there´s a water reservoir from where a trail leaves, on the right side, and leads to the **Quitumbê Mountain**. The 20-minute hike is in the shade and from the top you can see the sea, the innumerable channels that meander through the mangroves, the Salto Morato waterfall and the sinuous vegetation-covered mountains.

Capuchin monkeys: threatened with extinction

★ Superagüi National Park

Access through chartered motorboats in Guaraqueçaba (🕒 50 minutes). In January and February, a boat leaves Paranaguá (🕒 3h) on Saturday and returns on Sunday. ☎ 482-1262

The history of Superagüi can be traced back to the time the first European immigrants arrived in Paraná, in 1852. The Swiss William Michaud is, for the most part, responsible for the preservation of the region. As a great naturalist in Superagüi, he portrayed the island in a bucolic way and expressed his wish to have it kept like that. Turned into national parks in 1989, the Superagüi, the Peças, the Pinheiro and the Pinheirinho islands, besides the Patos River Basin, make up a total of 33,988 hectares. The Islands are also home to two species threatened with extinction: the *papagaio chauá* (the red-browed parrot) and the *mico-leão-da-cara-preta* (the black-faced lion tamarin). Most visitors prefer the Superagüi, an artificial island created in 1953 with the opening of the Varadouro Channel to border on São Paulo, and thus boost commerce in the region. For those who come to the park, the entrance is at the Superagüi Barra. There you can find the biggest

◀ Guaraqueçaba Bay: a preserved area

The Superagüi village: the largest village on the island has some inns near the beaches

village on the island and also some inns. You can hike through the only trail on the island that is open to visitors, going from the small village to **Deserta Beach**. During almost one hour, visitors can observe the native vegetation, such as moss, and the river that acquires a reddish tone because of the mangrove swamp, synonymous with fish nursery and subsistence for the locals – fishing is a strong trait in the region. Deserta Beach has a 37-kilometer stretch of sand to the Barra do Ararapira, on the border of Cardoso Island, in the State of São Paulo. You can either hike or go by bike and camp along the way. Between the months of August and November, some migrating birds such as long-billed terns use the beach as a resting place.

The boats that take visitors for one-day outings to Superagüi, when returning to Guaraqueçaba, make a stopover on Pinheiro Island, where, at around 5 o´clock in the evening, there´s the flight of thousands of red-browed parrots that return to the island to sleep.

★ Salto Morato Natural Preserve

20 kilometers from Guaraqueçaba along a road full of potholes.
482-1506/ 978-2140, fundacaoboticario.org.br Visits from Guaraqueçaba for those who aren´t driving. From Tuesday through Sunday, from 8:30 am to 6 pm.

In 1994, the O Boticário de Proteção à Natureza Foundation created the preserve in a 23 square kilometers area to protect this section of the Rainforest. Visitors are greeted at the entrance of the park and then taken to the Visitors Information Center, where the ecosystem is shown in detail, through videos, talks and panels. A model of the terrain around the Guaraqueçaba region gives visitors an idea of the size of the area. From there on, there are two options to visit the park: the first is a mild hike, to **Salto Morato** waterfall. A large portion of the hike is along the river that flows down to the waterfall. You should stop by the **Aquarium**, a huge clear natural pool, formed by a curve in the river, and where you can dive in the company of an incredible variety of fish. As you approach Salto Morato, vegetation gets denser and the volume of the water along the trail gets

Orchids bloom in the park ▶

The fig tree ▶ has roots over the river

larger. That´s where you´ll come across the 130-meter waterfall, a true invitation to contemplation. The other option is a guided tour that takes visitors to an old fig tree. The tree, on the riverbank, has large roots that cross to the other side of the river, forming a natural bridge – a perfect ecosystem for the growth of several species of bromeliads, orchids and other regional plants. If you want to visit both places, you should get there really early in the morning. The park has excellent camping facilities.

Sebuí Ecological Preserve

Access on a speedboat from Guaraqueçaba. 7 hours. Info.: Pousada Chauá, 482-1265. Only guided tours.

The trip on a speedboat is worth the visit. It goes through many river villages, where you can see a great variety of birds. But the best part is the five waterfalls that are formed on the Sebuí River.
To reach the first waterfall, you´ll have to walk an hour and a half on an easy trail along the course of the river. The trails taking to the other waterfalls are more slippery and difficult because the forest becomes denser. But the first waterfall is already worth the visit, because there you can swim in a refreshing well.

Salto Morato: a 130-meter waterfall

TIPS

• You´ll need at least 3 days to get to know the region and calmly appreciate all the attractions.
• Don´t miss the Bronze mountain (4 natural observatories with a view of Guaraqueçaba, Superagüi, Ilha do Mel and the border on Cardoso Island) and the Tromomó mountain (with caves and huge stone blocks on the top of the mountain). Hire a guide at Pousada Chauá, 482-1265.
• To go to Superagüi and Sebuí, try to form a group of at least 4 people to share the cost of the boat.

Ilha do Mel

The small island on Paranaguá Bay became an ecological preservation area

Pontal do Sul 30 minutes (boat)
Paranaguá 1h45 (boat)
41
www.ilhadomelonline.com
Paranaguá District

It´s one of the most sought-for outings in Paraná. The island offers a combination of wild nature and desert beaches – a rarity on the Brazilian coast, especially in the South. In order to reinforce the idea of deserted place, a lighthouse stands on one of the mountains and cars are not allowed. To go from one side to the other, you have to walk on sandy trails sided by native vegetation and it gets really dark at night – make sure you bring a lantern. But the urban areas have plenty of inns, camp sites and restaurants. And almost every night there´s a party in a bar. Walking past these hubs brings back the sensation of being on a desert island. In 1992, around 95% of the 27 square kilometers of Rainforest, mangroves and rocks on the island became part of the Ecological Station and, in 2000, the place was declared a World Historical site by Unesco.

There are two ways to reach the island. From Pontal do Sul (455-1144) the trip takes 30 minutes, and from Paranaguá (422-6882) one hour and a half. A good option is to go down the Serra da Graciosa by train to Paranaguá, visit the historic downtown and from

Conchas Lighthouse: the best view of the inlet

there on, take a boat to the island. To return, take a boat to Pontal, which is faster, and from there a bus to Curitiba. From Paranaguá, there are more buses going to Curitiba (the two sections along BR-277 to Curitiba are the same in distance). There are parking lots near the trapiche in Pontal do Sul. From the continent, the boats leave to two different places on the island: Nova Brasília (same bus stop for those going to the lighthouse or to the fort) and Encantadas. The island is divided into two well-defined portions, and you can observe the sea bater on both sides from a sand stripe. Researchers fear that erosion might break the island into two, because in the past the sand section was completely under water.

★ Nova Brasília and Farol das Conchas

The section that comprises both places is where most of the small hotel are concentrated. Boats arrive in Nova Brasília and on the right

The Fort´s cannons were used only once, against an English ship

The Cormorant episode

Nossa Senhora dos Prazeres Fortress was built in 1780 to defend Paranaguá Bay from an eventual attack from Spanish corsaries. However, its cannons were used only once, during the episode involving a British ship, called the Cormorant. It happened in the 19th century, when England started pressuring, and Brazil, along with some other countries who also used that kind of workforce, agreed to abolish the traffic of African slaves. Paranaguá was an important port in the South of Brazil and, despite the agreement, continued to receive clandestine slave ships. In 1845, the British Parliament passed the Aberdeen Law, according to which British ships could search and imprison slave ships at any point of the coast. In 1850, the Cormorant entered Paranaguá Bay and suspected that there was a slave ship ready to anchor. The Cormorant took the suspected ship and also sank other ships that were decked. Local inhabitants were angered at the arbitrary measure and convinced the fortress commander to open fire at the ship. One of the British sailors who was on the Cormorant died, but the ship itself resisted. Because of the sad episode, the Brazilian imperial government had to officially apologize to England. That episode made abolitionist tendencies stronger and was the base for the approval, in the same year, of the Eusébio de Queiroz Law, forbidding the traffic of slaves in Brazil.

Miguel Beach: surrounded by rocks and native vegetation ►

Conchas Lighthouse, Ilha do Mel ▶

there´s a tourist information center. The inns are near and just by looking where the people are going you can tell where the restaurants, bars, stores and the charming rustic-style art shops are located. There are many inns, and the best thing to do is to visit as many as you can and choose the best (book beforehand for New Year and Carnaval). **Farol das Conchas** is about 20 minutes from the boat house. Go up the stairway to the lighthouse and enjoy the view: the small inlet on the right, **Fora Beach**, is a favorite with surfers; on the left, **Farol das Conchas Beach** is calm, a great place to swim. On the same trail leading to the lighthouse, there are signs indicating **Grande Beach** – a deserted, long beach with high waves (access through bushes that form an interesting labyrinth).

Nossa Senhora dos Prazeres Fortress

From Nova Brasília, another 40-minute hike. You can also hire a motorboat-taxi that takes you to the fortress in 10 minutes.

This is the most isolated place on all the island. There are very few inns and all very far away from one another. The fortress that named the beach or the fort is the only 18th-century military construction in Paraná. Atop the main façade, there´s a huge shell sculpted in a stone block. Inside the fort, there´s a steep 600-meter trail leading to the top of the Baleia mountain. That´s where the cannons are, built in 1909 to protect the bay, and it´s also an observatory that affords a view of the Peças Island (read Superagüi). Going north from the fort, there´s a place called **Ponta do Hospital** (hospital place). At the time, slave ships made a stopover at this point because of the many slaves who had scurvy and lack of vitamin C. The place was perfect because of the many lemon trees and orange trees, rich in vitamin C.

Encantadas

On the southern tip of the island, there are many inns. The main attraction is

◀ Gruta Encantada: inspiration for legends

the **Gruta Encantada** (enchanted cave), formed by a huge crack in the rock, right in front of the ocean. According to legend, mermaids lived inside the cave, and lured sailors with their irresistible singing, thus making their boats sink. The top of the mountains near the cave affords an impressive view of the whole area.
On **Fora Beach**, near the cave, there´s a food court with several bars.

TIPS

• The section that separates Nova Brasília from Encantadas (◔ 4 hours) can´t be missed. It´s a beautiful road with parts including going up mountains that form natural observatories and then going back down to desert beaches. If it´s raining, be careful because the rocks become really slippery.
• You can go to the island and come back on the same day. An option is to leave Nova Brasília early in the morning and go straight to the fort (◔ 3 hours). When coming back, see the village, the lighthouse and follow the signs indicating Grande Beach and walk to Encantadas (◔ 3 hours). From there, take the boat back to Paranaguá or Pontal do Sul.
But the best thing to do is to sleep over on the island and enjoy the sights calmly.
Another good option for those looking for beauty, quiet and green areas is the Miguel Island. Surrounded by native vegetation, it can be reached on foot from Encantadas or Nova Brasília.
• There are no drugstores on the island. Bring everything you need from the continent, especially bug repellent.
• When packing, try to take as few items as you can. But if your bags are too heavy, there´s a shuttle service to the inns.

Lapa

The Casa Vermelha, currently a museum, exemplifies the architecture of Lapa

Curitiba 71 km
Paranaguá 162 km
Joinville (SC) 178 km
41,777
41
lapa.pr.gov.br

The city houses the best-preserved historic site of all the historic towns in Paraná. Streets, houses and monuments are witness to the golden age of cowboys. Historic downtown consists of 14 blocks, and staged a bloody battle in the end of the 19th century, the Federalist Revolution (see Maragatos versus Pica-paus). Hundreds of Republican soldiers died trying to resist the attack to the city, in what became known as Cerco da Lapa (the Lapa siege).

It´s very easy to see the whole town. If you are driving, park far from the old buildings façades. It´s better to walk through the small and inviting historic downtown. In every detail of the colonial façades, the scrollworks, the old lamps and the gardens permanently in bloom take us back to the past. To a time when only horses and carriages rode the narrow streets.

The Pantheon next to the Memória House

★ XV de Novembro Street and Historic Downtown

The city seems to be permanently ready for a period movie.

As if the beauty of the housing complex, carefully painted, wasn´t enough, the place is full with history. Number 67 on XV de Novembro Street, for example, known as **Casa Lacerda** (Tuesday through Sunday, from 9 am to 12 noon and 1 pm to 5 pm), was restored as a wealthy home of the time, where the Capitulação da Praça letter was

S. João Theater house: Elizabethan style ▶

signed. That was a letter from the 1894 revolutionaries to honor the heroic form the city was defended. On the other side of the street, the most important civic monument in Paraná, called the **Heroes Pantheon**, is where the mortal remains of General Carneiro and hundreds of soldiers who fought the Cerco are kept. Next to it there´s a small 1888 building, known as Casa dos Cavalinhos, that houses **Casa da Memória** (Tuesday through Sunday, from 9 am to 5 pm), a museum that documents the history of Lapa and displays old photographs and books. There are 10 winged horses sculpted on the façade of the house, and it´s said that the man who built the house won the lottery. Apparently, he had dreamed of horses the night before and, as a winner, decided to pay homage to the animal that brought him such good luck.

General Carneiro Plaza

622-1616

A meeting place for locals, the square has a bronze bust in honor of the general who defended the city in the Cerco episode. On both ends stand the theater and the church, which were used as hospital wards and even as graveyards during the Cerco. Built in the 1870´s by a local entity in charge of literary studies, the **São João Theater** (daily, from 9 am to 5 pm) is the only Elizabethan-style theater in the South. Its interior is covered with wood, including the arcades and the floor, and up to now there is an intense cultural programming. The Matriz de Santo Antônio Church was the first building

Lapa´s Siege: a museum tells the story

Maragatos versus Pica-paus

The Cerco da Lapa was a symbol of the resistance of the Republican government – led in Lapa by Cel. Antônio Ernesto Gomes Carneiro – to the advancement of the organized federalist troops in Rio Grande do Sul. The Gaúchos (from Rio Grande do Sul) were against the military government of marshal Floriano Peixoto. Also called *maragatos*, they intended to reach Rio de Janeiro to oust the government. Lapa´s Republican forces were composed of less than a thousand men, the so-called *pica-paus* (woodpeckers), who resisted bravely against an army made up of over 3 thousand soldiers. With Cel. Carneiro´s death, Lapa surrendered on the 26th day of battle. That time was enough for Floriano´s government to organize itself in São Paulo and try to stop the federalist impetus.

Gregorian chant in a Trappist pyramid

The chapel resembles a wooden pyramid and many colorful glass windows appear right in the middle of a prairie full of groves. This is the setting where a group of Trappist monks lives, in Lapa. Trappist monks represent a dissidence of Benedictine monks. This is the only nucleus of Trappist monks in Brazil. All they do, from the wee hours of the morning till evening, is to work and pray. Besides planting corn and soy, they make mouthwatering desserts: jams, cakes and delicious biscuits. But, during Corpus Christi and Christmas time, what brings hordes of faithful to the Mosteiro de Nossa Senhora do Novo Mundo chapel are the Gregorian chants. The monks have been in the country since 1977. They got permission to purchase the land in 1982 and the pyramid was built two years later.

Trappist monks say Mass with Gregorian chants

in town, and its interior displays the tombs of General Carneiro and of another revolution hero, Cândido Dulcídio.

Casa de Câmara and Jail

David Carneiro Avenue. Open daily, from 9 am to 5 pm

Currently, it´s home to the **Weapons Museum**, displaying several war-like artifacts used in the Lapa Siege and also some used by Brazilian soldiers in World War II. The ground floor, where today the exhibition halls are located, was used as a jail. The second floor, today the City Council, used to be the hearing rooms and the administration.

Monge State Park

Take Getúlio Vargas Street and go up the hill, following the signs.

This is a pilgrimage place, where the faithful light candles in honor of Priest João Maria. It´s located inside a beautiful cave where the devout João Maria is supposed to have lived. The faithful considered João Maria a miraculous saint (read The Miracle Cave next page).

TIPS

- Make sure you eat the typical cowboy dishes in the city´s

On one of the oldest stone walls in Paraná, the faith of pilgrims

restaurants: arroz de carreteiro (rice with chunks of several kinds of meat), feijão tropeiro (beans with pork cuts) and the traditional quirera lapeana (made with broken corn, accompanied by fried pork ribs, fried bacon, sausage and eggs). Quirera lapeana is a highly caloric dish that was also very energetic to sustain cowboys during the long and tough journey.

- In Historic Downtown, visit the Casa Vermelha, actually a museum displaying the attire and artifacts used by cowboys.

The miracle cave

The belief in the miracles performed by the Italian monk João Maria de Agostinis, who lived in Paraná from 1847 to 1855, takes hundreds of people to the Monge Cave, a little over 3 kilometers from Lapa, every month. The Catholic Church never acknowledged his miracles, but he´s regarded as a saint by the people who were cured or had relatives cured when they resorted to him in prayer. He was called João Maria by many people in Paraná, and he visited several cities in the State. He studied the power of herbs and was also a psychic and used to recommend natural formulas for those who coudn´t afford to buy medicines. .

People pray to the Italian priest ▶

Morretes

Historical buildings in Morretes, a city cut by the Nhudiaquara River

Curitiba 78 km
Paranaguá 35 km
Guaraqueçaba 116 km
15,273
41
462-1024
morretesturismo.com.br

It´s the main city by the Serra da Graciosa and its fame is due to the production of ginger, Brazilian *cachaça* and banana. From Curitiba, there are at least 3 ways to reach Morretes: the first two include going down Serra do Mar along the Curitiba-Paranaguá railroad or by car along the winding Graciosa Road. The third way is along BR-277, a double highway in good condition. Those coming through the Graciosa Road will reach Porto de Cima, a stopover for going down the Nhudiaquara River. When you get really hungry, remember that it´s only 8 kilometers to Morretes, where the famous clay pots are always hot, full of the typical dish *barreado*. Those who come by train will get off at the station, close to the historic downtown.

★ Serra da Graciosa

50 kilometers from Curitiba along BR-116 towards São Paulo

A colonial-style arcade stands at the entrance to Serra da Graciosa. Drivers should tackle the 28-kilometer ride slowly, for the road is winding (149 curves) and slippery on rainy days, and in many parts you can´t drive at over 20 km/h. Along the way, you´ll see many hydrangeas, bromeliads, heliconias, orchids, banana trees and native vegetation, and also places with kiosks, grills and bars that sell traditional banana candies and cachaça. At **Recanto Rio Cascata**, you can bathe in a small waterfall on hot days. At **Recanto Bela Vista**, it´s worth to go down the 500-meter trail to see the magnificent view from the top of an observatory.

Historic Downtown

The road from Porto de Cima to Morretes is completely straight in the last 5 kilometers and at the end you´ll get a glimpse of the tower of the 1765 **São Benedito Church**. The railroad cuts the asphalt a few meters before the church. Turn left and go ahead until you see a metallic bridge

Graciosa: from sidewalks to the railroad

Serra do Mar was of vital importance for the colonization of Paraná. The Indians were pioneers in opening the first trails because they had to go from the plateau to the coast in order to fish. Later on, it was the slaves who paved the same trails, on which cowboys rode mules along their steep and slippery parts, taking gold, silver, wood, tobacco, fabrics and matte to other parts of the country. That´s how the first commercial route between the prairies and the Paraná coast began. There were three possible routes along the Serra do Mar: Arraial, Itupava and Graciosa. All were paved with river pebbles and, thanks to them, the Graciosa and the Itupava trails can still be used today, in some parts. With time, a wider and paved road became necessary, and Graciosa Road was built in 1873.
It was Emperor D. Pedro II´s wish to consolidate the route from the prairies to the coast for good. The solution was to build a r ailrod linking Curitiba to the Paranaguá Port.

Graciosa Road: historical trail

on which only one car at a time can pass (On the other side are the restaurants serving *barreado*). That´s where the historic houses begin. At the **Lamenha Lins Plaza** there´s a bandstand and a little farther ahead, **Artes da Terra** shop sells art and serves coffee. Go to the **Rua das Flores** sidewalk, with more restaurants, and rent a bike to enjoy the city, located in a flat area. To the left is the **Casa Rocha Pombo** (open daily from 10 am to 4 pm), that tells the history of the city and was named after a writer from Morretes. There you can learn about the lives of important people, as painter Frederico Lange de Morretes, whose love for the city was so great that he incorporated the name of the city to his own. The stylized pine tree seeds, already a symbol of Paraná, were designed by him and are present on the downtown sidewalks. Go ahead to **Nhudiaquara River**, with tables and benches on its banks. In April the sidewalk is taken with the stands of a street market selling farming products and typical art. At the end of the street stands the 1769 **Nossa Senhora do Porto Church,** with a Way of the Cross painted by Theodoro de Bona. There are many colonial-style buildings along the way from General Carneiro Street to the church. One of them was visited by Emperor D. Pedro II.

Old houses encircle Largo Lamenha Lins

SURROUNDINGS

Porto de Cima

8 kilometers from Morretes

The district was very important in the 18th and 19th centuries – with the gold mining and the Nhudiaquara River navigation – as an important

A dish for festive days

Barreado is synonymous with partying. That was the pretext used to create a dish, now present for over 200 years in Antonina and Morretes, that was, at the same time, tasty, nutritious and that could take women away from the kitchen so that they too could take part in a festival that is said to have originated Carnaval. It´s basically made with other than prime cuts, as the shoulder, accompanied by bacon, onions, garlic and bay leaf. It takes from 16 to 24 hours to cook just right. The secret is to not let vapor out of the pan, so the meat doesn´t get dry. At the time, cooks used to make a mixture of manioc meal and water, and seal the lid of the pan perfectly. The accompaniment is a manioc mush made with the *barreado* broth, banana, orange and the traditional banana-flavored *cachaça* from Morretes.

Carnaval originated the dish

outlet for the goods being taken from the Antonina port to the prairies. Still standing is the small **São Sebastião Church**. Well-kept inns can be found on the road leading to Morretes. In most of them you can hear the sound of rivers and streams that cut the properties and form an dense net of water courses. Beautiful waterfalls can be found in this part, such as the **Redondo Falls**, inside a hydroelectric plant, and the **Macacos Falls**, forming 4 natural pools from where the Marumbi complex can be seen. There are guided tours to the 2 falls, because the region is quite isolated.

The most traditional thing to do in Porto de Cima is to go **down rivers** (☎ 462-1925). You have to go up 3-kilometer Prainhas Road by car and, from there, go down the river. Along the way, some curves, small falls and a green corridor formed by the Rainforest. The finishing line is at the metallic bridge, some 2 hours later. Also on the riverbank, you can visit the **Nhudiaquara Sanctuary** (Saturdays, Sundays and holidays, from 9 am to 6 pm, ☎ 323-3724, www.nudiaquara.com.br), a thatched house decorated with fiberwood

furniture and an extensive deck over the river. At km 2 of Prainhas Road.

Marumbi State Park

There are two ways to get to the park´s headquarters: either take the train in Curitiba and get off at Marumbi station (🕒 2 hours); or go along Prainhas Road in Porto de Cima for 5 kilometers, leave the car at IAP and go on foot for 2 hours. Only 4-WD vehicles can tackle this route. Before going, call the park administration to know the road conditions (☎ 333-5044). Turned into a State park in 1990, Marumbi is a traditional climbing region, with 8 peaks: **Abrolhos**, **Torre dos Sinos**, **Esfinge**, **Ponta do Tigre**, **Gigante**, **Boa Vista**, **Facãozinho** and **Olimpo** (with a 1,539-meter highest point). Trekkers have to register before leaving and also register when they get back, so that rescue teams are not put into action without the need to do so. The park has camping facilities and a museum that tells the history of mountain climbing in Marumbi. There are 4 main access routes, with different-color signs. All of them are tough and guides are required. There´s also **Rochedinho** (🕒 30 minutes), a small elevation above the Carvalho viaduct, from where you can have a view of the range and the train. Other options: the **Marumbinistas Waterfall**, a 50-meter almost vertical fall, and some **natural pools** formed along the rivers.

Antonina

16 kilometers from Morretes

Together with Paranaguá, Antonina was one of the most important ports in the South of Brazil. The heyday of matte production lasted until the 1930´s, and the port became the 4th largest in Brazil. The main constructions of the time are still standing, such as the richly adorned **Municipal Theater**, on Carlos Gomes da Costa Street, and the old **railroad station** (restored in 2002), at the city entrance, currently housing exhibitions, restaurant and art shop. Antonina Historic Downtown has two-store houses and stone houses, many in ruins. On XV de Novembro Street, check the façades of buildings as the **City Hall** (see the panel

◄ Marumbi, a mountain climber´s paradise

Antonina preserves houses from the 1930s

depicting Antonina Bay), the **O Boticário** shop and **Pharmacia Internacional**, opened in 1926. On the way up to **Nossa Senhora do Pilar Church**, there are other period buildings. In the Laranjeiras district, next to the fountain by the same name that supplied the city with water for a long time, there´s a trail amidst the thick vegetation leading to **Morro da Pedra**, the highest point in town.

The most sought-for places to see the bay are **Ponta da Pita** and the **municipal boat house** where there are catamaran rides on weekends and holidays. Antonina is resuming its port activities with the construction of the Ponta do Félix terminal. At the old abandoned Barão de Tefé port, the imposing warehouses of the **Matarazzo Industrial Complex** are witness to a wealthy time of intense port activity. The Winter Festival, in July, attracts visitors with its artistic-cultural workshops.

TIPS

- 12 kilometers from downtown, along Anhaia Road, **Fortuna waterfall** can be reached through a mild hike inside the woods.
- Go to **Engenho da Serra** (☎ 9978-2150), in América de Cima, to see the production of *cachaça*. From Friday through Sunday taste Italian food at a restaurant near the river.
- To visit the falls or go up the Marumbi, call the Marumbi Guide Association (☎ 462-2934).

Paranaguá

The Paranaguá Port, in the old town, important for Paraná's soy

Curitiba 96 km
Ilha do Mel 1h30 (boat)
Morretes 43 km
127,171
41
422-6882
paranagua.pr.gov.br

Founded in 1684, Paranaguá is the oldest city in the State and today houses one of the most important ports in the country. Settlement started a little earlier, in 1550, after rumors that there was gold in the region. In the beginning of the 16th century, the first exploiters visited the city sporadically, to trade tools, fishhooks and fabrics for the cotton planted by the Indians. When the news that there was gold there spread, hordes of adventurers from Cananéia, São Vicente and even Rio de Janeiro took the city. The Municipal Chamber was installed and the Pelourinho was erected, and is currently displayed on XV de Novembro Street, behind the Coffee Market. In 1660 it became a province and in 1842 a city, a time when most of its buildings and manor houses were built, today its biggest attractions.

★ Historic Downtown

The highlights are easy to visit on foot. If you arrived in town by train, go along Arthur de Abreu Avenue till you find the river. See the architectural details of the **railroad station**, built in 1880. The opening of the Curitiba-Paranaguá line triggered

a very economically prosperous time. Before reaching the river, at the corner of XV de Novembro Street, watch the Baroque-style **Ordem Theater**, previously Ordem Church, on the right. On **Praia Stree**t, see the colorful façades of the mansions by the Itiberê River. Some remain just as they were built, in an interesting contrast to the ones that were restored and painted in bright colors. On the river, it´s possible to see the boats leaving to Mel Island, Guaraqueçaba and other places in the bay.
On the right side stands the **Coffee Market**, a mandatory stopover to taste *barreado*, shrimp balls, seafood or fried banana covered with cinnamon. Don´t miss, on the other side of the street, the shops with handcraft baskets. Go to an imposing building, previously a Jesuit school, that today houses the **Archaeology and Ethnology Museum**. Right beside it is the **Paranaguá Historical and Geographical Institute**, displaying historic documents on the founding of the city, as the **Memória Histórica de Paranaguá**, written by "the father of Paraná History," Vieira dos Santos as well as decorative pieces. Nearby you can see the bridge that crosses the Itiberê River and links Paranaguá to **Valadares Island**, where fandango players can be heard (see sidebar). Go up the Historical Institute street and turn left to observe old houses and the 1578 **Nossa**

Clogs and instruments to dance fandango

A pretext to meet friends

The fandango is a combination of all of Paraná´s folkloric dances typical of the coast of Paraná. Its origin is uncertain, having been attributed to the Spanish, the Portuguese, and there are people who sustain it´s originally Brazilian. Whatever the origin, the fandango has always been a pretext to party after long working hours, whether to put a house up or to help with the crops. The rhythm is marked by the violin, a kind of drum called *adufo* and the tapping of clogs on the floor. The instruments are made by the fandango players themselves, who go to the woods to find the right wood. Valadares Island, linked to Paranaguá by a bridge, is the place that most keeps this tradition, especially in places like Casa do Fandango, Mangue Seco and the bar of "seu" Pedro Pereira.

◀ The train goes from Curitiba to Paranaguá

Large mansions on the Itiberê River banks, a busy harbor for boats

Senhora do Rosário Church, the first built in the State.

Paranaguá Archaeology and Ethnology Museum

575, XV de Novembro Street
422-8844, www.proec.ufpr.br.
Open from Tuesday through Sunday, from 12 noon to 6 pm
Built in 1755, it was a Jesuit school until 1769, when the Jesuits were banned from Brazil by Marquês de Pombal. Then it housed the customs and was also used as the headquarters for troops. In 1963 it became a museum directed by Paraná Federal University. In its interior, there´s an extensive collection of archaeological findings such as prehistoric shellmounds, funerary urns, weapons and ceramics, found in the interior and coastal cities of Paraná. The ethnological collection comprises body adornments, fabrics and plumes from several Indian peoples in Brazil. There´s also a reproduction of a sugar mill and shows of fishing techniques.

SURROUNDINGS

Pontal do Paraná, Matinhos,

Paranaguá Bay

Caiobá and Guaratuba

Leaving from Paranaguá, take PR-412 (parallel to the main spas). If you´re leaving Curitiba, take BR-277 and follow the signs for about 120 kilometers. The southern beaches of Paranaguá are favorites with Paraná inhabitants. From Pontal do Paraná to Caiobá there´s a long line of beaches: Pontal do Sul Beach, for those willing to go to Mel Island (boats leaving at different times during the day); Leste Beach, and Matinhos Beach to the south, with 36 spas along 17 kilometers and bordering on Caiobá;
Caiobá is the most popular, with hills, such as the Boi hill, trails leading to the sea, and the Escalvado, or Morro da Cruz, from where you have a bird´s-eye-view of all the beaches in the region. And the last one, Guaratuba Beach, the second largest and with the best urban planning on the coast – a ferryboat crosses Guaratuba Bay every 20 minutes. The place has different options of outings, taking visitors to archaeological sites, ostrich nurseries, and also to the Parati Waterfall and the Boguaçu Park.

TIPS

- Take the train to go down Serra da Graciosa to Paranaguá and from there take a boat to Mel Island. In high season, traffic is very heavy until you get on BR-277 (a double highway to Curitiba). There are many spas nearby.
- On Saturday mornings (only in the months of January and February), there´s a boat that leaves to the Superagüi Park and returns on Sunday afternoon. For information: Praia Street, 422-6882.

◄ **Praia de Leste, one of the Paraná's people favourite**

Prudente

Prudentópolis

The city is known by the number of waterfalls: ten are over 100 meters tall

Curitiba 207 km
Ponta Grossa 101 km
Guarapuava 72 km
46,323
42
prudentopolis.pr.gov.br

Waterfalls and the Ucranian culture are the highlights of Prudentópolis. The municipality is home to over 100 waterfalls, 50 of them are considered to be large, and 10 are over 100 meters high. It´s one of the main Slavic colonies in Brazil. From the almost 47 thousand inhabitants, 73% are of Ucranian descent and the remaining 27% of Russian and Polish descent. Most of the communities have a typical round-tower church and worship two saints: John the Baptist, representing the "Latin" Catholics, whose church bears an imposing Gothic tower; and Saint Josafat for the Slavic, in hexagonal churches with round gleaming domes. The city also has a 60-member group that performs folkloric dances, the Vesselka.

The new land

A former republic of the now-extinct Soviet Union, Ucrania is home to a people who has always struggled to maintain their identity, even after centuries of oppression by other Slavic peoples. Around 1890, in search of better life conditions, hundreds of Ucranian citizens came to Brazil to work and conquer the dream for the freedom they didn´t have in their own country. They arrived in Paraná between 1894 and 1898 and, thanks to an agreement with former President Prudente de Moraes (later honored by naming the city), they received land in exchange for the workforce to build telegraph lines. One of the traditions that is still kept up to now is the delicate work of the *pêssanki* eggs (*pêssanka* in singular form). They were probably created by gypsy communities around 2,000 years ago, and were used in guessing ceremonies. According to legend, the *pêssanki* should be given at Easter time.
The geometrical precision of the paintings are present in colorful drawings that intend to represent love, abundance and the Christian faith.

The painted Easter eggs have a Gypsy origin

★ São Josafat Church

São Josafat Street, Downtown. Daily services in Ucranian at 7 pm.
This Bizantine-style temple is formed by 3 domes and, by the altar, exquisite sacred images – called *ikonostás* – stand for Catholic saints and tell Jesus´ life. The golden and colorful images were painted at the Fine Arts Academy, in Vienna, Austria.

Millenium Museum

Ucrânia Plaza, Downtown. Tuesday through Friday, from 8:30 am to 11:30 am, and from 1:30 pm to 5:30 pm; Saturday, from 9:30 am to 11:30 am, and from 2 pm to 5 pm; Sunday, from 9 am to 11:30 am.
Its name honors the one thousand years of Christian faith in Ucrania. The museum displays pictures, documents and objects that tell the saga of the first immigrants that came to Paraná around 1895. Look for Meroslawa Krevei, a theologist and the museum´s administrator, who will tell you everything about the history and culture of Slavic people, and show you the colorful perfectly symmetrical embroideries.

★ São Francisco Waterfall

On the road to Jaciaba, km 55, only for 4-WD vehicles. Excursions organized at the Mayná Hotel, 446-2091.
This is Prudentópolis postcard, present in all the promotional leaflets, under the slogan "land of the gigantic waterfalls." Access is difficult, after about an hour on a road full of potholes and another half-hour hike to a cliff. The reward is a vertiginous 196-meter-high waterfall.

★ Recanto Perehouski

On the road to Jaciaba, km 24. Access through dirt road in good condition.
It´s formed by only one watercourse, the Barra Limpa River, that flows narrowly and safely at the beginning of the trail and then goes into a series

◄ **The Bizantine-style Saint Josafat Church**

of curves until it drops over small waterfalls. Along the way you can bathe in the falls and dive into the natural pools. An interesting geological formation, along most of the way, is a rock wall eroded by water, forming a long corridor of concave walls. In some parts, you´ll have to walk on slippery rocks, climb hills with the help of ropes till you reach the place you came here for: where the water falls down from a canyon. "Dona" Isabel Perehouski, the owner, makes and sells delicious biscuits and cakes.

★ Salto São Sebastião and Salto Mlot

Road to Jaciaba, km 29, about 5 kilometers past Recanto Perehouski. Access through a dirt road in good condition.

The trail that leads to both falls is slippery and dangerous at some points. As soon as you start going down, you can already see, on the other side of the cliff, a huge wall and the 135-meter-high São Sebastião Waterfall. As you continue your descent, it´s possible to hear the noise of another waterfall, a lot closer than the first: it´s the Mlot fall. At first you think it´s a small waterfall, but along the way you´ll see that the real Mlot waterfall actually falls a little farther down, along a rock wall, and forms a 114-meter-high waterfall. This is a very unusual sight: two waterfalls, one in front of the other. You need to be very careful if you want to go down to the well where the two waterfalls meet.

Salto São João

Road to Barra Bonita, 20 kilometers. Follow the signs to Recanto Cassiano.

The 84-meter fall can be seen from the road. To reach the top, make a left on the main road and take the trail inside the jungle. Near there, at the Recanto Cassiano, the two arms of a river form small waterfalls and natural pools, where you can rent barbecue grills.

TIPS

- In the surroundings of Prudentópolis, there are 32 Bizantine-style churches, many in faraway communities. It´s a common sight to glimpse,among many trees, a round and gleaming dome.
- To visit the most famous falls in Prudentópolis, allow at least three days. There are dozens that can be visited with the help of locals.
- Have a taste of Ucranian cuisine. Typical dishes such as *peroghê*, similar to the Italian dish raviolli, is a pasta filled with ricotta cheese or beans; the *borchtch*, a hot soup accompanied by beets and pork meat; and the *uzvár*, a dessert made with dry fruit.

Immigrants´ descendants still keep old traditions

◀ The 196-meter-tall São Francisco Waterfall

Vila Velha

A ship´s bow is one of the rock formations "sculpted" by the passing of time

Curitiba 113 km
Castro 45 km
Foz do Iguaçu 548 km
273,469
42
220220-1314
pontagrossa.pr.gov.br

Furnas: over 100 meters deep

The prairie region displays a geological formation that dates back to 600 million years ago. At the time, the whole area was part of the ocean, and innumerable volcanic eruptions and the shifting of tectonic plates produced huge mountain ranges, changing the landscape completely. In the following 200 years, extensive glaciers melted down and took with them large deposits of sand and rock. With the passing of time and by force of wind and water, the sandstone formations acquired their present shape in Vila Velha. Several other attractions in the region, like the Guartelá Canyon (see Castro), Lagoa Dourada and the Buraco do Padre Waterfall date back to the same time.

Ponta Grossa

The city is the starting point to visit all the interesting spots in the region. It was first founded as a district of Castro, by the cowboys. In the following years it became independent and currently is one of the most economically prosperous cities in Paraná. In Ponta Grossa, there´s the **Mosteiro da Ressurreição** (Km 9, Souza Naves Ave. Reservation is required), where Benedictine monks produce licquor, handmade candles and became famous when they put out a CD with Gregorian chant. The **Época Museum**, next to the Sant´Ana Cathedral, on Roosevelt Plaza (Monday through Friday, from 8 am to 11:30 am; and from 1:30 pm to 7 pm; Saturday, from 6 pm to 12 pm) is in an art nouveau house built in 1880. The collection of the museum displays old coins, swords used in the Argentina War, radios, weapons and several period utensils.

★ Vila Velha State Park

26 kilometers from Ponta Grossa through BR-376 ☎ 228-1138
Sandstone formations: daily, from 8 am to 6 pm; Caves: daily, from 8 am to 4 pm.

Huge rock formations are what makes Vilha Velha famous. Some got nicknames, like the Boot, the Sphynx, the Camel, the Indian and the Cálice. Bordering the rock formations, there´s also a trail inside a grove. The park was restored in 2002 and up to the finishing touches of this guide it was still closed. The trails were marked with signs and two other excursions, to **Furnas and Lagoa Dourada**, which could only be reached by going back to BR-376, now can be taken from the same entrance and by paying only one ticket fare. The caves are circular sanstone craters that can be over 100 meters deep. In the largest, there´s an elevator that takes you down 54 meters to a platform built over a water mirror. From down there, you have the exact notion of its immensity. Air is more humid, there´s water flowing from the walls where birds build their nests.
Lagoa Dourada has the same geological origin as the Caves. Surrounded by an immense green area, Lagoa Dourada (golden lagoon) got its name because its bottom is covered by a mineral that reflects sunlight. If you walk by the riverbank, you can see several types of fish.

★ Buraco do Padre Waterfall

26 kilometers from Ponta Grossa downtown. Take the road to Itaiacoca. Wednesday through Sunday, from 8 am to 5 pm.

20 kilometers away from the city.

Lagoa Dourada, formed at the same time as Vila Velha, reflects the sunlight

After driving for 20 kilometers outside of the city, half way on a dirt road, always along vast plantation fields, signs indicating the waterfall alert you to the upcoming of a unique setting. When you get there, you´ll have to open a farm´s gate, park the car and walk for 10 minutes on a trail that becomes narrower, and finally goes into a dense forest. The stream, present from the beginning of the trail, at first mild, becomes strong and molds its course according to the rocks that have become to serve as trail by now. The noise of the water becomes ever more intense and suddenly the stream flows like an immense rug spread out from rock formations that look like a passageway into another dimension. What looked like a cave now is revealed as an immense *furna* (a crater), from where a waterfall goes down 45 meters from a hole in the rock . In the afternoon the show is even more beautiful, with the sunlight coming in through a crack at the entrance of the crater and bringing light into the cave and the water. As you go up the crater, do so on the right side, and,with the help of a rope, reach the top and watch the waterfall from yet another perspective. From up there, it´s possible to observe the contrast of the scarped rocks with the huge prairie land, forming huge walls.

TIPS

- If you wish to spend a whole day in the Waterfalls, leave early in the morning and go to Itaiacoca, passing through the **Rio de São Jorge Canyon** and the **Capão da Onça**.

Huge rocks that form figures are part of the Vila Velha Park complex

Buraco do Padre: a 45-meter waterfall ▶

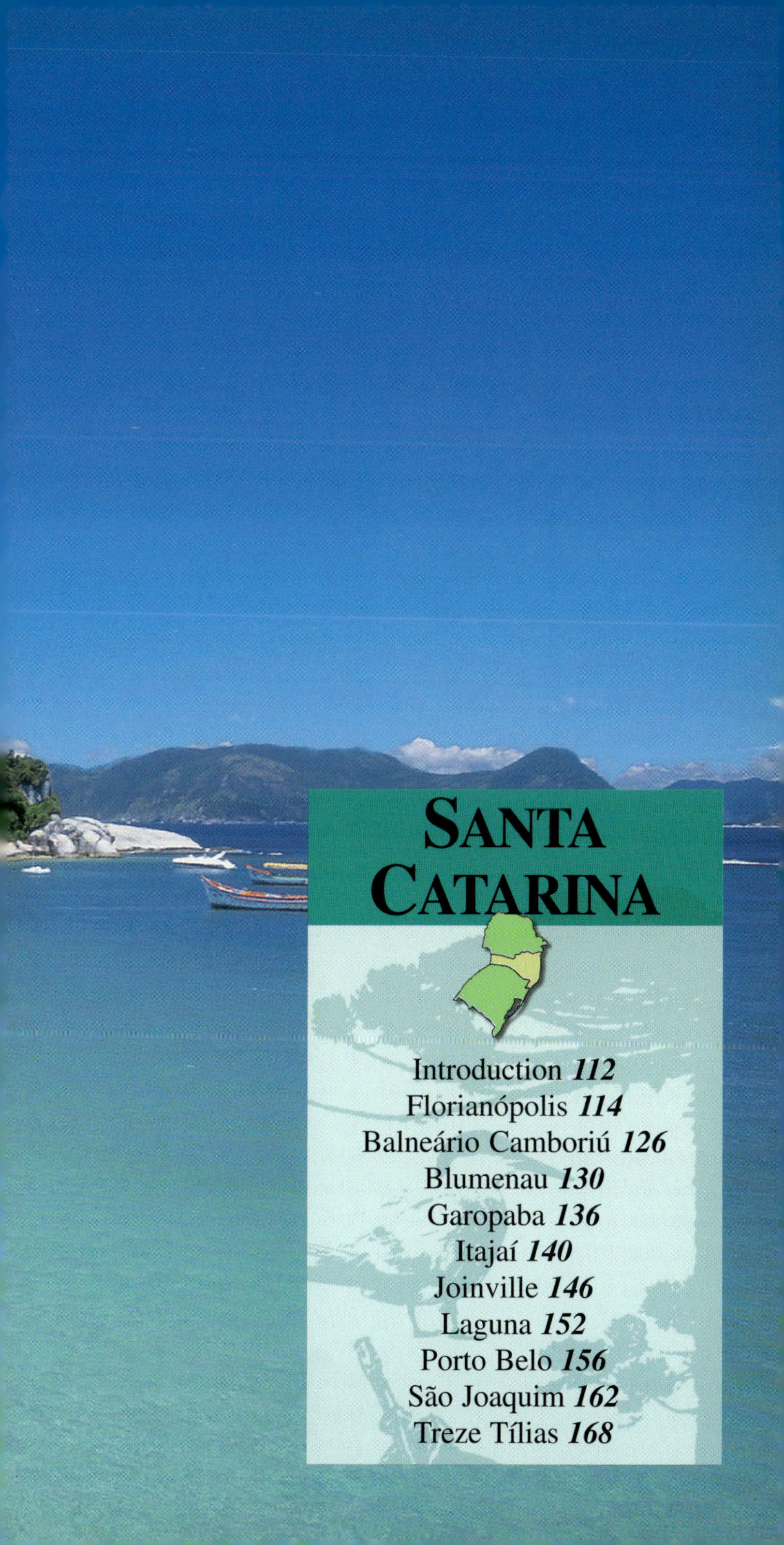

Santa Catarina

SANTA CATARINA

It' s the only Brazilian State that honors a saint in its name. There are people who say it' s an homage to Saint Catherine of Alexandria, and there are those who say the Italian Sebastião Caboto, who arrived on the Santa Catarina coast around 1526, chose the name to honor his wife, Catarina Medrano. Santa Catarina is located in the South of the country and covers an area of 95,400 square kilometers (the approximate size of countries such as Austria, Hungary, Ireland or Portugal). The State borders on Argentina to the west and stands in the geographical center of the southern and southeastern regions. Santa Catarina welcomes both those who look for the beauties found on its 500-kilometer coast as well as those who search for the bucolic setting of the 18 cities that make up the Serra Catarinense (Santa Catarina mountain region). In the mountain region, there are hundreds of walking trails, river rapids, several free-flight spots, mountain-climbing areas and farm-hotels that are in the rural tourism sector. In addition to all that, Santa Catarina is home to the Serra do Rio do Rastro road, which goes down the mountain in winding curves from an altitude of 1,467 meters to sea level. The capital, Florianópolis, is 1,850 kilometers from Buenos Aires, 712 kilometers from São Paulo, 1,144 kilometers from Rio de Janeiro, and welcomes visitors from all these places. Floripa, short for Florianópolis, has 100 beaches, in part responsible for the title the city shares with neighboring Balneário Camboriú, as the city with the best quality of living in all Brazil. It' s also considered one of the best places for the mating of the southern right whale, and for that reason, the Santa Catarina coast gets all the attention between the months of May and November, when it' s

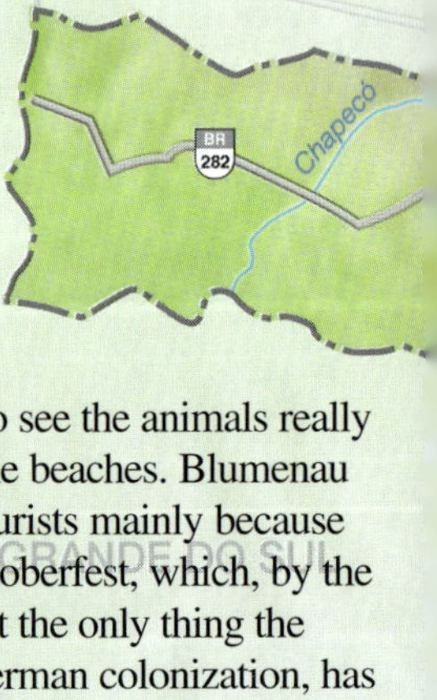

possible to see the animals really close to the beaches. Blumenau attracts tourists mainly because of the Oktoberfest, which, by the way, is not the only thing the city, of German colonization, has to offer. The small Nova Trento draws visitors because of Madre Paulina, the first Brazilian saint. For those who prefer the thermal water spas, the main destination is the Great Florianópolis area, to the south and west of the State.

Highlights

1. Florianópolis
2. Blumenau
3. Porto Belo

◀ **Bombinhas, one of the beautiful beaches of Santa Catarina**

N
O
L
S
0
35
70 km
River
State Capital
City
State Boundary
Park
Paved Road
Dirty Track
Airport
CURITIBA
BR 476
BR 101
BR 280
SC 301
BR 153
SC 453
BR 116
SC 418
BR 470
BR 486
BR 282
SC 438
SC 430
BR 101
São Francisco do Sul
Porto União
Schroeder
Corupá
Jaraguá do Sul
Joinville
Barra Velha
Piçarras
Penha
Treze Tílias
Fraiburgo
Timbó
Pomerode
Itajaí
Blumenau
Brusque
Balneário Camboriú
Itapema
Bombinhas
Nova Trento
Porto Belo
Gov. Celso Ramos
SANTA CATARINA
Canoas
Santo Amaro
da Imperatriz
FLORIANÓPOLIS
Palhoça
Lages
PARQUE
NACIONAL
DE SÃO
JOAQUIM
Urubici
PARQUE
ESTADUAL DA
SERRA DO
TABULEIRO
Garopaba
Imbituba
São Joaquim
Bom Jardim
da Serra
Orleans
Laguna
Urussanga
Tubarão
Criciúma
Araranguá
Mampituba
PORTO ALEGRE
1
2
3

Floripa

Florianópolis

Despite being a modern metropolis, the biggest attraction of Floripa are its natural beauties

Curitiba 304 km
Porto Alegre 474 km
São Paulo 712 km
342,000
48
244-5822
pmf.sc.gov.br
guiafloripa.com.br

The city, founded in March of 1726 and settled by Azoreans, thrives on commerce and tourism. Settlers left their marks which can be mostly seen in the districts of Ribeirão da Ilha and Santo Antônio de Lisboa: narrow streets, houses that open right onto the sidewalks and the typical accent. Much of the city´s popularity now is attributed to tennis player Gustavo Küerten, the city´s favorite son. Temperatures ranging between 20ºC and 30ºC all year long are an invitation for the 42 beaches that line the island (there are as many as 100, but access to most is only through trails and tourism is still incipient). The northern section has a better tourist infrastructure; the eastern side attracts surfers and the southern coast has rustic beaches that still preserve the flora and fauna.

Hercílio Luz Bridge: 819 meters ▶

Hercílio Luz Bridge

This is one of the longest suspension bridges in the world, 819 meters long, with two 75-meter tall towers, considered to be Florianópolis postcard. It´s closed for traffic and pedestrians, and at night it´s even more beautiful because of the hundreds of lamps.

Public Market

At the corner of Conselheiro Mafra Street and Largo da Alfândega, Downtown. Monday through Friday,

Santa Catarina Island

The neoclassical Customs building now houses institutes and art shops

from 9 am to 10 pm; Saturday from 9 am to 3 pm.

The construction of the building started in 1898, and the market consists of 144 stands with vegetables, fruit, fish, handcrafts and bars. Be sure to go to Stand 32, 224-5588, to taste some ostriches.

XV de Novembro Plaza

On the way to the **Metropolitan Chapel**, the **Santa Catarina Historical Museum**, the **Mercado Municipal** and the **Customs House**, you´ll come across the plaza, with a fig tree dating from 1871. According to legend, going round it four times is a surefire way to find a great love.

The Customs House

141 Conselheiro Mafra Street, Downtown, 224-6082. Monday through Friday, from 9 am to 6:30 pm; Saturday, from 9 am to 12:30 pm.

Public Market: its building dates from 1898

When it was opened, in 1876, this neoclassic building used to be a mandatory stopover for people and goods arriving to Florianópolis. Currently, the second floor houses the National Historic and Artistic Heritage Institute (Iphan). On the ground floor, there are the Santa Catarina Fine Arts Association, an art shop and the Alfândega Bar.

Nossa Senhora do Desterro Metropolitan Chapel

XV de Novembro Plaza, Downtown. Daily, from 6:30 am to 6:30 pm.

This is a 1773 building that best defines the eclectic architectural style of the city. In its interior, a sculpture of John and Mary fleeing to Egypt, sculpted by artist Demetz. One of its seven altars belonged to the first church of the former Desterro.

★ Santa Catarina Historical Museum

228 XV de Novembro Plaza, Downtown,. 221-3505 and 221-3504. Tuesday through Friday, from 10 am to 6 pm; Saturday, Sunday and holidays, from 10 am to 4 pm.

Located inside the Cruz e Sousa Palace (named after a Paraná symbolist poet). The building was declared a Historical State Heritage in 1984 and is a symbol of the neoclassical eclectic architecture of the 19th century. The collection includes furniture, art objects and documents. The highlight is the inlaid floor, with a Portuguese influence.

São José Fortress, erected in 1740

Also deserving attention are the wall paintings and the plaster details of the ceiling, as well as the art nouveau glass window of the central nave. The ground floor is used for temporary exhibitions, mainly on themes related to the culture and history of Santa Catarina.

★ Fortresses

The 11 fortresses located in strategic points of the island were built by the Portuguese to defend the land south of Brazil from Spanish invaders in the 18th century. The three main fortresses – Santa Cruz de Anhatomirim, São José da Ponta Grossa and Santo Antônio de Ratones – have been restored. The largest fort in the South, **Santa Cruz de Anhatomirim** was also the first to be built to protect the capital and was concluded in 1744. The 2,678-square-meter island became, 150 years later, an arresting and execution site for politicians who didn´t abide by the laws established by Marshall Floriano Peixoto´s government. At the fort, bearing a majestic portico with Eastern traits, the colonial-style two-storied house, the gunpowder storehouse and the troop´s headquarters are open to visitation. The architectural style of **São José da Ponta Grossa Fortress** has the influence of Italian Renaissance and was built on an unleveled land in 1740. That´s why there are ramps connecting the chapel, the Commander´s house, the gunpowder storehouse, the kitchen, the troop´s headquarters and the weapons

Lagoa´s attractions

The district Lagoa da Conceição is 20 kilometers from downtown Florianópolis and is, by far, the most popular place in town. During the day, all the agitation is on the neighboring sands of Mole and Joaquina beaches. At night, it is bars and restaurants that throb with action. The popularity of Joaquina started with surfers in the 1970s, but the neighborhood still keeps its traditions. Rendeiras Avenue, the main avenue in Lagoa, is where 10 embroiderers show their work.
The tradition of fishing and folklore present in tales of witches, werewolves and the *boitatá* are also part of the locals´ lives. The Terno de Reis, Ratoeira, Cantoria do Divino, Pau-de-Fita and the Boi-de-Mamão festivals are some of the artistic-cultural expressions that were preserved.
The Carijó Indians of the Tupi-Guarani tribe were the first to live in the area that surrounds the 21 square kilometers of water that make up the Lagoa da Conceição.
Later came the Azoreans, who founded the Freguesia de Nossa Senhora da Conceição da Lagoa in 1750, together with Santo Antônio de Lisboa. In 1845, an illustrious visitor, Emperor D. Pedro II donated a silver piece to the Lagoa church. Upon returning to the island, in 1861, he´s said to have donated two bells.

The district still keeps its Azorean traditions

The island with Rupestrian inscriptions

This 381,648-square-meter land was declared a National Artistic and Historic Landmark in 2000 by IPHAN. The Campeche island in southern Florianópolis, with crystal-clear waters, was named after a plant – identified at the time of the Spanish invasion – and certainly deserves a visit. It´s located thirty minutes south of Armação Beach by boat. On the trails that are open to visiting tours, all guided, there are awesome archaeological remains. On Campeche, you can find the most numerous Rupestrian inscriptions on the southern coast of Brazil, totaling 167, or 53% of all known inscriptions on Santa Catarina Island. On walls and isolated blocks found in the western side of the island are concentric circles, parallel winding lines, parallel broken lines, solid triangles and squares, spirals and stylized figures of men and animals. There are also places probably used as shops to produce, sharpen and polish rock instruments. The 10-meter-high so-called "pedra fincada"(stuck rock) is the most interesting rock formation on the whole island.

warehouse. It´s located atop a hill, between Jurerê Internacional and Forte beaches. The **Santo Antônio Fort** was built on Ratones Island, also in 1740, and was designed to complete the triangular cross-fire system with the other two fortresses. There, you´ll see what´s left of the military quarters, the gunpowder storehouse and the flour warehouse. Scuna Sul (www.scunasul. com.br, ☎ 224-1806) has daily excursions from the boathouse under Hercílio Luz Bridge, and from Canasvieiras Bridge. In summer, artisans make bilro embroideries at the fortresses.

★ Ribeirão da Ilha

In the southwest of the island, 27 kilometers from Downtown, Ribeirão da Ilha is the main district with reminders of the Azorean colonization in the South in the 18th century. Houses that open right onto the sidewalks and small calm beaches make up the setting of this traditional place to taste oysters. Other outings: **Matriz Nossa Senhora da Lapa Church**, **Ribeirão da Ilha Ecomuseum** ☎ 237-8148 or 222-4573 and **Ostravagante Farm**, the only in the city to have the Federal Inspection Seal (SIF) to produce oysters and

◀ Beaches and archaeological remains

mussels. (ostravagante@matrix.com.br, ☎ 237-8374).

BEACHES

North of the island

The spas that offer the best tourist and entertainment infrastructure are located in this section of the island. **Ingleses Beach** is one of the most sought-for and **Canasvieiras** is one of the largest spas on the island. Together, they have the largest number of hotels and apartments for rent in summer. Fancier places can be found on **Brava** and **Jurerê Internacional** beaches. Brava Beach is a favorite with the young crowd, and has high waves and a "costão" to the left worth visiting. **Jurerê** and **Daniela** beaches attract mostly families. Those in search of quiet should go to **Forte Beach**, where São José da Ponta Grossa Fortress is located. Surfers prefer **Santinho Beach**, that houses the Costão do Santinho, the largest resort and spa in the South. Next to it is the **Open Air Archaeological Museum**, with a 600-meter-long trail leading to the site of many rupestrian inscriptions. ★ **Santo Antônio de Lisboa** and **Sambaqui** are attractions in themselves. In these districts, sea bathing is not recommended but the scenery – history is told in every corner – is worth the visit. In Sambaqui, don´t miss the Art Center and the many labs for oyster breeding at the Federal University of Santa Catarina. In the neighboring district, it´s worth visiting the Casa Açoriana, ☎ 235-1262. Feira das Alfaias (an art center) is near the Roldão da Rocha Pires Plaza, and is open on weekends.

Azorean architecture in Ribeirão da Ilha

East of the island

Florianópolis comes alive on Lagoa da Conceição Beach and on the neighboring beaches. Some of the finest restaurants can be found in this part of the island, with a nightlife filled with action. To the south are Canto da Lagoa and Rendeiras Street, also lined with popular restaurants and through which you´ll have to pass to go to the beaches. "Joaca," or **Joaquina Beach**, is best approached through Rendeiras Avenue. Take a right, and enter the beach that offers the best infrastructure. **Mole Beach** is so called because of its fluffy sands, and it´s a favorite with surfers and

Santinho Beach: infrastructure, fun and high waves, to the delight of surfers

The beaches in the south of the island, like Campeche, are for those who seek calm

paragliding buffs. It´s located atop Morro da Lagoa, on the opposite direction of Joaquina. The hill takes you to **Barra da Lagoa**, a calm beach from where an unforgettable view extends across the lake – and it´s a better view than the one from the Tourist Observatory when you arrive from the Florianópolis downtown area. Barra is located at the southern tip of **Moçambique Beach** (the longest, 13 kilometers of almost untouched clear soft sands), next to the channel that links Lagoa da Conceição to the Atlantic Ocean. In July, there´s the traditional Tainha Festival. Between Barra da Lagoa and Mole, **Galheta** is a desert beach that can only be reached through a 300-meter trail, with no bars or restaurants, attracting nudists.

South of the island

Those searching for rest and contact with nature should look for the beaches on the southern coast. **Morro das Pedras Beach** is rustic and has high waves, a surfer´s paradise. Also a heavy-seas beach,

Traditional fishing communities live on Matadeiro beaches and on others in the south

◄ Brava Beach: ideal for young people who like high waves

Mole Beach, along the way to Morro da Lagoa, acquired its name because of the soft sands

Campeche made an impression on French writer Antoine de Saint-Exupéry in the 1920s. The author of *The Little Prince* was a pilot for the French airline Ligne Latécoère and landed many times on the Campeche airfield. The main avenue leading to the beach from highway SC-406 was named Pequeno Príncipe (Little Prince). **Armação Beach** is also very popular, and has many restaurants and bars. Lodging options are limited, but you can stay there and from there go to **Campeche Island** (read The island of the rupestrian inscriptions); **Matadeiro Beach; Solidão; Pântano do Sul**, home to a traditional fishing village; Caieira da Barra do Sul; **Tapera**, ideal for those who have children in tow; **Lagoinha do Leste**, one hour on foot, or **Naufragados**, three hours on foot or 20 minutes by boat with access through Caieira da Barra do Sul Beach, at the end of Baldicero Filomeno Highway, or **Lagoa do Peri** – the largest freshwater lagoon on the Santa Catarina coast.

SURROUNDINGS

Palhoça

Access through BR-101, km 235, in the Great Florianópolis area, www.palhoca.sc.gov.br, 242-3202.

As a great producer of shellfish, oysters and shrimp, the city also has

Pântano do Sul: a fishermen´s place

Serra do Tabuleiro: entrance to the park with beautiful waterfalls is via Palhoça

one of the largest breeding grounds for scargots in Brazil. Having been colonized by Azoreans, this 102,000-inhabitant city is known for its natural beauties. **Guarda do Embaú Beach** is the prettiest in town and has rustic inns, mainly for surfers. **Baixo Beach** offers better infrastructure, but good surprises await visitors on **Sonho, Pinheira, Pontal, Fora** and **Cima** beaches. **Pedras Altas Beach** is a favorite with nudists and is located at the Serra do Tabuleiro State Park (the largest preservation unit in the South). Part of its 90 thousand hectares belongs to Palhoça. The other part comprises the municipalities of Santo Amaro da Imperatriz, Águas Mornas, São Bonifácio, São Martinho, Imaruí, Garopaba, Paulo Lopes and Florianópolis, in addition to some islands and beaches. The park has a rich array of flora and fauna species and has also beautiful waterfalls and a zoo, but only a small part of its beauty is open to guided tours. For tours, call ☎ 224-8299. Another spot worth visiting is **Papagaio Island**, located between the Pinheira and

Sonho beaches, with 142 thousand square meters and 80% of native vegetation. It belongs to the Sehns, who keep a luxurious inn there. Access is through Sonho Beach or by boat from Veleiros Yacht Club, in Florianópolis. The 250-year-old **Brito Inlet** was declared a Historic Landmark because of its colonial houses. **Nossa Senhora da Conceição de Araçatuba Fortress**, built in 1742, is part of the Inlet setting. In February the city is home to the Navegantes Festival, and in June it´s time for the Bom Jesus de Nazaré and Divino Espírito Santo festivals.

Santo Amaro da Imperatriz

BR-282 towards Lages, www.portalsantoamaro.com.br.

The municipality is located 37 kilometers from Florianópolis and is visited by those looking for **thermal waters** to relieve stress and cure certain illnesses and by adventurers who look for the **rapids** of the Cubatão River. At the place, a hospital was built in 1818, and became the first thermal hospital in the country. Since 1993, a festival has been held every March to divulge the place as the largest corn producer in the State.

TIPS

- There are very few parking spaces on the island of Santa Catarina. Of all the beaches, Joaquina has the best infrastructure for cars.
- Stores open only after 9 am and until 1 pm on Saturdays. Museums and public agencies close for lunch.
- Going down rapids on the Cubatão River can be arranged in Santo Amaro da Imperatriz, 245-7021/ 245-1673.
- In Águas Mornas, the temperature of the water from the springs can reach 42° C. Those who can get by without luxury can go to the bathtubs of the Rancho Alegre Bar.

Floriano´s city

Florianópolis started as a modest fishing village called Nossa Senhora do Desterro and gained political emancipation in 1726. Between 1748 and 1756, the village attracted hordes of settlers from Azores and Madeira. In 1823, Desterro became the capital of Santa Catarina and was renamed Florianópolis in October of 1894, in honor of Marshall Floriano Peixoto, President from 1891 to 1894. The change was very polemical, since the Anhatomirim Island had been used to shoot thousands of opposition leaders. Desterro then became the setting for deaths during the Federalist Revolution. In April 1894, Marshall Floriano´s followers regained control of the capital.

Anhatomirim: a ground for shootings

◀ **Guarda do Embaú, the most beautiful beach in Palhoça**

Camboriú

Balneário Camboriú

The city has a good infrastructure, parks and charming beaches

Florianópolis: 90km
Joinville: 80km
Blumenau: 58km
100,000
47
367-8122 and 363-4439
camboriu-sc.com.br

The city known as the Wonder of the South Atlantic was emancipated from Camboriú in 1964. It draws a great number of tourists in the summer months, when the population reaches 1.6 million inhabitants. Colonized by Azoreans, the region already showed its tourist vocation even when it was called Arraial do Bom Sucesso and was still a district of Camboriú. The first hotel was built in 1932, and today there are hundreds of good hotels and inns, most of them lined along Brasil and Atlântica avenues. According to a poll conducted in 2002 by the Santa Catarina Urban and Environmental Development Secretary, it boasts the title of the city with the best quality of living in the State, before Florianópolis and Blumenau, second and third places.

Estaleiro: rough sands and crystal-clear waters ▶

★ Cyro Gevaerd Park
BR-101 towards Florianópolis, km 137, 367-0033. Daily, 9 am-7:30 pm December to February; closes at 5 pm the rest of the year.
More popularly known as Santur park (the official tourism department of the State), the park covers an area of 116,000 square meters and boasts a zoo with over 1,200 animals, a mini-farm, an aquarium with 50 freshwater fish species and 45 marine species from the Santa Catarina coastal region. It´s also home to the Flora and Fauna Museum, and the Gea, an archaeological museum and the only one to have 716 pieces displaying the typical art of the Azorean settlers.

Cristo Luz
800 Indonésia Street, www.cristoluz.com, 367-4042. Daily, 10 am-midnight.
The 33-meter-tall statue and weighing 528 tons was blessed by Pope John Paul II in October of 1997, when he visited Brazil for the second time. Every day of the week the Christ displays a different color, with the help of a headlight. On Monday it´s white (representing peace and faith), on Tuesday it´s yellow (peace and energy), on Wednesday, blue (peace and health), on Thursday it´s time for violet (peace and reflection), on Friday the color is red (peace and love) and on Saturday the statue becomes pink (peace and happiness). Besides the statue, the complex comprises two observatories, a cave that pays homage to Nossa Senhora Aparecida, an open square for events that can accommodate 2,500 thousand people, a restaurant that affords a bird´s-eye-view over the city, a snack bar, cafeteria, ice cream parlor, shops and a parking lot for 500 cars. From Atlântica and Brasil avenues, there´s free transportation to the Christ.

Beaches
There are ten, each with a different calling. Central Beach is 6.8

The cablecar at the Unipraias Park affords a spectacular view of the region

kilometers long and is where most of the hotels, bars, restaurants and nightclubs are located. It´s sided by Atlântica Avenue and its full charm is revealed in the streets closed for traffic along the shore. To the south is **Laranjeiras**, set apart by history, with pre-historic shellmounds and over 5,000-year-old animal fossils. This 750-meter-long beach is only 6 kilometers from Downtown and is best approached along Linha de Acesso às Praias (LAP), leaving from BR-101 or via Barra Sul on the

The Christ changes color every day of the week

cablecars (read Unipraias Park). **Taquarinhas** and **Taquaras** are fishing villages and are located 2 kilometers after Laranjeiras. Still in the south is **Pinho**, the first official nudist beach in the country, 9 kilometers from Downtown. **Estaleiro** is 2 kilometers ahead and keeps its own characteristics for cast fishing. It has 1,450 meters of rough sands and boasts crystal-clear waters. **Estaleirinho** is one kilometer ahead via Linha de Acesso às Praias. The beaches north of the city are **Canto** (only 50 meters long that can be reached by trails), **Buraco** (high waves and having almost all the area taken by a hotel) and **Amores** Beach (ideal for surfing, on the border of Balneário Camboriú and Itajaí via Osvaldo Reis Highway).

★ Unipraias Park

6006 Atlântica Avenue, Barra Sul, www.unipraias.com.br, ☎ 367-0493. Daily, 9 am-8 pm December-March; the rest of the year, closed on Tuesday.

The tourist complex opened in August 1999 and is one of the most famous sights in town. It covers an area of 85,000 square meters in the middle of the Rainforest. It has 47 cablecars and three stations, from which you can enjoy a majestic view of the beaches of the region. The cablecars can seat six people, and take visitors from Central Beach to Laranjeiras Beach. **Barra Sul** is the boarding station for visitors. It covers an area of 1,500 thousand square meters and has a parking lot, restaurants, bars and shops. The **Rainforest** is the second stop and stands at 240 meters high atop Aguada Hill. There, an environment park was created with a 60,000-square-meter preserved area. Adventure buffs can face the challenges presented by arvorismo (suspended trails between the crowns of 15-meter-tall trees). Five hundred meters of catwalks take visitors to observatories and reading spots. In one of them, there´s an oratory with the image of Santo Antônio da Guarda, sculpted in bronze by Italian artist Franco Fiabane and blessed, in 1999, at the Basílica de Santo Antônio de Pádua. According to legend, those who touch the saint´s head will find his or her soulmate. **Laranjeiras** Station is the next stop, located 100 meters from the beach by the same name.

TIPS

• There´s a Tourist Information Center at the main entrance to the city. It´s worth stopping by, mainly to get the city map. Almost all streets are known by numbers and many end on Brasil Avenue, Downtown, that has intense traffic.
• By the way, visitors are quite surprised at the traffic. Be prepared to face the same difficulties to park as in Florianópolis. Parking on Brasil or Atlântica avenues is almost impossible.
• Lodging options are mostly on Atlântica and Brasil avenues, but it´s possible to find better prices on Estado Avenue, with access to BR-101.
• In addition to visiting the beaches by car or in cable cars, you can do the same on a schooner, Barco Pirata. The boat leaves daily, starting at 10:30 am. The excursion takes an hour and a half. 367-3258 and 367-2815.
• The Helisanta company offers 5-, 7- and 10-minute helicopter tours, leaving from Heliporto Esplanada das Marinas, at 1366 Beira Rio Avenue, Barra Sul (www.helisanta.com.br, 361-0880).

Laranjeiras Beach is very well-known and is located 6 kilometers from Downtown

Blumenau

The city of German origin boasts a different architectural style and many parks

Florianópolis 139 km
Joinville 90 km
Itajaí 49 km
270,000
47
326-6901 and 326-6968
blumenau.sc.com.br

Home of the largest beer festival outside of Germany and the biggest popular event in the country after Carnaval, the city was founded in 1850 by German immigrants and has much more than the Oktoberfest to offer. Regarded as the financial capital of Santa Catarina, Blumenau is the most important city in the Itajaí Valley and its economy is based on the industrial sector. The agroindustry sector, computer technology, the metal-mechanics sector and the production of handcrafted crystal are also very developed areas. It ranks third among the cities with the largest population and is also among the cities with the best quality of living in the country. The European style and the German traditions are easily noticed by visitors. There are 35 hunting and gun clubs spread all over town and the city is home to the Santa Catarina Target Shooting Federation.

The city is famous for its beer

Beer Museum

On the corner of XV de Novembro Street and Hercílio Luz Plaza, Downtown. Monday-Friday, 7 am-7 pm; Sun, 9 am-3 pm.

Located at the plaza where Cervejaria Continental is, the museum has two rooms that display equipment used in the making of beer from the 1940s to the 1960s. Besides the casks, fermentation pots, bottle filler, a decimal scale and pasteurizing measurement scales, the place shows old photographs of the city and of Cervejaria Brahma.

Water Museum

Lages Street, Boa Vista, 323-3116. Daily, 9 am-8 pm.

Located, since September 1999,

At the Glas Park, handmade crystal ▶

where the water treatment plant used to be, opened in 1943. Visitors are allowed to watch the proceedings, from the purification of the waters of the Itajaí-Açu River to its distribution. Old equipment and self-explanatory pictures are part of the museum, which also has an observatory that affords one of the most stunning views of the central region of the city.

Glas Park

147 Rudolf Roedel Street, Salto Weissbach, 327-1261.Monday-Friday, 9 am-6 pm; Saturday, 9 am-1 pm.
About 10 kilometers from Downtown, lies the museum opened in 1997 and belonging to one of the companies that produce handmade crystal. It displays pieces brought from Germany, some dating back to the 18th century, that help tell the history of the manufacture of crystal. The museum is part of the shop Glas Studio, where there are about 600 items that were produced there. Visitors are allowed to watch workers mold the pieces.

Vapor Blumenau

66 Paraguai Street, Ponta Aguda. Daily, 9 am-5 pm.
An original of the boat built in Germany that was used as a cargo ship for years, between Blumenau and the Itajaí Port. Its maiden trip was in 1895. It took four hours to go to the port and six to return to Blumenau. It now houses a museum. Entrance is through the Moinho do Vale restaurant or on Juscelino Kubitschek Plaza, popularly known as Prainha

Vila Germânica

Alberto Stein Street (an annex to the

The Beer Festival

Typical attire at the German festival

It's in October, for 18 days, that Blumenau locals have the chance to show to all the country the cultural richness inherited from their German ancestors.
The Oktoberfest started in 1984 to raise funds for the reconstruction of the city, which had suffered two devastating floods. Since then, the Oktoberfest has become the main tourist destination in all Santa Catarina State in the month of October. More than that: it became one of the largest beer festivals in all the world, second only to Munich's festival.
In 2002 alone, the festival drew a record number of visitors: 503,000 people went to the two pavilions of the Blumenau Exhibition Foundation (Proeb) and drank approximately 224,000 liters of draft beer. Between the years of 1988 and 1992, the festival gathered over 1 million visitors.

Proeb pavilions). Daily, 10:30 am-6:30 pm.

The center of Oktoberfest is open all year round. There are ten shops in buildings that are reminders of an authentic German village and sell good-humored T-shirts, beer mugs bearing the symbol of the traditional German beer festival, chocolate, wine and several other items. The village boasts restaurants with typical German food.

Vila Itoupava

378-1170.

Located on the Massaranduba River basin, 25 kilometers from Downtown, the 5,000-inhabitant village occupies an area of only 91 square meters with 7 kilometers of urban area. The typical German buildings are only part of the attraction. The rural area lures visitors with fishing lakes with the fish-and-pay system, cheese, yoghurt, chocolate, licquor and jam manufacturers. Blumentur 323-3951 takes visitors to the village, leaving daily, always in the morning, from the main hotels in town. The visit lasts about 4 hours.

German immigration

Dr. Blumenau´s house, currently a museum

The northern region of Santa Catarina has three important cities colonized by Germans and founded more or less at the same time: Blumenau (1850), Joinville (1851) and Brusque (1860). Blumenau was founded by the doctor and pharmacist Hermann Bruno Otto Blumenau, who was granted the land to start an agricultural colony for European immigrants. In the first few years, the colony was a private property of its founder, but financial difficulties made him ask the government to take over the land. Dr. Blumenau directed the colony until 1880, when it was declared a municipality. The old territory that in 1934 covered an area of 10,510 square kilometers was downsized to the current 531 square kilometers.
In the remaining area, 31 other towns emerged.

Spitzk Ecological Park

3777 Bruno Schreiber Street, Progresso, 336-5422. Daily, 7 am-7 pm.

The district is located 15 kilometers from Downtown, and it´s home to headwaters, cascades, natural pools and walking trails. One of them takes visitors to the highest point of the park, at 936 meters high. Its infrastructure includes chalets, a snack bar, grills and camping sites. Some scientists from the main natural history research institutes have already come to the Spitzk (meaning sharp-pointed head).

Nascentes Park

Santa Maria Street, Nova Rússia, 340-7574. Daily, from 2 pm on.

A Preservation Unit, intended to

In Brusque, the architecture of the ▶ City Hall shows its European influence

develop ecoturism, researches and environmental education policies. It´s located 21 kilometers from Downtown, in a 52-square-meter region of rainforest donated to the municipality by the Artex company. It has 50 kilometers of trails and roads and a large number of headwaters.

São Francisco de Assis Natural Park

Ingo Hering Street. (back to Neumarkt Shopping Mall), ☎ 222-2137. Daily, 8 am-5 pm.

It´s the third largest continuous original area of the rainforest in Santa Catarina, and declared an environmental protection area. It has typical secondary rainforest vegetation, distributed along 656 thousand square meters. The area belongs to the region´s native forest complex and houses a large number of animals.

Parque Horto Botânico Edith Gaertner

78 Alameda Duque de Caxias, Downtown, ☎ 3221676. Tuesday-Friday, 9 am-5 pm; Saturday, 9 am-12 am; 2 pm-4:30 pm; Sunday, 9 am-12 am.

The park, also known as the cat graveyard, was named after a lonely woman who lived there, surrounded by centuries-old trees. Her cats kept her company. When they died, her favorite ones were buried with pompous ceremonies, for which her neighbors were invited. The graveyard is in a bucolic part of the 4,000-square-meter park that has a small native forest and a mini-zoo that is home to 15 animals and 60 birds.

Fritz Müeller Ecological Museum

2195 Itajaí Street, Downtown, ☎ 326-7106. Monday-Friday, 8 am-12 am; 1:30 pm-5:30 pm; Saturday, 9 am-12 am; 2 pm-4:30 pm; Sunday, 9 am-11:30 am; 2 pm-5 pm.

This is where the German researcher Fritz Müeller, a collaborator of the English scientist Charles Darwin, lived. Müeller came to Brazil to study the Brazilian flora and fauna and dedicated part of his life to the city of Blumenau. The house, turned into a museum in 1939, displays small collections of natural history.

SURROUNDINGS

Brusque

Access through SC-411 from Nova Trento or through BR-486 leaving BR-101, ☎ 251-1833, www.brusque.sc.gov.br.

Settled by Germans in 1860, the city on the Itajaí Valley also has strong influences by Italians and Polish. The

Fenarreco: a gastronomy feast in Brusque, where the main dish is the teal

city was named after Francisco Carlos de Araújo Brusque, president of the Santa Catarina Province in 1890, the official founding of the colony. Commerce is the main drawing card of the tourism industry, but Brusque offers other attractions to visitors. The **Azambuja Valley**, 2 kilometers from downtown, are the sanctuary, the cave with a water fountain that houses an image of Our Lady of Caravaggio, Morro do Rosário and the **Dom Joaquim Arquidiocesano Museum**, considered to be the most complete sacred art museum in the South, displaying a collection of 4,000 works. The **Matriz São Luiz Church**, located in front of Barão Von Schneéburg Plaza, Downtown, is the most modern religious temple in Brusque. Its construction started in 1961 and 25,000 granite stones were used. The **Padre Raulino Reitz Ecological** and **Zoobotanical Park** is another attraction in town. The 216-thousand-square-meter park is home to 650 animals of 130 different species, an orchid nursery and a bromeliad nursery. The chair lift of the zoobotanical garden leads to the **Leopoldo Moritz Municipal Park**, a 22,000-square-meter model farm that depicts the colonization

Madre Paulina, the only Brazilian saint

Amabile Lucia Visintainer was only 10 years old when she left Vigolo Vattaro, in Trento, in northern Italy, to follow her family and other 102 immigrants who arrived in Santa Catarina in 1875 to found Nova Trento. In 1890, the young lady began her religious mission. With two friends, she created the Imaculate Conception Sisters Congregation, which currently gathers 600 sisters in 11 countries. In December 1895 she became a nun and adopted the name Paulina do Coração Agonizante de Jesus. Until her death, in 1942, she worked in homes for the elder, charity homes and hospitals in Santa Catarina and São Paulo. She was canonized and received the title of saint – the first in Brazil – on May 19, 2002.

Mother Paulina´s Portal in Nova Trento

Santa Paulina Sanctuary:
☎ (48) 267-0250

period. In October, Brusque is the site of the **Marreco Festival (Fenarreco)**. The event was created in 1986 by the Tourism Municipal Commission to divulge the teal, with its popular *ente mit rotkohl*, a typical dish of the German cuisine.

Nova Trento

Access through SC-411 on BR-101, (48) 212-6300.

In 1875 the city welcomed its first immigrants coming from Trento, in northern Italy. Currently, it has less than 10,000 inhabitants, but over 30,000 faithful come to the town because of Santa Paulina, the first Brazilian saint (read Madre Paulina, the only Brazilian saint). The city has several churches, chapels and monuments and is famous for producing good wines, but it is the Vígolo district, where the saint lived, that draws almost all the pilgrims who come to Nova Trento. At the **Santa Paulina Sanctuary**, there are 20 visitation spots that include a replica of the house where she lived, chapels, memory rooms, a photographic memorial, a museum and restaurants. Halfway from Downtown to the sanctuary stands the house where she spent her childhood, which is a must-see stopover. The top of the hill is the farthest point on the visitation route, where visitors will see a statue of the saint with a hoe in one of her hands and a cross in the other, representing work and prayer.

Casa do Imigrante: a museum in Pomerode

◀ Restaurants serve German fare

★ Pomerode

Access via BR-470 and SC-418, www.pomerode.com.br

The city bears the title of the most German city in Brazil and it couldn´t be any different. Of the 22,000 inhabitants, almost 80% have a German origin and still speak German. The first immigrants arrived in 1863. The 217-square-kilometer area, situated on the Medium Itajaí Valley, has houses typical of northern Germany, combining exposed bricks and wooden poles. The houses can be seen on **Rota do Enxaimel**. The cultural memory is preserved also in the 5 folk dance groups, 19 hunt and shoot clubs and the museums **Casa do Imigrante Carl Weege, Pomerano, Erwin Curt Teichmann** and **Hotel Fazenda Mundo Antigo.** The zoo, opened in 1932 by the German industrialist Hermann Weege, is still another attraction in Pomerode.

TIPS

- The German identity of Blumenau has a strong link to German cuisine. Dishes having pork, sausage and poultry as the main ingredients are present in all the restaurants´menus.
- Having a colonial coffee lunch in the afternoon in Blumenau or Pomerode can take you to Germany without having to leave Brazil.

Garopaba

The city founded by Azorean immigrants today receives hordes of tourists

Florianópolis 75 km
Laguna 62 km
Araranguá 156 km
13,000
48
254-3106
garopaba.sc.gov.br

The city is known in all of Brazil for the beauty of its nine beaches and for being visited, between the months of June and November, by dozens of southern right whales, who come to Garopaba´s calm waters to feed their babies. Garopaba is home to the Southern Right Whale Environmental Protection Area (APA), and tourism is its main economic activity. At least 100,000 visitors flock to its beaches in the summer months. A surfer´s paradise, the city covers an area of 111 square kilometers in southern Santa Catarina. It emerged early in 1666 with the arrival of the first Azorean immigrants, but it was only in 1846 that Freguesia de Garopaba was founded. The building of the Matriz São Joaquim Church dates from this period. It stands at the top of a hill, in Historic Downtown, and affords a magnificent view of Garopaba Beach. The city was officially founded only on December 19, 1961.

Beaches

Garopaba´s nine beaches are the city´s main attraction. The most urbanized and having the best infrastructure in terms of restaurants and lodging is the

An old Indian burial site on the beach

The southern right whales come to the Santa Catarina coast to breed

Whales in sight

From May to November, the southern right whales go to the coastal region of Santa Catarina to breed and feed their babies. In this region of crystal-clear waters and many protected inlets, the females and their babies get very close to the beach, some just 20 meters away from the sands, and can be easily sighted. In 2000, the Federal Government created an Environmental Protection Area (APA), an area of 156 square kilometers along a 130-kilometer stretch, in the southern coast of Santa Catarina. Its headquarters are in Imbituba and the objective is to protect the region and boost sustainable whale-watching tourism. Itapirubá Beach, in the same municipality, is home to the Southern Right Whale Project, which has the Species Preservation National Center. The southern right whale is still threatened with extinction, with only 7,000 animals on the planet. The project gives information to visitors on how to watch the whales, ☎ 255-2922. For information, check the site www.baleiafranca.org.br, updated constantly and with information on the species and the region. The Center also supports whale-watching in high seas. Visitors can make reservation on boats, ☎ 9907-5852. In Imbituba, there´s the Whale Museum, at the restored building of the last whale station in the south of the country, on Porto Beach.

one that bears the name of the city. **Garopaba Beach** is approximately two kilometers long, is frequented mainly by families and blends smartly and harmonically its quiet fishing village with the hectic lifestyle of bars, restaurants and shops. In order to maintain the natural beauty of the place, city laws forbid the construction of buildings more than two floors high. **Preguiça Beach** is located at the end of Garopaba Beach, and is a small and calm spot of the district of Vigia. Vigia is a strictly residential area and boasts magnificent houses that offer a striking contrast to the natural beauties of the place, among them the **Nossa Senhora de Lourdes Cave**. To the south of Garopaba Beach, two kilometers from Downtown, is **Silveira Beach**. It´s surrounded by mountains and is famous for the waves, among the best in the country for surfing. It´s also the place to go if you´re an amateur fisherman or a diver. A surfer´s paradise, however, is **Ferrugem Beach**, the second most developed beach in the city. It´s 5 kilometers from Downtown, and access is via a dirt road, but the real action happens at night, when the bars are crowded with young people. There´s a shellmound at the place, a Carijó Indian graveyard, from the time of the colonization of the coastal region of Garopaba. The 800-meter-long **Barra Beach** is located between Ferrugem and Ouvidor beaches and is a peaceful hub where the setting formed by the ocean is broken only by the few inns and rental houses that host mainly families and couples. **Ouvidor Beach** has white sands, dunes and hills, and is also only 800 meters long. It´s surrounded by a green oasis and keeps an air of wilderness, with only a few houses. From the top of the dunes, visitors can see all the beach and the **Costão da Caranha**, where you´ll find some caves and Rupestrian inscriptions. In the southernmost part of Garopaba, bordering on Imbituba, **Vermelha Beach** is a private beach. It´s practically wild and is also sought-for by surfers. But to go there you´ll need a special permit. On the northern tip, **Gamboa Beach** is 15 kilometers away from Downtown and access is through hills. The sea is open and is very dangerous. It´s the most urban beach after Garopaba and Ferrugem. Neighboring Siriú Beach is part of the Serra do Tabuleiro State Park and keeps its native vegetation intact.

SURROUNDINGS

Imbituba

Access via BR-101, ☎ 255-0281.

It has the second largest port in the State that accounts for most jobs offered in the 32,000-inhabitant city. Other important economic activities are the trading business, industry and the tourism industry. The city, officially founded in 1958, is 87 kilometers away from the capital city, Florianópolis. Imbituba covers an area of 182 square kilometers and still has traces of the Azorean colonization, but tourists flock to the region because of the waves on **Rosa Beach** and **to see the southern right**

Among the many attractions of Imbituba and surroundings, Rosa Beach and whale-watching

Five kilometers from downtown Garopaba, Ferrugem Beach is the second most crowded

whales. Rosa Beach has five-star waves (according to a rate established by the State environmental agency) that are close to perfect and, during the summer months, its population – essentially made up of fishermen – gets three times larger. It becomes almost impossible to drive on the narrow streets, full of potholes. The only two roads lead to the beach and to **Alto do Morro**; the other goes to **Barra da Lagoa de Ibiraquera**, one of the most beautiful settings in the region, well-known for shrimp fishing. Another attraction in Imbituba is **Itapirubá Beach**, also famous for preserving nature. Also part of the route are the **Sant'Ana de Dentro, Sant´Ana de Fora, Araras, Tacami and Ouvidor islands**, in addition to **Ilhota do Batuta**. A schooner is the best option to visit the islands.

Siriú is part of the Serra do Tabuleiro Park

TIPS

• If you´re driving, the best access route is SC-434. Enter SC-434 at the 273 km marker on BR-101. It´s 15 kilometers to Downtown on a paved and well-marked highway. There´s another option, passing through the city of Paulo Lopes, at the 252 km marker on BR-101. This is a dirt road, with lots of going up and down hills.

• Turismo Vida, Sol & Mar ☎ 255-1222 and ☎ 254-4199, offers excursions to whale-watching spots, on an inflatable boat for 20 people. The excursion takes 🕒 3 hours. You can also see the whales from fishermen´s boats, and if you´re lucky, you can see them from the beach, with your two feet planted firmly on the sand.

Itajaí

Despite the calm appearance, Itajaí is the largest fishing port in the country

Florianópolis 90 km
Balneário Camboriú 10 km
Schroeder 92 km
148,000
47
348-1080
itajai.com.br

The city boasts the largest fishing port in the country, with four places to dock ships, a 592-meter pier, the only one in Brazil designed exclusively for tourists. Itajaí is also where the second largest university in the State is located. Its architecture still has traces of the German and Azorean colonization period and the city still has a quiet country-style quality of living. It has beautiful beaches, good hotels and restaurants, but the economy is based on the port and fishing, despite the industrial sector having a great importance on the city´s income. The city was officially founded on June 16, 1860 on the Itajaí-Açu riverbanks. According to data by the Itajaí Fishing Industry Union (Sindipi), in 2002 there were 336 fishing boats registered in the city, totaling 3,700 jobs on board.

October is the month for the city´s main event. The Marejada, created in 1986, is considered to be the largest Portuguese and fish festival in Brazil, gathering some 200,000 visitors in 17 days. The Colono Festival, in July, is another feast that brings thousands of visitors to the city.

Matriz do Santíssimo Sacramento Church

Irineu Bornhausen Plaza, Downtown.

The church is regarded as the most important artistic and cultural monument in town. Designed by the German architect Simão Gramlich, also the creator of several other churches in Santa Catarina, its construction started in 1940, but was finished only in 1955. The architecture has several romantic and Gothic elements and the interior of the building houses beautiful paintings by Italian artists Emílio Cessa and Aldo Locatelli. The stained glass windows have eucaristic and biblical motifs and the ceiling has a huge painting of Virgin Mary. The altar boasts an imposing statue of Moses sculpted by artist Teichmann, from Pomerode.

The tourist pier receives merchant ships too ▶

Municipal Public Market

Ministro Victor Konder Avenue,Downtown. Monday-Friday, 8 am-7 pm; Saturday, 8 am-4 pm

Also known as Center for the Popular Culture, the market keeps the beauty of its 1917 construction. The highlight is in the roof rigging and the internal fountain. Inside the market, you´ll find fishing products, regional art, Azorean spices and Azorean cuisine. It also serves as grounds for a variety of cultural events throughout the year.

Itajaí Historical Museum

233 Dr. Hercílio Luz St., Downtown, 348-1335. Tuesday-Friday, 9 am-5 pm; Saturday-Sunday, 1 pm-6 pm.

It´s located inside the Marcos Konder Palace building, built in 1925 to house the City Hall, where it stayed until 1972. Currently, the museum is kept by the Genésio Miranda Lins Foundation, which is responsible for preserving the historic memory of Itajaí. The museum´s art nouveau architecture is its biggest attraction, but inside the building, the collection made up of furniture, artworks and photographic panels document the main periods of the region´s history, from the colonization period to the mid-20th century.

At the Cathedral, paintings by Aldo Locatelli

Tourist Pier

Vidal Ramos Plaza, Downtown, 341-8000, www.portoitajai.com.br.

In September 2000, the pier gained the only terminal exclusively dedicated to ocean liner passengers in Brazil. It was created by the Itajaí Port Superintendency in conjunction with the City Hall in order to attract ocean liners and to boost tourism in the city and the vicinity. The port is often used by the Brazilian Navy and by oceanography research ships, in addition to merchant ships that need repair, when the pier is empty.

Beto Carrero World

One of the first theme parks to open in the country and the largest amusement park in all Latin America, Beto Carrero World has been visited by over 8 million people since its opening, on December 28, 1991. It´s the main destination of people who go to Balneário Penha, and receives an average 7,000 visitors per day, going up to 20,000 on high-season weekends. Located on Armação Beach, Beto Carrero World was idealized by businessman João Batista Sérgio Murad, more popularly known as the cowboy Beto Carrero. It covers a vast area of approximately 2,000 square kilometers, divided into seven theme spaces, with 85 attractions for all age brackets, including a zoo with 800 animals of 171 species. At the Medieval Castle, the entrance to the park, there are 110 outsourced commercial stands plus eight shops that sell Beto Carreiro and Betinho Carrero designer items. In order to make visiting all the attractions easier, there´s a train that takes visitors around the park to all the different rides. In February 2003, the park opened the highest free-fall tower in the world, 100 meters high, equivalent to a 30-floor building. Another new attraction is the Lost Continent, a river with rapids, full of surprises, where visitors will find caves and whirlpools on boats for up to 10 people, ☎ 261-2354, www.betocarrero.com.br.

The park has 85 different attractions

Sodegaura Way

A friendship landmark between the cities of Itajaí and Sodegaura, in the province of Chiba, in Japan, Beira-Rio Plaza has many Japanese cherry trees. The construction of the plaza was a joint venture made by both towns, sister cities since 1979. From 1993 on, Ministro Victor Konder Avenue, where the square is, has become a Tourist Support Zone (ZAT), thus collaborating for the place to become known as a gastronomic and entertainment space. And that´s where some of the best restaurants in town are located.

The waves of Atalaia Beach make the place one of the hottest spots for surfers

Beaches

Some of the fancier beaches in the State of Santa Catarina are located in the city of Itajaí. **Cabeçudas Beach**, for example, is considered to be one of the most sophisticated in the country, boasting streets lined with trees and surrounded by sumptuous mansions. In addition, the beach stages several free-flight and yachting competitions. The **Cabeçudas Lighthouse** can be seen from the beach sands. The clean and calm waters of **Geremias Beach** are synonymous with tranquility and are the ideal spot for those who have children in town. Geremias Beach is where the exotic **Bico do Papagaio** (parrot´s beak) is located. It´s a rock sculpted by nature and whose shape resembles a giant bird. The Tupi-Guarani name of the rock may have influenced the Indians when choosing the name of the Itajaí River. Another mecca for those dedicated to having some calm and quiet is **Amores Beach**, located at the base of **Morro do Careca**. Its 160-meter-high platform is used by free-flight pilots. The large quantities of iodine present in the waters of Morcego Beach are an added attraction for those people who are looking for the cure of respiratory or digestive illnesses. Surfers prefer the high waves of **Brava** and **Atalaia** beaches. On Brava Beach, all the bars and restaurants are furnished in a rustic style, which fits in well with the young atmosphere and the agitated nightlife the region offers.

SURROUNDINGS

Penha

Access via BR-101, 9 km from the Navegantes Intersection, ☎ 345-3428.

The largest producer of shellfish in the country, with an average yearly output of 3.5 tons, the city became known in 1991, when businessman Beto Carrero opened the first theme park in the country (read Beto Carrero World). Colonized by Azoreans, the 18,000-inhabitant city still has very few hotels, most of them located around the park. Penha has 19 beaches, spread along 31 kilometers, and three festivals a year that draw visitors in ever increasing numbers. February is the month for the **Shellfish Festival**. In its 18th edition, in 2003, the 10 days of the festival gathered 90,000 people. For over 160 years, The **Divino Festival** has taken place, always in May. June is the time for the **São João and São Pedro Festivities**, the oldest festivals in town, that have been celebrated for almost 250 years. Among the beaches, **Alegre Beach** is the calmest. **Saudade Beach** has clear waters and high waves, ideal for surfing. Also good for surfing, **Grande Beach** boasts many restaurants and bars, besides a fine view of **Ponta da Vigia**. Quilombo Beach is also a favorite with surfers. **Paciência Beach** still keeps its natural beauty, enhanced by rocks jutting out into the ocean. There´s no infrastructure on the beach and access is difficult,

◀ The rock sculpted by nature resembles a parrot´s beak

but it´s worth the effort because of the stunning view if offers. Access to **Vermelha Beach** is also difficult, but divers love the place. **Armação Beach** boasts the title of the noblest beach in the region, where you´ll see the most valued real estate properties. On **Armação do Itapocoroí**, there are many amateur and industrial fishing boats along its 800 meters and this is where the first settlers arrived. Boats leave from here and from Alegre Beach to **Feia Island**, where the **Caverna do Diabo** (Devil´s Cave) is located. Surrounded by fishing and diving spots, 20 minutes from the coast, the island has nothing to do with its name. The oldest building in town is worth a visit. It´s the **São João Batista Church**, built in 1759.

Piçarras

Access via BR-101, 9 km north of Itajaí, ☎ 345-0222, www.picarras. com.br.

The Azoreans were the first to arrive in Piçarras in 1758, due to a shipwreck, according to the town´s history books. The settlers found a large quantity of clayey rocks called *piçarro*, the origin of the name of the city, founded officially in 1963, after being part of São Francisco do Sul and Penha. Boasting only 7 kilometers of beaches, tourism is the city´s main source of revenue, followed closely by fishing and agriculture. In summer, it gathers some 100,000 visitors, ten times its population. **Piçarras Beach** is the most popular in the region. Located in the central region, it´s proper for swimming and popular with water sports addicts. **Palmeiras Beach** is also very good for swimming, with very calm waters. It borders on **Itajuba Beach**, in Barra Velha. At night, beautiful people gather in bars or restaurants on Nereu Ramos Avenue. In the month of February, Piçarras is home to the Jet Ski Brazilian Championship.

Barra Velha

Access via BR-101, ☎ 456-0055, turismo@netgio.com.br.

Tourism in Barra Velha occupies the third position among the city´s main economic activities. The first and second places are, respectively, fishing and agriculture. It´s one of the most sought-for places on the State´s northern coast. It has a good hotel industry system, and its beautiful beaches draw visitors during all the summer. One of the most popular beaches is **Central Beach**, where the colorful boats full of fish and shrimp make for an unforgettable sight, mainly at dawn. The beach with the best infrastructure is fancy **Itajuba**. And **Tabuleiro Beach**, together with Itajuba, are the favorite beaches with surfers. However, there are many other beaches as popular: **Pedras Negras** and **Pedras Brancas** beaches, **Grant** and **Península** beaches, parallel to **Lagoa da Barra Beach** and stage for fishing tournaments. The lagoon is an attraction in itself. As the meeting place of the Itapocu River with the ocean, it is 6 kilometers long and forms a 200-meter-wide peninsula, full of fish. The 14,000-inhabitant city also has festivals that draw thousands of visitors. In February it´s time for the maritime procession of **Our Lady of Navegantes**. Between the months of May and June, the biggest event in town takes place, the **Divino Espírito Santo Festival**. And since 1997, in September, Barra Velha has been the venue for the **Pirão** (Manioc Mush) **National Festival (Fenapir)**.

TIPS

- You can reach Itajaí via Balneário Camboriú or via the intersections Itajaí-Brusque (linking BR-101 to Downtown), or the one on Adolfo Konder Avenue, or the Itajaí-Blumenau. Navegantes Airport is 7 kilometers away via the highway or a 20-minute ride via the ferryboat.
- In Itajaí, don´t miss the Morro da Cruz, near Downtown, from where you´ll have a stunning view of the city and the meeting of the Itajaí-Açu River with the ocean.
- Still in Itajaí, go to Morcego Cave on Morro do Farol. The cave is about 5 meters long and only 50 meters deep. It´s 7 kilometers from Downtown.
- Capitão Gato Schooner, ☎ 9977-1851, leaves daily to Feia Island from Penha.

In Penha, 31 kilometers of sea and beaches ▶

Joinville

Modern Joinville invests on its German origins

Florianópolis 184 km
Curitiba 135 km
Porto Alegre 698 km
437,000
47
453-2663
joinville.sc.gov.br

The city boasts a large number of industries and is one of the most populous in Santa Catarina. It´s also the third industrial hub in the southern region, after Porto Alegre and Curitiba, in revenues to the State. The land was donated, in 1843, to Joinville Prince, François Ferdinand Philipp (France´s Luis Felipe´s son), as dowry, when he married Princess Francisca Carolina, Emperor D. Pedro II´s sister. The colony, called Dona Francisca, at first received Norwegian, Swiss, but mainly German immigrants. Today, the modern city of Joinville boasts the title of Latin American Center for Tourism and Events. Centreventos Cau Hansen, built as an arena and inspired by high-tech American and European projects, seats 10,000 people. It houses the only ballet school of Bolshoi outside of Moscow. Before its opening, in March 2000, Joinville was already a reference center for the arts in the country, thanks to its Dance Festival. It has taken place every July since 1983 and is the biggest festival for dance students, amateur and professional ballet dancers in Brazil and the fourth in Latin America. Another traditional event is the Flower Festival, in November. In October, the city hosts the Fenachopp (draft beer festival), the second largest German festival in the country.

Alameda Brustlein

Historic Downtown. Also known as Palmeiras Street.
It´s the entrance to the Royalty´s old summer house, a palace that currently houses the Imigration and Colonization National Museum. The giant imperial palm trees were planted by Frederico Brustlein, in 1873, and were declared National Historic Landmark in 1982.

★ The Immigration and Colonization National Museum

229 Rio Branco Street, Downtown,

433-3736. Tuesday to Friday, from 9 am to 5 pm; Saturday, Sunday and holidays, from 11 am to 5 pm.
It´s located in the old palace used by the Royalty as a summer house. It´s mandatory for those who wish to learn more about the immigration and colonization periods in the South of Brazil, starting in March 1851, the year European immigrants started to arrive to the then-colony Dona Francisca. The collection includes furniture, weapons and transportation means used at the time.

Sambaqui Archaeological Museum

600 Dona Francisca Street, 433-0114. Tuesday to Friday, from 9 am to 5 pm; Saturday, Sunday and holidays, from 11 am to 5 pm.
Over 10,000 archaeological items found in the region and neighboring cities are on display in this museum, a unit of the Joinville Cultural Foundation. At the venue, visitors will learn about Brazilian food and costumes from a time prior to colonization. In Joinville alone, there are 42 archaeological sites, classified as sambaquis (shellmounds or middens, remains of Indian villages and burial sites).

★ Bicycle Museum

Monte Castelo Plaza, Railroad Station, 455-0372. Tuesday to Sunday, from 9 am to 12 noon and from 2 pm to 6 pm.
It´s the only museum of its kind in South America, and displays over 16,000 pieces owned by collector Valter Fernandes Busto, in a cargo warehouse at the old Railway Station. The collection goes from candy wrap paper with bicycle pictures to miniatures, accessories and hard-to-find equipment.

Firefighter´s National Museum

13 Jaguaruna Street, Downtown, 431-1112. Daily, from 8 am to 10 pm.
It´s located at the headquarters of the Voluntários de Joinville Fire Station, the oldest Fire Department in the country. The collection includes equipment that tells the story of the Fire Department in the city and in the State.

Príncipe de Joinville III Boat

Board on Baltazar Buschle , Espinheiros, 455-0824, www.barcoprincipe.com.br.
Daily, 9 am on, from December to March; Saturday and Sunday, 9 am on, from April to November.
A three-floor modern luxury ship, having a swimming pool, two bars and capacity for 350 people. It leaves Joinville in the morning and visits 14 islands before arriving at São Francisco do Sul, where passengers disembark to visit the city. The trip lasts an average of 6 hours. In the summer months there are stops for swimming on Flores Island.

In the Piraí region, a rural area in Joinville, the typical farms are the highlight

The Bolshoi Theater School

It´s gratifying to enter the only Bolshoi Theater School outside of Russia. Visits are allowed only on Fridays, preferably on a scheduled tour. About 300 students were granted scholarships, and follow the technique and methodology of the choreography school in Moscow. The teachers and pianists are Brazilians, Russians, Armenians and Ucranians. At least 85% of the students come from poor families and study at public schools in Joinville. Besides learning classic ballet and popular dances, having rhythm and music classes, and doing breathing exercises, among other classes that make up the technical education, children have hygiene and nutrition lessons, have access to a library with computers connected to the Internet, can use a cultural space where they watch dance videos in between classes and have pedagogical activities, that range from caring for nature to performing theater acts. The school has an area that covers six square kilometers, and what is seen all around the school is young-talented kids in contact with a form of art they had never dreamed of before. The social philosophy behind the Brazilian school is the same as in the Moscow school.
☎ 422-4070,
www.escolabolshoi.com.br

Entrance to the Bolshoi: ballet, Moscow style

Zoobotanical Park

Pastor Guilherme Rau Street, Boa Vista, ☎ 431-5016.Tuesday to Sunday, from 9 am to 6 pm.

The Zoobotanical Park covers a 40-square-kilometer area, and is located at the base of Boa Vista Hill. It is the right place for visitors to have a direct contact with Mother Nature. Among the many animals present in the park, there are several species of monkeys, alligators, wild teals, macaws, toucans, owls and capybaras that can be watched.

Morro de Finder Ecological Park

Antônio Horitsch Street, a cross-street of Piratuba Street, Bom Retiro, ☎ 431-3452. Daily, from 8 am to 6 pm.

Specimen from the rainforest flora and fauna are spread all over the 500,000-square-meter area. Visitors can walk or go biking along the marked trails and observe all the beauty of headwaters, groves and lakes. From there, visitors have a bird´s-eye-view of Babitonga Bay.

From Morro do Boi, in Corupá, it´s possible to see the ocean, on clear days

SURROUNDINGS

Corupá

Access via BR-280, passing through Jaraguá do Sul or São Bento do Sul, 375-1171, turismo@corupa-sc.com.br.

Besides being the largest banana producer in Santa Catarina, Corupá is a must-see city for those who enjoy extreme sports. The 477-square-kilometer city has circa 12,000 inhabitants and 67 waterfalls, dozens of rivers and streams, many groves and a vast area of preserved rainforest. At **Emílio Batistela Ecological Park,** 375-2232, also called **Rio Novo Municipal Park**, there are as many as 14 waterfalls, on a 2-kilometer route. Just a one-hour hike away from Downtown is **Morro do Boi**, at an altitude of 920 meters, from where you can see the ocean on clear days. At **Braço Esquerdo,** there are two waterfalls that are good for the practice of canyoning, besides many trails leading to beautiful waterfalls and groves. The city´s many natural attractions include **Morro da Igreja** (Church Hill), **Véu de Noiva Waterfall**, **Omã Beach** and the **Recanto da Água Verde**. Allow some extra time to visit the **Natural History Museum**, an learn more about science and history by observing stuffed animals. It´s located inside the **Sacred Heart of Jesus Seminary**, an exposed-brick building with an iron structure, built in 1929.

Jaraguá do Sul

The city is crossed by BR-280, 372-8096, www.jaraguadosul.com.br.

If you go to Jaraguá do Sul and don´t visit the Malwee Park, you haven´t been there at all. The park was created in 1978, in a 1.5-million-square-meter preserved area, and boasts 35,000

Corupá Waterfall: attraction to sports fans

trees, a 100-square-kilometer lake, two museums and 15 kilometers of decorated roads. Other attractions include Morro da Boa Vista, the Malwee, Jaraguá, Serra Preta and Serra do Funil peaks, the Rio do Júlio Fall, and waterfalls that beautify the city of the Itapocu Valley. In the last few years, many clubs for the practice of extreme sports have sprung up. Sports include free flight, acquariding, mountain-climbing and canoeing. The city was settled by Germans, Italians and Hungarians and strives to keep its traditions. The most important festival in the city is the Schützenfest, a meeting of hunt and shoot clubs held in October. The best way to understand the city and its costumes is to pay a visit to the Emílio da Silva Municipal Museum. It´s located inside the building of the old City Hall and displays a collection of photographs and objects belonging to the first settlers.

Miniature pieces at the Sea National Museum

★ São Francisco do Sul

37 kilometers from Downtown Joinville, on a paved road, 471-2222, www.saofranciscodosul.com.br.

It´s the third oldest city in Brazil and has the fifth largest Brazilian port in number of containers shipped. São Francisco do Sul combines history and nature. On the narrow streets of the Historic Downtown, declared National Artistic and Historical Landmark, the highlight are the charming houses that can be traced back to the Portuguese colonization period. Among the calm-water beaches and the strong-wave beaches, **Enseada Beach** is the most popular with visitors. It has the shape of a horseshoe looking at the open seas and is 20 kilometers from Downtown on SC-280. Mullet fishing can be found on **Molhe Beach**, in the winter months. Molhe shares with **Saudade Beach**, where there´s a 6,000-year-old shellmound, the preference of surfers. **Grande** is practically a desert beach and is the most distant from Downtown. In January it hosts the largest net fishing championship in the south of Brazil. Be sure to visit the islands on the Babitonga Bay archipelago, that can be reached by boats, leaving from Downtown São Francisco do Sul. **Rita Island** was a Navy fuel base and supplied fuel to Brazilian squad ships during World War II. In the town´s historic quarter, visit the **Matriz Nossa Senhora da Graça Church**, built in 1699 with a mixture of lime, shells, sand and whale oil. Inside the church, tourists are able to see an image of the patron saint, left there in 1553 by some

Spaniards who built a chapel to honor the saint after being saved from a storm. **The National Museum of the Sea** is also located in Historic Downtown. It´s the only one in Brazil dedicated to preserving the Brazilian sea heritage and displays collections of artwork and naval modeling, and includes a library, a shipyard, a rafts exhibition hall and even a space dedicated to sailor and adventurer Amyr Klink. Check it out. In April, the city hosts the **Fishing National Festival (Fenapesca)** and the **Traditions of the Island Festival (Festilha).**

Schroeder

Access via BR-280, ☎ 374-1191.

With a little over 10,000 inhabitants and having been emancipated only 39 years ago, Schroeder is known as the ecological capital of Santa Catarina. Half of the 149.5-square-kilometer town is formed by hills covered with the green areas of the Rainforest. To the north of the city settled by Germans is the **Bracinho Ecological Station**, a sanctuary set amidst the Serra do Mar, covering an area of 46 million square meters. Created in 1988 next to the Bracinho Hydroelectric Plant, 12 kilometers from Downtown, the station was the first conservation unit to be inside a hydroelectric plant area in the State. The station is open to small groups who call in advance. For mountain bike lovers, the city offers the **Kamikaze Track**. It´s located in the **Rio do Braço Sul Valley**, and is considered to be the best Down Hill track in South America. Those who prefer rappelling can choose the Rio **Macaco Waterfalls**. The rapids of the **Bracinho River** are sought by those who enjoy canoeing and acquariding. Off-road adventurers should go to **Duas Mamas Road**, in Rio **Júlio Valley**. Every October the city holds the **Schroederfest**, a festival to celebrate the anniversary of the city.

TIPS

• Joinville has many options for those who are looking for rural tourism. Most attractions are located from 10 to 20 kilometers from Downtown. In the Piraé region, for example, small roads lead to water parks, fishing lakes and places to buy bread, biscuits, jams, cheeses, cakes and artwork. Bonita Road is another good option, with rustic restaurants and small preserved houses.

• Visit Piazza Itália, a kind of Little Italy in Joinville. It´s a gastronomic and cultural complex boasting typical architecture, at 79 Antônia Garibaldi Street, ☎ 455-3991.

• To go to some waterfalls and peaks in Jaraguá do Sul and Schroeder, you have to hire a guide. Ação Livre Turismo e Aventuras takes groups for rappelling, rafting, jeep tours and hikes in both cities (acaolivre@netuno.com.br or ☎ 372-0604 and 371-8341).

Historic Downtown in São Francisco do Sul, the third oldest city in Brazil

◀ Visits are allowed on the islands of Babitonga

Laguna

The city colonized by Azoreans has a well-preserved Historic Downtown

Florianópolis 110 km
Lages 247 km
Imbituba 30 km
47,408
48
646-0533
lagunagolfinho.com.br

The city was declared a National Historic and Artistic Landmark by IPHAN in 1984. It was founded in July 1676 and made history even before its colonization, by the Azoreans. It´s the southernmost point of the imaginary line created in 1494 to divide America between Portugal and Spain, in the Tordesilhas Treaty. Laguna staged the Farrapos Revolution and the Juliana Republic, and is proud to be the home of Anita Garibaldi, and of having the best street Carnaval in the South. Laguna is also where bodyboard two-time champion Soraia Rocha was born. The memories of a distant past live side by side with the beauty of the beaches. In low season, fishermen go to Laguna to catch mullet and shrimp. Between the months of April and July it´s possible to see porpoises pushing whole schools of mullets to fishermen´s nets. Shrimp fishing is a spectacle worth seeing, especially at night. Fishermen attract shrimp with gas lamps, making the Imaruí and Santo Antônio lagoons look like illuminated carpets.

Carioca Fountain

Largo da Carioca, Historic Downtown.
Built in 1863 by slaves and enlarged in 1906, the fountain supplies the whole city with water. As legend goes, the couple that drinks that water will never part and will look 15 years younger. It´s also believed that those who drink the water end up returning to Laguna. By the fountain is **Casa Pinto d´Ulysséa**, built in 1866 and having its walls covered with Portuguese tiles.

Morro da Glória

It´s the highest point in town. At 126 meters, it affords a bird´s-eye-view of the Historic Downtown, several districts, the southern and northern beaches, lagoons and the Santa Marta Lighthouse. Since 1953 it has housed an image of Our Lady of Glória, 12 meters high (the pedestal only is 4 meters high), built by the German

Laguna´s heroine

Anita Garibaldi

The woman who became known as the heroine of two worlds – for participating in the Farroupilha Revolution and in the struggle for the unification of Italy – was born on August 30, 1821 in Morrinhos, a county in Laguna, under the name of Ana Maria de Jesus Ribeiro. She is said to value freedom since an early age. Ana enjoyed riding horses and bathing in the sea, taboos for a woman at the time. In 1833, her father, Bento Ribeiro da Silva, died and her mother, Maria Antônia de Jesus, gave her daughter´s hand to shoemaker Manuel Duarte Aguiar because she was worried about Ana´s reputation and also in hopes of improving the family´s financial situation. Ana was only 14 years old when she got married at the Matriz de Santo Antônio dos Anjos Church. The marriage didn´t work, and Manuel left Laguna and Ana to join the imperialist army. In August 1839, the 18-year-old girl met the love of her life, Italian Giuseppe Garibaldi. Just two months later, the bold and fearless Ana went with him on the Captain ship Rio Pardo. Anita, as Garibaldi called her, had her fire baptism in the battle of Imbituba, on November 4, and never stopped fighting side by side with the man with whom she had four children. They got married on March 26, 1842, in Montevideo. In 1848, she was acclaimed by the Italians who waited for them on the Geneva Port.

couple Alfredo Staege and Elisa Faccio Staege. You can go by car, leaving Voluntários Benevides Street, from Mar Grosso Beach or via the Historic Downtown.

Santo Antônio dos Anjos Church

Vidal Ramos Plaza, Historic Downtown.

It´s a Toscany-style church, built in the 17th century with Minas Gerais Baroque altars. It has a canvas depicting the Imaculate Conception, painted by Santa Catarina artist Victor Meirelles in 1856, an image of patron saint Antônio dos Anjos de Laguna, sculpted in Bahia on a cedar wood trunk in the 18th century, and the Santíssimo Sacramento Chapel, all covered with a layer of gold.

★ Anita Garibaldi Museum

República Juliana Plaza, Historic Downtown Daily, 9 am-7 pm

The building that houses the museum

In addition to a valuable historical heritage, Laguna has beautiful beaches

Anita´s home revives History

was built in 1747. The ground floor was used as a public jail and the upper floors were used as the City Council. It was from this building´s windows that the Juliana Republic was proclaimed. Despite the name of the museum being in honor of Anita Garibaldi, there are only a few photographs and documents. The collection includes mostly items from the Farroupilha Revolution and the Juliana Republic (read Man from the South). A statue honoring Anita Garibaldi stands in the middle of the plaza where the museum is located.

Anita´s Home

On the corner of Conselheiro Jerônimo Coelho and Vidal Ramos Plaza, Historic Downtown. Daily, 8 am-12 am; 1 pm-5 pm.

The building dating back from 1711 was where Ana Maria de Jesus Ribeiro got dressed for her first wedding, on August 30, 1835. The name Anita Garibaldi was adopted after she married Giuseppe Garibaldi, four years later. In the house there´s a small collection with items that tell their story.

Beaches

There are a total of 16 beaches, some still deserted. The one that is most sought-for is **Mar Grosso**. Having only 3 kilometers in length, it´s regarded as the noblest in the region and is very popular among tourists. The modern buildings and the centuries-old architecture Downtown offer a striking contrast. **Gi Beach**, another favorite in summer, is located 6 kilometers from Downtown and offers a beautiful setting together with the many rocks along the sands. One of the rocks, the **Pedra do Frade**, is quite intriguing: it´s a little inclined, and it may have been placed there as a landmark to the Tordesilhas Treaty. Some people say its name is derived from its shape, that reminds of a Franciscan brother. To reach **Farol Island**, a surfer´s paradise, you´ll have to take the ferryboat and cross the Balsa channel. Ten minutes later, you´ll come to the 14-kilometer dirt road that leads to the **Santa Marta Lighthouse**. Built by the French with stone, sand, mud and whale oil in 1891, the lighthouse is 29 meters high and the view spans a distance of 92 kilometers.

SURROUNDINGS

Araranguá

Access through BR-101, 522-1143.

Araranguá is one of the most beautiful settings of the Atlantic coast, having ★ **Morro dos Conventos** as its landmark and the spa by the same name as the destination of almost all tourists who visit Araranguá in summer. The lighthouse atop the hill affords a stunning vista of the dunes and the **Araranguá River** mouth. The city has one of the best infrastructures for camping in the country, and also many other points of interest. Five minutes on the ferryboat and another 5 kilometers on a dirt road, and you´re at **Balneário de Ilhas**, the oldest fishing village on the Araranguá River mouth, where the city founded in 1880 emerged. There are no hotels or restaurants,

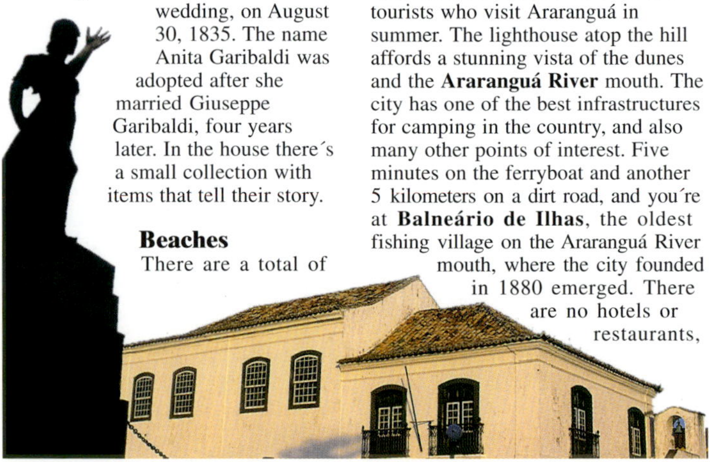

The building where the Republic was proclaimed now houses the Anita Garibaldi Museum

The Santa Marta Lighthouse, built by the French, is 29 meters tall

and it´s worth visiting the **Nossa Senhora Mãe dos Homens Church**, Downtown, the main religious monument in town. In February, the **Balneário Arroio do Silva**, frequented by locals, comes alive with the **Quilômetro de Arrancada de Caminhões**, a truck race on the beach sands. In the month of May, it´s time for the **Nossa Senhora Mãe dos Homens Festival**.

Criciúma

Access through BR-101, ☎ 431-0001.
The city is known as the Brazilian capital of charcoal and tiles. Tourism isn´t a strong call in the city, but going to **Mina Modelo** is a must for those who are in town. The only charcoal mine open to visitation in Brazil, ☎ 431-0157, it was active between 1920 and 1955 and became a model mine because nobody ever died at the place. The guided tour is on a cart and takes about 30 minutes.

Tubarão

66 km from Criciúma on BR-101. For those coming from the west, access is via BR-116 to Lages and then BR-282 and SC-438, ☎ 621-9081.
Founded in 1836, the city´s tourism potential is in its thermal waters. Comfortable hotel complexes have pools with average temperatures of 36º C. It´s possible to tour the whole city in **Maria-Fumaça** locomotives on the Thereza Christina Railroad. The city is located between hills and the sea, on the Tubarão riverbanks, and has several bridges that draw attention. A boat tour on the Tubarão River to Laguna relives the route taken by Italian, German and Azorean settlers. The lagoons **Manteiga**, **Garopaba, do Sul**, **Camacho**, **Gamboa Grande**, **Lino** and **dos Paus** are the highlights of the region.

TIPS

- When leaving Araranguá towards Laguna, or the other way around, be prepared to face several sections of BR-101 in terrible shape.
- Driving on the streets of Laguna requires a good dose of attention. There are no traffic lights and traffic is intense. In Historic Downtown, prefer to walk.
- Don´t leave Laguna before visiting Molhes da Barra, Lagoa de Santo Antônio dos Anjos and part of Downtown on board a schooner. Flipper ☎ 9986-0596 and Possenti ☎ 9987-9739 have tours that leave daily from the pier next to the public market.
- In Araranguá, the nearest hotel to Morro dos Conventos is open only in the summer months. On Araranguá Municipal Highway, which links the spa to BR-101 there are some cheaper hotels.

Boats contribute to the picturesque scenery of Bombinhas Beach ▶

Porto Belo

Stopover for 90% of the ships that cruise along the south coast of the country

Florianópolis 55 km
Balneário Camboriú 25 km
Blumenau 90 km
47
10,682
369-5638
portobelo.com.br

Beaches are the greatest attraction in Porto Belo, founded in 1832 by Azoreans. The city has a very good infrastructure and receives over 60,000 visitors in the summer months, but docks and jet ski rental companies, motorboats and sailboats contribute to making the nautical activities more attractive than the terrestrial part. Porto Belo is considered to be one of the most beautiful regions on the Brazilian coast, and is the stopover point for 90% of the ocean liners that pass through the South seas of the country. The Travessia de Porto Belo is an event that celebrates the city´s anniversary, on October 13, and is the most important event of the year. In its 11th edition, at the end of summer in 2003, 597 swimmers crossed the 1,200-meter stretch.

Beaches

Porto Belo Beach is an inlet with calm waters and moderate winds. It´s the favorite setting for sailmen and water skiers. It´s from its docks that boats and

schooners leave for the beach by the same name and others in the region. Sailmen from all over the world come to Porto Belo through the **Caixa D´Aço Beach**, a natural port in which floating bars are attractions in themselves. **Estaleiro Beach** has crystal-clear waters that are ideal for swimming and diving. It´s a rural beach, and to get there you´ll have to take the road that leads to the Yacht Club. It´s a narrow dirt road that passes by the Araçá Village and Caixa D´Aço Beach. **Araçá Beach** – a fishing village – still retains the habits of its first settlers, and there you´ll find the first fishing port of the region. Those looking for calm and quiet should go to **Costão das Vieiras**. Set amidst Perequê and Porto Belo beaches, the Costão has the three calmer beaches in the region.

Porto Belo Island

www.ilhadeportobelo.com.br, ☎ 369-4146, Daily, from 8 am to 7 pm.

The Amateur Fishermen´s Association boats take visitors to the island in 20 minutes. The nearly 40.000 square-meters island is 1,400 meters long and 400 meters wide. It´s administered by the grandsons of businessman Ernesto Stodieck Júnior, who bought the island in 1953 and began a restoration project, including the planting of native vegetation. The island has two kiosks that sell juices and snacks, a restaurant, an ecological 40-minute walking trail where you´ll find Rupestrian inscriptions, underwater trails and several nautical sports. The island used to be the headquarters of the Adventure House – the home of the Schürmann family when on land – now in Bombinhas.

A diver´s paradise

The Arvoredo Marine Preservation unit is the only one in the South and one of the three in Brazil. It covers an area of 178 km^2 and became a preservation unit in 1990. Since 1995, it has been the site for several research programs to supply information to an environmental education project, which aims at informing the population on the importance of the preservation unit. It´s formed by the Galé, Macuco, Deserta and Arvoredo islands. Arvoredo is the largest, covering an area of 2,7 km^2. The preservation unit also houses the Calhau de São Pedro, a rock formation with no vegetation in the middle of the ocean. Located 3 km from the coast and surrounded by water with a 40-meter-deep visibility, it´s a diver´s paradise.

Diving on the largest island: Arvoredo

SURROUNDINGS

★ Bombinhas

It´s 10 kilometers from Porto Belo on SC-412, ☎ 369-2350.

Bombinhas is the headquarters of the Arvoredo Marine Biological Reserve and is regarded as the divers´ paradise on earth. It was emancipated from Porto Belo in 1992 and has about 11,000 inhabitants and 19 beaches in an area of only 36.6 square kilometers. Some of the beaches are just small strips of sand, like the 100-meter **Sepultura Beach**, a landmark in town. As underwater tourism is strong, due to the proximity of the four islands of the preservation unit, there are several diving courses in the city. They are responsible for arranging most of the excursions to the islands. Despite being only one kilometer long, **Bombinhas Beach** is the most crowded of them all. This is where you´ll find most of the agencies that organize diving tours and most of the restaurants and lodging options. The open-sea **Bombas Beach** is two kilometers long and has clear sands and a perfect infrastructure for families and tourists in general. **Quatro Ilhas Beach** has only 800 meters of open seas and a wide stretch of sand. It´s one of the favorite beaches among surfers.

Another favorite is the 4-kilometer-long **Mariscal**, which is regarded as one of the most beautiful in the city, with good hotels and restaurants. **Zimbros Beach** is among the most sought-for beaches and its charm is fully revealed in the picturesque scenery it offers: fishing boats adorn the shore. The base of the Schürmann family on land is in Bombinhas. **Adventure House** (☎ 369-4940) was based in Porto Belo Island from 1997 to March 2003 and soon this year will open a space on **Ribeiro Beach,** between Bombas and Bombinhas Beach. The eco-cultural center will display objects, photographs and videos telling the story of the Santa Catarina family who has sailed the world over for more than 10 years. The Center also works with schools from Santa Catarina, Paraná and Rio Grande do Sul. Another attraction in the city is the **Bombinhas Museum and Marine Aquarium** (museumarinho@terra.com.br). With the largest collection of the Santa Catarina Sea Studies Center, the museum displays whale bones, shark teeth, relics from shipwrecks and seven aquariums.

Marine species at the Bombinhas Museum

Governador Celso Ramos

Access via BR-101, ☎ (48) 262-0141.

Governador Celso Ramos is located inside the environmental protection area of the Anhatomirim Island and another positive aspect is its proximity with the Arvoredo Marine Biological Preservation Unit. The typical setting of a fishing village is combined with the Rainforest natural beauties, giving visitors the impression of a backlands beach. There are good lodging facilities right on the beach and others a little farther, amidst green vegetation, with access via dirt roads. **Palmas** is the largest beach in town and one of the most beautiful in the region. On **Armação Beach** stands the **Nossa Senhora da Armação da Piedade Church**, built over 200 years ago. **Grande Beach** is the one with choice waves for surfing. **Costeira Beach** is a former whale fishing resort and up to now visitors can see dolphins in the ocean. In all, the coastal region has 23

In Zimbros, many boats and all the charm of amateur fishermen ▶

◄ Mariscal, the most popular with surfers

beaches between the sea and the mountains. In February, the city hosts the **Nossa Senhora dos Navegantes Festival**. In May, it´s time for the **Divino Espírito Santo Festival**, and, in June, the São Pedro Festival is held in the city.

★ Itapema

Access via BR-101, ☎ 368-2400.

Beautiful beaches and a first-rate hotel system contribute to making Itapema one of the most beautiful cities on the Santa Catarina coast. The tourism industry is the main economic activity, drawing 120,000 visitors in the summer. The city was settled by Azoreans in 1748, and belonged to Camboriú and Porto Belo before being emancipated on April 21, 1962. At present, the city has approximately 26,000 inhabitants. The main attractions are the beaches and nautical activities. The largest and most famous beach is **Meia**, providing tourists with an excellent infrastructure. **Itapema Beach** is the most popular and also boasts very good services. It is also the ground for sports and nautical events. Another very popular beach is **Costão Beach**, regarded as one of the most beautiful in town. The best waves for surfing are on **Cabeço Beach**. **Estaleiro** and **Ilhota** beaches are still very rustic and also attract surfers. Fisherman flock to **Canto da Praia**: net fishing is the subsistence means for most part of the population.

TIPS

- Don´t leave Porto Belo without having lunch or dinner at Pier 98, ☎ 369-4694.
- The Porto Belo Amateur Fishermen´s Association promotes daytime and nighttime fishing excursions. For information and reservation, call the Porto Belo fishermen´s boathouse, ☎ 369-4815.
- There are four diving schools in Bombinhas: Pata da Cobra Adventures, ☎ 369-2119, www.patadacobra.com.br; Hy Brazil Diving School, ☎ 369-2545, www.hybrazil.com.br; Trek & Dive, ☎ 369-2137, trekdive@trekdive.com.br; and Submarine, ☎ 369-2473, www.submarinescuba.com.br.
- To go to the Bombinhas Museum and Marine Aquarium, go off Leopardo Zarling Avenue, on Bombas Beach, and take Leopardo Street. It´s located in the district of Zé Amandio.
- In Itapema, allow some extra time to see the period buildings from the time of the Azorean colonization. They are large richly detailed houses with stone walls, high ceilings and wooden doors.

São Joaquim

View of the São Joaquim National Park, one of the main attractions in the mountain region

Lages 76 km
Serra do Rio do Rastro 54 km
Tubarão 145 km
22,790
49
233-0411

Located on one of the highest points of the Santa Catarina mountain range, São Joaquim is considered to be the coldest city in Brazil. Snow is almost always present in the harsh winters, with temperatures ranging between 10º C and 15º C below zero. Founded in 1887 by the trailblazer Manoel Joaquim Pinto, it covers an area of 1,888 square kilometers and preserves traditions from the German, Italian, Japanese and African cultures. São Joaquim is the second largest apple producer in the State, and every October hosts the National Apple Festival, which is its biggest attraction, right after the snowfall.

Igreja Matriz

João Ribeiro Plaza, Downtown, 233-0015. Daily, 8:30 am-6 pm.

The biggest attraction of this church, built between 1918 and 1935, with basalt stone taken from the nearby hills, is its architecture. On the exterior walls, there are images of Biblical prophets and of Adam and Eve sculpted in rocks. A Nossa Senhora da Serra sculpture, by artist Elson Outuki, decorates a flower bed near the church.

Snow Valley

SC-438, 10 km from São Joaquim Downtown towards Bom Jardim da Serra, www.valedaneve.com.br, 233-3447 and 9983-8586.

It´s a 30-hectare area, with four water cascades and three trails. The main one (1h10) takes you to a 1,300-high spot. The beauty of the place is in the vegetation, with lots of pine trees and ferns, some over 300 years old and up to 5 meters tall. The place has rustic cabins and a restaurant.

National Historical Museum

168 Major Jacinto Goulart Street, Downtown, 233-2798. Daily, 9 am-11 am; 1:30 pm-5 pm.

The museum tells the history of the city through pieces dating from the cycle of the wood, documents and photographs from the time of the settlers and items related to the cowboys´time. Besides the permanent

Serra do Rio do Rastro: one of the most beautiful settings in the interior of Santa Catarina

collection, the museum periodically displays theme exhibitions that document the history of São Joaquim.

SURROUNDINGS

Bom Jardim da Serra

Access via Highway SC-438 from BR-101, BR-116 or BR-282. Another way to reach the city is via SC-430 from BR-282 or via SC-444 from BR-101, 232-0197.

Located between the cities of São Joaquim and Lauro Müller, the town is home to one of the most beautiful settings of Santa Catarina, the **Serra do Rio do Rastro**. The road from the coast to the mountain region is 12 kilometers wide, located at an altitude of 1,460 meters, and was opened by the first families who arrived at the region. Cowboys rode the Serra Geral trail, at first called Serra dos Doze, with mules carrying leather, cheese and pine seeds to exchange for sugar, flour and fabrics. São Jardim da Serra was founded only in 1905. In 1921 it became a village and in 1967 it became a town. The city has 14 rivers that spring up and flow into the **Pelotas River** and at least 30 water cascades with over 10-meter falls and more than 30 other smaller cascades. Another natural attraction is the 490-square-meter **São Joaquim National Park**. The **Laranjeiras Canyon** is also part of the tourist route, at an altitude of 1,540 meters on the Santa Cândida Farm, 20 kilometers north of Downtown. Access to the canyon is via walking trails or on horseback.

Lages

Access via the intersection of highways BR-116 (going from north to south) and

Rural Tourism

Lages was one of the first cities to promote rural tourism in the country, by opening its farms, so that tourists could have a taste of the hospitality and the habits of the locals. The first farm to offer infrastructure for visitors was the Pedras Brancas Farm (access via km 10 on SC-438, 223-2073), in the 1990s. The Boqueirão Farm Hotel (access via km 225 on BR-282, 226-0354) has very good facilities, with heated swimming pools, saunas and insulated rooms. The Barreiro Farm (access via the 43 km marker on SC-438, 222-3031) reproduces the daily life in a kitchen with a dirt floor, and the SESC Rural Inn (km 4.5 on SC-425 in the Índios district, 224-9988) combines horse riding with walking tours to attract visitors.

Pedras Brancas Farm, a pioneer in Lages

With the first snowfall, locals and tourists take to the streets in São Joaquim ▶

BR-282 (going from east to west), 221-1000, www.cidadelages.com.br.
Lages is the largest city in the State in terms of extension, covering an area of 2,651.4 square kilometers. It´s located between the east and the west part of Santa Catarina and boasts the title of "national capital of rural tourism." The 157,000-inhabitant city is known by the large quantities of pine trees. The **João José Theodoro da Costa Neto Ecological Park** alone concentrates more than 8,000 native pine trees, some over 20 meters tall, in an area of 2.34 million square meters. In June, Lages is home to the **Pine Tree Seed National Festival** (Festa do Pinhão), one of the largest cultural and gastronomic events in the South. Another big event in the region is the **ExpoLages**, the largest farming festival, held in October. Among the tourist attractions, visit the **Jonas Ramos Park** and the **Thiago de Castro Historical Museum**. The park was built in 1771 so that women had a safe place to do their laundry. It´s also home to the Public Library and to the Ida Schmidt Environmental Education Center. The historical museum, regarded as the largest private collection in the State, displays 18th and 19th century items, such as war weapons, clothing, objects, documents and photographs.

Orleans

Access via SC-438 Highway, from BR-101, through the intersections to Gravatal and São Ludgero. Another option is via SC-446, from Criciúma, (48) 466-0178.
What projects the name of the city both in Brazil and in South America are the sculptures of artist José Fernandes, depicting Biblical themes. ★ The **Esculturas do Paredão** (Wall Sculptures) are located on a hillside on Etieni Gardieni Stawiarsk Street, Downtown. The action of the sun and the rain has washed away many of their characteristics, but they still attract many visitors. Orleans was settled by Italians in 1884, and currently has a little over 20,000 inhabitants. Another tourist attraction is the **Open-Air Museum**, located at km 33 on SC-438 Highway, (48) 466-0011. It´s the only one of its kind in Latin America, and seeks to give a clear picture of the settlements, displaying manioc flour and sugar mills, a still, a brick factory, a saw mill, a carpenter´s shop, a warehouse showing several types of transportation means and a chapel. The mills are run by animals and by waterwheels.

Urubici

Take SC-430 at the 132 km marker on BR-282 or follow the Serra do Corvo Branco on SC-439, 278-4245.
The city is one of the coldest in the country and its natural wealth includes over 80 waterfalls and cascades. It´s known as the vegetable capital, ranking first on the Santa Catarina production line, putting out some 74,000 tons of vegetables a year. In February, Urubici holds the **Vegetable National Festival** (Fenahort), in April it´s time for the **City´s Motorcycle Endurance**, and on the second Sunday of May, it holds the Our Lady Mother of Men Festival. The **Morro da Igreja** (Church´s Hill) is a landmark in town, and also the highest point in the South, at 1,828 meters. There, the **Pedra Furada** (Rock with a hole) calls attention because of the 30-meter crack. The place offers cascades and canyons, but it´s advisable to check weather conditions before going.

Urubici: breathtaking waterfalls ►

Esculturas do Paredão: the artwork is a cultural highlight of Orleans

Urussanga

Access via highways BR-101, SC-444, SC-445 and SC-446, through Criciúma and Cocal do Sul (south access) or Gravatal and Orleans (north access), (48) 465-1188, www.urussanga.sc.gov.br

Located in the south of the State, 18 kilometers from Criciúma and 24 kilometers from the beginning of the Serra do Rastro, the city founded by Italians in 1878 keeps the traditions of the immigrants who first came to the city. There are a series of cultural manifestations, always with a lot of wine, that celebrate the immigrants´ culture. The **Wine Festival** and the **Rittorno Alle Origine** are the most popular festivals, and are held in alternate years, in August. Homemade wine and rhum production isn´t the main economic activity, but answers for most of the local income. The main tourist attractions are the wineries and the historical buildings and monuments located Downtown, the only collection of urban Italian architecture declared historical heritage by the Santa Catarina Cultural Foundation. Another pride and joy of Urussanga is the marble work **La Pietà**, an original-sized replica of Michelangelo´s sculpture, given as a present to the city by Pope John Paul VI at the celebrations of the first centennial of Italian colonization, in 1978.

TIPS

• The view afforded by the observatory on Serra do Rio Rastro, on SC-438, can´t be missed. From there, it´s possible to have a bird´s-eye-view of the region and see the beautiful setting of the curves that surround the mountains. On clear days, you can also see the ocean.

• On the way to São Joaquim, those leaving Lages can go to the Araucárias Observatory, which affords a view of a large concentration of pine trees. There´s another panoramic view of São Joaquim from the 89-step Belvedere Stairway, at 1,450 meters high.

• While still in São Joaquim, make sure you visit the Pirata Cascade, a 15-meter-high free fall on Refúgio do Pirata Farm.

• In Lages, go to the Caveiras River Fall. About 20 kilometers from Downtown on BR-282, the place is ideal for fishing, with a large lake, a dam and a cascade, all in the middle of a green oasis.

Grapes that Urussanga turns into wine

• The view of Urubici from Morro do Oderdeng, 3 kilometers from the city, is awesome. The hill is 1,400 meters high and has one of the best free-flight ramps in the State.

Treze Tílias

Treze Tílias, the most Austrian of all Brazilian cities, cultivates its European roots

Blumenau 400 km
Florianópolis 450 km
Fraiburgo 71 km
5,029
49
537-0166

As the largest Austrian colony in Brazil and the birthplace of wooden sculptures in Santa Catarina, Treze Tílias resembles a city in Tyrol. The Tyrolese tradition is present in the gardens, in architecture, in decoration and even in the clothes of hotel and restaurant employees. Located in the Midwest of the State, covering an area of 178 square kilometers, the city founded in October 1933 has also an Italian section. The Linha Pinhal community is located 10 kilometers from Downtown and preserves traditions as the descendants of the first Austrian immigrants do. On the second Saturday of July, the Associazione Veneta throws a party for the community, the Italian Evening, a festival with lots of music, dancing and typical food. The Tyrolese Festival (Tirolerfest) is held in October, celebrating the anniversary of the Austrian immigration.

Andreas City Museum Thaler Cultural Center

São Vicente de Paula Street, Downtown. Monday-Friday, 9 am-12 noon; 2 pm-5 pm.

Better known as Castelinho (Small Castle), the building that houses the museum was built in 1937 to be the home of the city´s founder, Austria´s Minister for the Agriculture, Andreas Thaler. It also housed an administrative center of the Dreizehnlinden colony and was

◀ Apples are the region´s typical product

Popular harvesting: hordes of visitors come to charming Fraiburgo because of the famous apples

declared a Historical Landmark in 1996. Divided into five visiting spaces, the collection keeps the belongings of the first settlers and a library with books on Tyrol.

★ Godofredo Thaler Studio

260 Leoberto Leal Street, Downtown, ☎ 537-0123.

Godofredo Thaler is the founder´s grandson and inherited from his father the talent to sculpt. He´s known mainly by the sacred works of art that he makes out of cedar and pine knots, some as high as four meters. The sculptor believes he has turned out over 300 images of saints, most sent to other cities, states and countries. The Christ at the Brasília Cathedral, for example, was sculpted by him. Austria also has some of his sculptures. The studio is beside his own house, turned into a small private museum, housing works by his father and his two daughters, also sculptors.

Art: Treze Tílias invests on sculptures

Vale das Tílias International Thermal Complex

585 Vidoira Stroot, Downtown, ☎ 537-0277, www.termasinternacional.com.br.

As part of the Treze Tílias Park Hotel complex, the park has thermal swimming pools, cascades, a water playground, a multi-use court, children´s and adults´ toboggan, a rapids river, sauna, chalets, bungalows and restaurants. Open only for hotel guests and those with passports.

SURROUNDINGS

Fraiburgo

71 quilometers from Treze Tílias, on SC-453, ☎ 246-2222.

It covers an area of 82 square kilometers, with around 10 million

Rio Bonito Waterfall, in Porto União ▶

apple trees and a yearly output of 350 tons, which give Fraiburgo the title of "apple town." Responsible for 40% of the national production and 60% of Santa Catarina production, the circa 35,000-inhabitant city is also an important honey producer, but its attractions are mainly because of the blossoming of the apple trees

Folklore: groups relive the traditional dances

in October and the harvesting of fruits, between February and May, a time when the city founded in the 1930s gathers as many as 100,000 tourists. **Bosque Rene Frey** is one of the places that tourists can actively participate in the apple crop. A 50-hectare property administered by Renar Hotel, the area has trails that can be tackled on foot, on horseback, by jeep or by truck. **Steiner Park** is an attraction in itself. The 150,000-square-meter ecological park, three kilometers from Downtown, right by SC-453, at the exit to Videira, offers a complete entertainment infrastructure.

Porto União

Access via SC-280, SC-302, BR-153 and BR-475 highways, ☎ (42) 523-1155.

A railroad is the dividing line between Porto União and União da Vitória, in Paraná. They used to be only one city until 1916, when a border agreement due to the Contestado War divided them into two cities, one in Santa Catarina and the other in Paraná. The different States is no obstacle for both to live as twin sister cities. The city in Santa Catarina has 32,000 inhabitants and

the one in Paraná has a little over 48,000. Together, they form an important university center with the Contestado University, the Cidade de União da Vitória College, the Philosophy, Sciences and Letters State College and the Unidade de Ensino Superior Vale do Iguaçu. The **União Railroad Station** is considered to be a true work of art for both States. The side that belongs to União da Vitória is exactly the same as in Porto União. Built in 1942 to serve both cities, it was deactivated. A project plans to make the station a cultural center. The twin-sister cities have another point in common: the calling for ecological tourism, boasting over 200 waterfalls, in addition to an endless number of trails that end in waterfalls and cascades. Most of its natural beauties are far from Downtown, though. And to reach them you have to use a dirt road.

TIPS

• In Treze Tílias, besides visiting the Godofredo Thaler Studio, it´s worth visiting the many other sculptors who live in the city. There are at least 15 artists who work with wood in their studios, spread along Leoberto Leal, Pioneiros and Presidente Kennedy streets.

• Those visiting Treze Tílias have to taste the typical fare of Kandlerhof restaurant, at 80 Videira Street, behind the City Hall, ☎ 537-0276.

• The Fraiburgo Receptive Tourism Center (Centraltur), ☎ 246-3326, takes visitors to apple orchards and to coolers that select and pack the fruit. At harvest time, tourists are allowed to pick the apples and pay when they return from the excursion. They charge by the kilo and it´s really cheap.

• In the land of apples, you can´t leave without tasting all the gastronomic variations made with the fruit. Estações restaurant is located at the Renar Hotel, ☎ 246-2133, and is one of the places that offer apples in several versions: jams, pies, spreads and also in non-sweet versions.

• Be very careful when driving in Porto União, because there are very few traffic lights. The streets of União da Vitória are better to drive.

• Those who want to check the dividing line between Santa Catarina and Paraná can visit the spot on the left bank of the Iguaçu River, under the railway bridge.

Rio Grande do Sul

Rio Grande do Sul

Situated in the southernmost part of Brazil, and bordering on Uruguay, Argentina and the Atlantic Ocean, the State of Rio Grande do Sul occupies 3.31% of the Brazilian territory and covers an area of 282,062 km^2. It´s a State that was settled in a slightly different way than the rest of the country. At first, it wasn´t even part of Portuguese domain. Later, came the Azoreans, and established themselves in Porto dos Casais Village, currently Porto Alegre. Then came the Italians, who settled in the northeastern part of the State, and the Germans who occupied the Rio dos Sinos Valley. The Pampas tradition was getting stronger on the border with Uruguay and Argentina. It´s in the Pampas (vast plains) that most of the cattle ranches are located, which is the base of the State´s economy.Today it´s the cattle industry that gives support to the textile and the food products industry in the metropolitan area of Porto Alegre. The landscapes attract visitors all year long. The beaches have dunes and lagoons. Stretching along part of the coast and separated from the ocean by a sandbank, is the Lagoa dos Patos (Patos Lagoon), the largest lagoon in Brazil. In the mountain region, cities like Gramado and Canela, of German tradition, are the highlights, and Bento Gonçalves and Caxias, the largest wine producers. The ruins of the Jesuit Missions were declared Historical Landmarks by Unesco. There is still Aparados da Serra, home to the longest canyon in South America.

◄ In Cambará do Sul, the typical Gaúcho

Highlights

1. Porto Alegre
2. São Miguel das Missões
3. Torres

2
3
RIO GRANDE DO SUL
Palmeira das Missões
Passo Fundo
Vacaria
São José dos Ausentes
Antônio Prado
Veranópolis
Jacuí
Taquari
das Antas
PARQUE NACIONAL DE APARADOS DA SERRA
Flores da Cunha
Bento Gonçalves
Cambará do Sul
PARQUE NACIONAL DA SERRA GERAL
Caxias do Sul
Garibaldi
Farroupilha
Nova Petrópolis
Canela
Gramado
Três Coroas
Torres
Santa Maria
São Pedro do Sul
Dois Irmãos
Sapiranga
Capão da Canoa
Osório
Rio Pardo
PORTO ALEGRE
Guaíba
Caçapava do Sul
Lagoa dos Patos
Piratini
Bagé
Mostardas
São Lourenço do Sul
Tavares
Pelotas
PARQUE NACIONAL DA LAGOA DO PEIXE
Rio Grande
São José do Norte
Balneário de Cassino
Estação Ecológica do Taim
Lagoa Mirim
Lagoa Mangueira
Chuí
Chuy
BR 285
RS 324
RS 122
BR 116
BR 158
RS 020
BR 287
BR 453
BR 471
BR 392
BR 290
BR 101
BR 293
N
O
L
S
0
35
70 km
River
State Capital
City
State Boundary
Park
Paved Road
Dirty Track
Airport

P. Alegre

Porto Alegre

Rio Grande do Sul capital city combines old buildings and the busy lifestyle of a metropolis

Florianópolis 474 km
Curitiba 711 km
1,360,590
51
0800 517-686 e 3333-1873
portoalegre.rs.gov.br

The Rio Grande do Sul capital is located on the right bank of the Guaíba River, in the place where five rivers form the Lagoa dos Patos (Patos Lagoon). It was founded in 1755 as a Portuguese post against the Spanish threats. The small village received Azorean immigrants, developed together with the State, and became one of the main commercial centers in the South. It could well be a rich and hectic metropolis, with no great attractions for tourists, but that is far from happening. In the 1960s and 1970s, Porto Alegre went through a modernization period, but many of its historic buildings were kept intact and the city still retains its charms. Visitors can walk around downtown Porto Alegre and visit most places of interest on foot in a single day. The Linha Turismo two-story buses leave from the Gasômetro Plant and take visitors along the tourist spots. The buses are comfortable and have both an audio system for information and guides. (1 hour, 30 minutes). Porto Alegre has a hectic nightlife at exotic Bom Fim, in the Bohemian district of Cidade Baixa and at the fancy Moinhos de Vento. However, just 15 kilometers from Downtown, the small farms in Belém Velho produce peaches, prunes and grapes. The city is home to the Lami Reserve, an important center covering an area of 1.8 square kilometers, where the red howler, which can only be sighted in this region, can be seen. Porto Alegre has over a million trees planted on the streets, making the city one of the towns with the most green areas in the country. With all that, the Gaúchos still keep strong traditional habits, such as going out on on the streets with the *cuia* (gourd) in hand to drink their *chimarrão* tea or going to Ipanema Beach or Beira Rio Avenue to enjoy a beautiful sunset on the Guaíba River. The city has two important festivals: the Farroupilha Week, from September 13 to 20, and the Nossa Senhora dos Navegantes Festival, on February 2, celebrated with a boat procession.

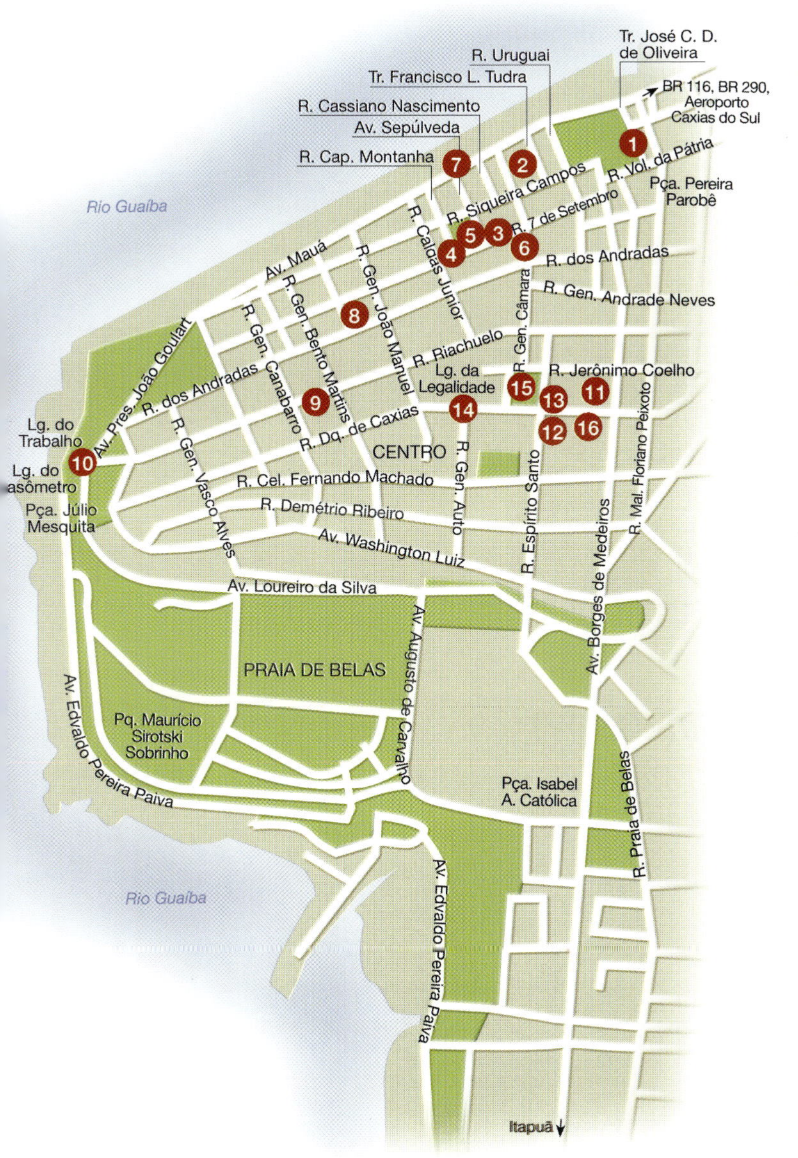

1 Public Market
2 City Hall
3 Alfândega Plaza
4 Santander Cultural
5 Rio Grande do Sul Memorial
6 MARGS
7 Central Portico of the Docks
8 Mário Quintana Cultural Center
9 Nossa Senhora das Dores Church
10 Gasômetro Plant Cultural Center
11 Matriz Plaza
12 Nossa Senhora Madre de Deus Church
13 Piratini Palace
14 Solar dos Câmara
15 Theatro São Pedro
16 Júlio de Castilhos Museum

Azorean origin

Porto Alegre owes its origin to its strategic position on the banks of the Guaíba River, an estuary of four rivers that is a natural route to the backlands of Rio Grande. In 1752, 60 Azorean couples camped on the riverbanks because they were waiting for transportation to the Missions. They were supposed to take the place of the Guarani Indians and the Jesuits who had been expelled by the Portuguese. But the war that erupted against the Indians led these couples to remain right where they were, in the so-called Porto dos Casais, the first name given to the city. In 1763, the village welcomed the Portuguese from Rio Grande, taken by the Spanish. This strategic position had to be secured against the Spanish advances. For that reason, besides being an administrative center, the city became a military area and Portuguese base in the South.

A stone bridge in the Azorean Plaza

★ Public Market

Glênio Peres Plaza, Downtown. Daily, from 9 am to 5 pm; closes on Sunday.

It was built to organize the commerce in the boathouses of the old Largo da Quitanda, where today the Alfândega Plaza is located. It was built in 1869, on the first dirt-fill in the city, and is said to be a replica of the Figueira Market, in Lisbon. A second floor, dating from 1912, built with Positivist airs (a French philosophical doctrine popular in the State after the Proclamation of the Republic) was added to the first floor, built in neoclassical style. This is one of the most traditional places in Porto Alegre, where you can buy fruit, vegetables, matte tea and artwork. There´s a tourist information center, restaurants and snack bars. Some streets are all-pedestrian zones, very popular in town.

City Hall

Montevidéu Plaza, Downtown, between Borges de Medeiros Avenue and 7 de Setembro Street.

It´s a neoclassical building with several statues of Positivism influence. It was open in 1901, and is going through a full-scale restoration. In addition to the Mayor´s cabinet, it will house a cultural center. Right in front is the **Talavera de La Reina** fountain, given as a present by the Spanish colony of Porto Alegre to celebrate the centennial of the Farroupilha Revolution.

★ Beach Street

The official name is **Andradas Street**. It was the place where Azoreans first settled, in the 18th century, and it´s also the oldest street in town. It has an intense commerce and imposing historical buildings, even in the all-pedestrian street. Highlights are the **Clube do Comércio**, built in 1938 in eclectic style; the 1913 art nouveau building that housed the first movie theater in the city, the Guarany, where today is the **Safra Bank**; and the buildings at the Esquina da Comunicação. The **Hipólito José da Costa Communication Museum** is located at the old building of the Republican newspaper *A Federação*.

Santander Cultural

1,028 Sete de Setembro Street, Praça da Alfândega, Downtown ☎ 3287-5500. Monday, from 12 noon to 8 pm; Tuesday to Saturday, from 10 am to 8 pm; Sunday, from 10 am to 6 pm.

Before becoming a cultural center in 2001, the building housed a bank. It was opened in 1932, and has an eclectic style, with the predominance of the French neoclassical style. The restoration project gave its original characteristics back. The building houses the **Coin Museum** and spaces for temporary exhibitions and shows. It still has a bookstore and design store, the **Santander movie theater**, where the safe used to be, the **Café do Cofre**, inside the old room for rental safes, and the sophisticated **Moeda Bar e Restaurante**, where the old vip agency was located. The cultural center is at **Alfândega Plaza**, where the traditional **Porto Alegre Book Fair** has been held since 1955.

Rio Grande do Sul Memorial

1020 Sete de Setembro Street, Alfândega Plaza, Downtown ☎ 3224-7210. Tuesday to Friday, 10 am to 7 pm; Saturday and Sunday, 12 noon to 5 pm.

The three floors of the former Post Office house a cultural center, on the history of Rio Grande do Sul. The building, dating from 1913, has a Baroque-style architecture and sculptures on the façade, by artists of the German community. Inside, a **bistro** and the **Post Office cultural space**. Next to the building, on

Buildings of the Mário Quintana Cultural Center

Sepúlveda Avenue, the **portico central do Cais do Porto** can be seen, with an iron structure and stained glass windows made in France in 1922. The **boat Cisne Branco** leaves from the portico to the Jacuí River Delta. On Sepúlveda Avenue, the highlight is the old headquarters of the Customs House, today housing the **Income Tax Department** and the **State Revenue Department**.

Rio Grande do Sul Ado Malagoli Art Museum (MARGS)

1010 Sete de Setembro Street, Alfândega Plaza, Downtown ☎ 3227-2311.Tuesday to Sunday, from 10 am to 7 pm.

The old building of the Fiscal Income Tax Department houses the MARGS, a museum that displays the largest collection of plastic arts in the State.

The cathedral was completed only in 1972

◄ The Public Market, a meeting place for Porto Alegre locals

There are approximately 3,000 works of art, by authors such as Portinari, Di Cavalcanti, Iberê Camargo and Xico Stockinger. The building has an eclectic style, and started being built in 1912. It houses a **bookstore** and a **store**, in addition to a **bistro**.

★ Mário Quintana Cultural Center

736 Andradas Street, Downtown
☎ 3221-7147.Tuesday to Friday, from 9 am to 9 pm; Saturday and Sunday, from 12 noon to 9 pm.
The old Majestic Hotel, a former meeting place of artists, intellectuals and politicians in the South, today houses a cultural center, with theaters, art galleries, libraries, a bookstore and a café. Poet Mário Quintana lived here and later named the building. In the golden age of the hotel, Getúlio Vargas, Vicente Celestino and Dalva de Oliveira were guests. The eclectic complex comprises two buildings with large domes, built between 1910 and 1933 and linked by bridges. The **Toy Museum** is located there, and also the **Lutzenberger Garden**. From the coffee shop, in the dome, the view of the Guaíba River is spectacular.

The two Veríssimos

Gaúcho Érico Veríssimo (1905-1975) is always remembered when people talk about the Rio Grande do Sul sage, which he described so well in his trilogy *O Tempo e o Vento*. The house where he spent his childhood today houses the Érico Veríssimo Foundation. He also named the cultural center on Praia Street. His ability to describe the man and his universe is a trait inherited by his son, but in a different way. Luís Fernando Veríssimo dedicated his art to humor and became known all over the country. In a funny way, he also unveiled the Gaúcho soul. His most popular book, *O Analista de Bagé*, is a satire to the roughness of the frontier Gaúcho.

Father and son: tradition in Porto Alegre

Nossa Senhora das Dores Church

630 Riachuelo Street, Downtown. Entrance on Andradas Street, between General Bento Martins and General Canabarro streets.
It´s the oldest church in town. Its construction began in 1833, but the towers took 97 years to be completed. It presents a combination of the Portuguese Baroque and the German style, with a statue on the façade representing faith, hope and charity. At Largo do Arsenal, a neoclassical building that housed the War Arsenal today is home to the **South Military Command Museum**.

★ Gasômetro Plant Cultural Center

551 Presidente João Goulart Avenue, Downtown. ☎ 3212-5979.Tuesday to Sunday, 10am to 10pm.
The old thermoelectric plant opened in 1928 was one of the first reinforced concrete buildings in the State. Since 1991, it has housed a cultural center, which holds exhibitions, workshops and art events. There are theaters, a café and a 117-meter-high chimney, declared Historical Landmark in 1982. The terrace offers a magnificent view of the sunset on the Guaíba River. The boat *Noiva do Caí* leaves from the plant.

Nossa Senhora Madre de Deus Church – Metropolitan Cathedral

1047 Duque de Caxias Street, Downtown, in front of Marechal Deodoro Plaza.Monday to Friday, 7:30 am to 6 pm; Saturday, 9 am to 7 pm; Sunday, 8 am to 7 pm.
The old church building, built from 1779 to 1820, used to be where today is the Matriz Plaza, the second place occupied by Azoreans in the city. It was demolished in 1920 to make room for the new building, which was completed only 52 years later. Inside

In the Jacuí Delta, a 30-island archipelago cut by channels

it, an Aldo Locatelli painting frames the patron saint image. In front, on Marechal Deodoro Plaza (Matriz Plaza), stands the **Monument to Júlio de Castilhos**, the founder of the State Republican Party, in power between 1889 and 1927. The work was sculpted in France by Décio Villares and brought to Porto Alegre in 1913. The sculpture has symbolic figures of the politician´s life. The Executive, Legislative and Judiciary palaces are on this plaza too.

Piratini Palace

Marechal Deodoro Plaza, Downtown, ☎ 3210-4100. Monday to Friday, 9 am to 11:30 am and 2 pm to 5 pm. It´s where the State government building is located, built in neoclassical style. The highlights are the French sculptures, the wooden furniture covered with a layer of gold, the Bohemian crystal chandeliers and the official cars. On the guided tour, every 30 minutes, 18 murals by Aldo Locatelli in 1951 can be appreciated. This is where the **Casa da Junta** is located, or what remained of the architectural complex that was the headquarters of the Azorean government building. Nearby, the **Solar dos Câmara**, built in 1818 by the first president of the province and later given to his son-in-law, Marechal Câmara. In 1981, it was bought and transformed into a cultural center. The former slave quarters house the State Chamber Library (Monday to Saturday, 8:30 am to 6:30 pm). On the other side of the plaza stands the current **Public Secretary**, which for some time housed the presidency of the province. There´s a café there now.

To the right, the Gasômetro Plant, from where Noiva do Caí leaves for a tour on the lake

Theatro São Pedro

Marechal Deodoro Plaza, Downtown
☎ 3227-5100. Tuesday to Friday, from 1 pm to 6 pm.
The oldest theater house in the city. The building started in 1833, but the Farroupilha Revolution presented some setbacks, and it was completed only in 1858. It was built in Portuguese Baroque style, and the inner décor is in velvet and gold. The biggest attraction is the 600-kilo chandelier, with 90 light bulbs and 35,000 crystal pieces. During most part of the year, the theater is open for free music presentations at lunch hour and late afternoon. The terrace at the **Café do Theatro** offers a panoramic view of the Matriz Plaza. At 1190 Riachuelo Street, the neoclassical-style **State Public Library**, finished in 1922, stands out. The busts in its interior pay homage to cult figures by Auguste Comte, Positivism´s mentor.

Farroupilha, the park that boasts more trees

Júlio de Castilhos Museum

1,231 Duque de Caxias Street, Downtown, ☎ 3221-3959. Tuesday to Friday, from 10 am to 7 pm; Saturday and Sunday, from 1 pm to 5 pm.
The house was built in 1897 as the official residence of the Republican Party leaders. Júlio de Castilhos lived here from 1898 to his death, in 1903. Its neoclassical style is a perfect example of the houses of the nobility in the 19th century. It displays documents and objects of the State´s history.

★ Farroupilha Park

Between José Bonifácio, Osvaldo Aranha and João Pessoa avenues.
It´s the oldest and most popular park in Porto Alegre, lined with trees. In 1807, the area called Várzea do Portão was donated to the city by the Governor. In 1884, when slaves were freed, it was named Campos da Redenção. In its 50,000 square meters there are lakes, a mini-zoo, an entertainment park, bronze and marble monuments and an illuminated fountain. A highlight is the Expeditionary Monument, a double granite Triumph Arch, inaugurated in 1953 to honor the soldiers who fought World War II. It houses the **Araújo Vianna Auditorium**, the **Café do Lago** and the **Bom Fim Market**. The park is home to **Brique da Redenção**, an artwork and antique fair. (Sunday, from 10 am to 4 pm).

Moinho de Vento Park

Between Göethe and 24 de Outubro avenues.
Located where the former horse racing track was, today in the district of Cristal. Up until 1836, there was a windmill that today names the park and the district. It has sports courts, a soccer field, a lake and children´s library. The administrative building is under a huge windmill. The neighboring streets have bars and restaurants. Walk around Goëthe Avenue and along Gomes and Padre Chagas streets, nicknamed "Walk of Fame."

★ PUC-RS Science and Technology Museum

6681 Ipiranga Avenue, building 40 on the PUC-RS campus, Partenon,

The windmill that names the park, built where there used to be a horse race track

☎ 3320-3903. Tuesday to Sunday, from 9 am to 5 pm.
In a fun way, visitors learn how the principles of physics, chemistry, math, biology, computer science and other sciences are present in our daily lives. Contrary to other museums, here everything can and should be touched. The experiments are divided into theme areas, like Universe, Planet Earth, Human Being, Electricity and Magnetism, Virtual World, Heat, Communications etc. The theme store is terribly enticing to kids. There´s a snack bar in the building.

Hills

In Porto Alegre, 65% of the area is formed by hills, distributed in several districts. Of the 44, some have urban characteristics, as the **Santa Tereza Hill** and the **Polícia Hill**, with good observatories facing the Guaíba River. On **Sabiá Hill**, on the banks of the lake, there´s a colonial coffee lunch and stairs that lead to the water. The **São Pedro Hill** is the largest in town. It´s home to several headwaters and animals threatened with extinction, like the red howler. It´s located in the rural zone, between the districts of Restinga and Lami. From up there, visitors can see the southern part of the town and **Lami Beach**, that, together with the **Belém Novo Beach** form the only two where you can swim. The 311-meter-high **Santana Hill** is the highest, and has lakes and cascades. The **Osso Hill** is located in the southern zone and is part of the Porto Alegre complex of granite hills with remains of the Atlantic Forest. It houses an important preservation area, the **Morro do Osso Natural Park**, partly open to visitation. It has an auditorium for educational activities, and rangers that guide visitors on the trails. Call before (☎ 3263-3769).

★ Delta do Jacuí State Park

The best way to visit the park and its islands is on boat. The *Noiva do Caí* (☎ 3211-7666) leaves from the Gasômetro Plant and the *Cisne Branco*

◀ Monument to Júlio de Castilhos

(☎ 3224-5222) leaves from the central deck of the Port and takes visitors on a one-hour tour along the margins of some islands and inside channels. The park was created in 1979 to preserve the Jacuí River delta, resulting from the meeting of the waters of the Jacuí, Sinos, Caí and Gravataí rivers, which form the Guaíba Lake. Contrary to what many think, the Guaíba is not a river. In Tupi-Guarani, Guaíba means "every water bay." An archipelago made up of 30 islands and cut by channels is also part of the area of the delta. It resulted from the age-old deposits of sediments brought by the rivers that form the Guaíba region. The islands, formed by porous sedimentary layers, absorb the waters and make floods less intense on the continent, and then, very slowly, like a sponge, they release the waters of the Guaíba Lake. Of the 30 islands, 16 are in Porto Alegre. The nearest and the only one to have legal occupation of the Jacuí Delta is the **Pintada Island**, with a 19th-century village. The *Turistinha* boat (☎ 9818-2274) leaves from the Gasômetro and offers, as an added attraction, lunch on Pintada, typical *peixe-na-taquara* (fish cooked on a bamboo) at the Fisherman´s Colony building Z-5, founded in 1921. The dish was created in the old fishing camps.

SURROUNDINGS

★ Itapuã State Park

57 kilometers from downtown Porto Alegre (4 kilometers on a dirt road). 1 Pombas Road, Viamão ☎ 494-8083. Wednesday to Sunday, from 9 am to 6 pm.

Created in 1973 to protect the last specimen of the original ecosystem of the metropolitan region of Porto Alegre. It´s 556 square kilometers of Atlantic Rainforest, granite hills, prairies, swamps, lagoons, three islands and eight beaches on the Guaíba Lake and Laguna dos Patos. At the place, 200 bird species, 40 reptile species, 300 plant species, as well as animals threatened with extinction, such as the otter and the red howler were catalogued. Only 10% of the park is open to visitation, the rest is used for preservation purposes. The open area has restrooms, snack bars, areas for barbecue, paved roads and parking lots. Five trails and three beaches are open – **Pombas**, **Pedreiras** and **Fora beaches**. The park has guides and tours on fishermen´s boats, and both tours are paid. At the Visitors Center, a 12-minute video is shown, besides panels that teach the importance of the conservation unit. The name of the park originated from the **Itapuã Lighthouse**, built in 1860 at the tip of

São Pedro Hill is located in the rural area of Porto Alegre

◀ Watching the sunset from the Guaíba is traditional in Porto Alegre

The red howler lives on the hills of the city

the peninsula where the Guaíba waters meet the Laguna dos Patos. The lighthouse can be seen from Pedreira Beach and on the boat tour. **The Fortaleza Trail** takes visitors to the ruins of the Farroupilha village, from where the imperial boats heading to the capital were bombarded. Outside the park, but still on the access road, is the **historical house,** which sheltered Farrapos leaders Davi Canabarro and Giuseppe Garibaldi. It´s currently a private home, but still keeps the original façade. The parks have a limited capacity for visitors on weekends, so you should buy the tickets in advance, at the Tudo Fácil (☎ 3227-6516), on Borges de Medeiros Avenue with Senador Salgado Filho Street.

★ Technology Museum of the Brazilian Lutheran University

101 Miguel Tostes Street, São Luís, Canoas ☎ 477-4000. Tuesday to Saturday, from 10 am to 8 pm; Sunday, from 10 am to 5 pm. Closes on holidays.

The museum, dedicated to technology, is divided into several theme areas. The main one is the **Automobile** area. It presents 98 years of the history of the car industry, with 250 cars, including sedans, vans and motorcycles. The collection includes vehicles of several makes and years, and has rarities such as the GM´s 1904 Oldsmobile and the 1908 Chase. An electronic system informs visitors about each model. The other museums that are part of the complex are smaller. There are the **Clock Museum**, the **Weapons Museum**, the **Post Office Museum** and the **Communications Museum**.

Sapiranga

61 kilometers from Porto Alegre, on BR-116.

Sapiranga is an industrial hub that exports shoes, in the Sinos Valley, of German colonization, that still retains many German-style houses. One of the oldest buildings is in Downtown. But its most important historic heritage is in the rural area, in centenary houses

The Gaúcho traditions

The Gaúcho figure became popular and it´s been a symbol of Rio Grande do Sul since the creation of the Gaúcho Traditionalist Movement (MTG). Until September 1947, there was no cult around it. In that year, eight students decided to receive, dressed in typical attire, the mortal remains of the Farroupilha leader Davi Canabarro, on Alfândega Plaza. That marked the beginning of a process that pays homage to the traditions and the Farroupilha ideals. In the same year, the first Gaúcho Center for Tradition, the 35 CTG (an allusion to the year of the Farroupila Revolution), was founded. The CTGs have spread around the country. In Porto Alegre, the Monument to the Lassoer, from 1954, stands as a symbol of the movement. The statue depicts a Gaúcho in typical attire. The model was folklorist Paixão Cortês, one of the eight founders of the movement.

***The Lassoer*, a monument to the Gaúcho ▶**

The meeting of the waters of the Guaíba River with the Lagoa dos Patos, at the Itapuã Lighthouse

around the **Ferrabrás Hill**. The hill affords a privileged view of the Sinos Valley and has a free-flight ramp. It was there that, in the 19th century, Jacobina Maurer, the leader of the religious sect of the **Muckers**, sought refuge. The story of the persecution of the Muckers is told in Fábio Barreto´s movie *Paixão de Jacobina,* filmed in the city. A great number of cascades is concentrated in **Picada Verão**. The highlight is **Recanto Ecológico da Família Lima** (☎ 3336-6759), owned by the music group, 13 kilometers from Sapiranga. The main attractions are the 5 waterfalls of the Cascata creek, forming natural pools. From the highest, at 35 meters, rappelling is practiced. It has sports courts, areas for barbecues and ecological trails where visitors can see howlers, squirrels and toucans. In Sapiranga, visitors can also parachute, accompanied by an instructor. Those interested should call the **Evolução Escola de Pára-Quedismo** (☎ 9988-7639, www.evolucaors.cjb.net).

A solar mansion houses a museum in Rio Pardo

Rio Pardo

143 kilometers from Porto Alegre on BR-290 and BR-471.

A historic town formed around the **Jesus Maria José Fortress**, built in 1750 to defend the territory against the Spanish and the Indians. What is left is three canyons, currently in the area of the water supply plant, open to visitors. Its rich Historic Downtown results from the economic heyday of the 19th century, when the city acted as distributor of goods that came from the capital. Start your visit by Solar do Almirante, a colonial building dating from 1790 that houses the **Santo Ângelo Municipal Museum**. The **São Francisco de Assis Chapel**, from 1812, keeps 18th-century life-sized images of Christ, representing phases of the Passion. An annex houses the **Sacred Art Museum**. The **Matriz N. Senhora do Rosário Church**, built between 1779 and 1801, has Baroque altars. The **Military School** building, from 1848, had Getúlio Vargas as a student and is being restored into a cultural center. Next to it is the **Senhor dos Passos Chapel**, from 1815. **Ladeira Street**, or Júlio de Castilhos Street, was the first paved street in the State. At number 257, **Casa do Turista** (☎ 3731-1274), eat the famous Sonho de Rio Pardo, a Portuguese donut filled with éclair. On the corner of Andrade Neves Street stands the house where Emperor D. Pedro II was a guest, in 1865. From 1798, the **Panatieri Cultural Center** is run by the family and is an homage to the father, the first black doctor in the State. Also worth a visit: the old City Hall building, from 1904; the first hotel, that today houses the **Tourism Bureau**; the **Barro Vermelho Cross**, site of one of the most bloody Farroupilha battles; and the **São Nicolau Chapel**, from 1763, with images having Indian traces. Rio Pardo has four spa regions, with entertainment infrastructure and interesting bars.

A historical house that welcomed leaders

TIPS

- Public transportation in Porto Alegre is fast and efficient.
- In summer, restaurants and bars located at the Public Market have live music from Tuesday to Saturday, from 6 pm to 10 pm.
- From March to December, the Solar dos Câmara (☎ 3210-2037) organizes free dance balls in the former dance hall of the manor house – in the same place where they were held in the past. Check out the hours.
- There are organized tours to the hills of Porto Alegre. Check it out at SAT.
- The best access route to the Itapuã Park is on the Guaíba Lake margin, until you get to Juca Batista Avenue. Then take Edgar de Castro Avenue and RS-118.
- You can visit Pintada Island by car, on Travessia Getúlio Vargas, built in 1958. The road complex, formed by four bridges, crosses three islands, goes through the city of Guaíba and goes to Pintada.

The origin of Gaúcho barbecue

The traditional *churrasco na vala* (barbecue in a pit) is a typical Gaúcho dish and is served at good barbecue restaurants in town. It's a heritage from the time of the cowboys.
At the time, cowboys cut the easiest-to-get cut of beef and roasted it on wooden sticks in a pit made on the ground.
With time, new techniques were incorporated. Cowboys put the two flaps of the saddle inside the pit too. They were drenched in horse sweat, and that helped salt the meat. Later, other cuts of beef were used, as the ribs, the shoulder and the *espanholado matambre* (hunger appeaser) – a tough cut that takes a long time to roast. The *charque*, on the other hand, is beef meat cut into slices, then salted and dried in the sun, so that it can be kept for a long time and sold in faraway places. It was one of the main products from Rio Grande do Sul in the 18th and 19th centuries.

Meat grilled on sticks

Bento Gonçalves

The 17-meter-tall stylized wine barrel welcomes visitors to the winemaking city

Porto Alegre 128 km
Santa Maria 287 km
Canela 117 km
Passo Fundo 186 km
88,932
54
453-2555
bentoonline.com.br

Right at the entrance gate you can notice the city´s historical connection with wine. A huge stylized 17-meter-high wine barrel welcomes visitors who arrive on the RS-470. Known as the National Capital of Wine, Bento Gonçalves boasts the title of Brazil´s largest fine wine and grape producer. In the general winemaking category, it takes second place, losing the title to neighboring

The best wines in the country are produced in the rich vineyards of Bento Gonçalves

Wine country

The Italians who came to Rio Grande do Sul in 1875, with the promise of fertile soil to plant, were poor farmers from the Trento, Veneto, Friuli and Lombardia regions. All they brought were some clothes, tools and grape seedlings. The Germans had already been given the best land in the valleys, for they were the first to be part of the project of the imperial government to occupy the southern territory. The Italians were granted the humid and small lands on the steep mountains, where they planted grapes and subsistence cultures. Despite the inadequate climate for the cultivation of grapes, they insisted – that was what they were used to doing and wine was what they enjoyed drinking. Perseverance paid off and, today, the Rio Grande do Sul mountain region is the largest winemaking region in Brazil.

The wineries are run by Italian families

Flores da Cunha. This tendency began in the end of the 19th century, when Italian immigrants arrived at Colônia Dona Isabel and brought techniques for the harvesting of grapes and the production of wine. But the techniques aren´t a privilege of the city that honors the main Farroupilha leader, Bento Gonçalves. The 80,000 Italians who came to the region spread their technique and mainly the passion for wine. Today, 25 cities are in the Wine and Grape Route, with wineries spread amidst the native vegetation of the mountain region. To get to know the gastronomic, wine-related and natural attractions of this region, the ideal place is Bento Gonçalves, with good hotels and restaurants. It´s also a furniture center and has had, for over 30 years, the only agrotechnical school in the country, where students major in Enology.

★ Valley of the Vineyards

Five kilometers from town on RS-470 and then RS-444.

It´s in the 81 square kilometers of mountains and valleys covered with native vegetation, on the border of Garibaldi and Monte Belo do Sul, that the best table wines in Brazil are produced. This feat can be attributed to the former wineries, created and administrated by members of a same family, like the **Don Laurindo**, the **Cordelier** and the **Villaggio Larentis**. Of the 29 wineries of the area, 23 formed an association, the Aprovale, and in 2002 got what they wanted: the Valley of the Vineyards is the first Brazilian region to have an indication of origin, a quality-control method. Most of the wineries are open to visitation and provide information on how the product is made. All this while visitors are invited to sample their produce. Many wineries also have restaurants open for groups, and where Italian fare is served together with the house wines. At **Casa Valduga** (☎ 453-3122), in addition to a restaurant featuring typical music, they opened an inn and a cafeteria in the middle of the vineyards. It´s worth visiting the **Cave de Pedra**, built from basalt blocks, resembling a Medieval castle, and the **Miolo**, dating from 1897, which offers an observatory that affords a unique view of the valley. But the best view can be seen from **Capela das Neves**, on the Linha Leopoldina Road. Seen from there, the vineyards look like a quilt, with several hues of green. It´s

Cave de Pedra is almost a castle

In Colônia São Pedro, most of the houses were made from stone, and they are being restored

said that while the chapel was being built, in 1907, there was a drought. In order to not stop the construction, workers used wine instead of water and finished the chapel.

★ Colônia São Pedro

13 kilometers from Downtown, on Linha Palmeiro towards Pinto Bandeira.

Along the 7 kilometers of road, there are colonial houses of the first Italians who came to Bento Gonçalves. The old gray stone and wooden houses are being restored to welcome visitors. Of the 105 buildings, 20 are already open to visitation. **Casa Bertarello** had its stones covered with plaster a long time ago, but has recently been given its original 1877 façade, and now visitors can taste its homemade-food. At **Ferraria dos Ferri**, visitors can see the the tools used in the beginning of the 20th century, run by waterwheels. At **Casa Vanni**, dating from 1935, visitors can buy sweets, artwork and pieces woven in manual looms. Visitors can also sample some wine in Colônia de São Pedro. The fourth generation of the **Strapazzon** family still makes wine. The house, was the backdrop for Fábio Barreto´s movie *O Quatrilho*. Make reservations for visitations.

★ Maria Fumaça

A 23-kilometer excursion between Bento Gonçalves and Carlos Barbosa 455-2788. Wednesday, at 2 pm; Saturday, at 8:30 am and 2 pm.

Maria Fumaça (Smoky Mary) – a coal-fired train composed of six cars pulled by an American vapor locomotive from 1941 – takes visitors on a route to some traditions and culture of the region. On the one-hour-an-a-half route, artists "invade" the train and perform funny acts, dance and sing Italian and Gaúcho tunes. At the stations where the train fired by mineral coal stops, there are shows and visitors can sample the main local produce. In Bento Gonçalves, it´s wine; in Garibaldi, champagne; in Carlos Barbosa, cheese. Make reservations in advance, but in high season there are extra trips.

★ Antas River

19 kilometers from Downtown on RS-470.

The Antas River separates Bento Gonçalves from Veranópolis and has its headwater in Serra dos Ausentes, in Bom Jesus. In Santa Teresa it acquires the name of Taquari. The animals which named the Antas (tapirs) River haven´t been seen for a while. It´s surrounded by 700-meter-high rocks and it winds through the hillsides of several cities. This makes for beautiful settings, which can be seen from the top of several observatories. At the 201 km marker on RS-470, 15 kilometers from Downtown, there´s one, the **Belvedere Ferradura**. Nova Pádua has an observatory with a hotel and a restaurant – the **Belvedere Sonda** is 5.5 kilometers from the city´s entrance on the road towards Travessão Mutzel. The river offers rapids, with rafting and canoeing as

Caverna dos Índios: 40-meter-high water cascade ▶

the major sports activities. The 12-kilometer descent takes two and a half hours and starts at the **cachoeirão,** 200-meter-long rapids. The rafting has a medium-difficulty level and is offered by many agencies, among them the Rio das Antas (☎ 451-2844) and the Radical Sul (☎ 453-6934). **The Júlio de Castilhos iron bridge**, where the rafting starts, is 35 kilometers from Bento Gonçalves. The 25-meter-tall German bridge, dating from 1932, is used for extreme sports.

SURROUNDINGS

★ Antônio Prado

95 kilometers from Bento Gonçalves towards Caxias do Sul, from RS-122.

The characteristics of the town were determined by commerce and not by agriculture, because the old village was part of the cowboys´ route. In 1989, it was declared National Historic Landmark for gathering the largest collection of urban wooden architecture, from Italian immigration. Walk along **Valdomiro Bocchese Avenue** and **Garibaldi Plaza**, and see most of the 48 buildings that were declared National Landmarks. Highlights are the **City Hall building**, a former jail, and the eclectic-style **Matriz Sagrado Coração de Jesus Church**, with a beautiful wooden bell-tower.

★ Caxias do Sul

42 kilometers from Bento Gonçalves on RS-470, RS-453 and RS-122.

It´s the second most populous city in the State, with 360,207 inhabitants, and it´s

an autoparts and car maker industrial hub. But you can still hear the dialect from Veneto. A tour reveals houses that belonged to Italian immigrants and many wineries. At **Cantina Zanrosso** (211-0730), visitors can taste the grapes picked at the time. At **Cantina Tonet** (224-1020), visitors help make their own wine. In the following year, the "producer" can buy the wine labeled with his own name on the site cantinatonet.com.br or by phone. In the urban area, there are reminders of the Italian colonization. A good example is the **Casa de Pedra Museum**, on Matteo Gianella Street. **The Diocesana Cathedral**, on Dante Alighieri Plaza, began being built in 1895 and boasts German glass windows and metal chandeliers with grape designs. **The São Pelegrino Church**, dating from 1953, Downtown, houses paintings by the Italian artist Aldo Locatelli. Among his frescoes, the *Way of the Cross* is considered his masterpiece. **Criúva**, 56 kilometers away, has traditions left by the cowboys, such as the *cavalgada* and the *churrasco-na-vala*. In Criúva, visitors can practice rappelling, rafting and go on trekkings (Operadora Criúva 267-8255). There´s still the **Palanquinhos** canyon, where the **Caixão River** flows, and the **Escondido** and **Mulada** cascades. In Santa Lúcia do Piaí, the Grutão Caverna dos Índios affords a beautiful sight: a 40-meter-high water cascade that forms natural pools.

São Pelegrino: Locatelli´s Final Judgement

Farroupilha

24 kilometers from Bento Gonçalves on RS-470, RS-453 and RS-122.

The city is the largest producer of the kiwi fruit in Brazil and the birthplace of Italian colonization in Rio Grande do Sul. In 1875, the first immigrants arrived in **Nova Milano**, 5 kilometers from Downtown, on RS-122 . What is left is **Casa Número Dez da Colônia** (268-2859), dating back from 1883 and built with mud by the first three families to arrive in the State. Today it´s a hotel where guests hang their clothes on ropes that fall from the ceiling. In the rural area, 14 kilometers from Downtown on Linha Müller, is the **Salto Ventoso**, a cascade over a cave where rappelling is practiced. It is a 52-meter-high fall, with a passageway used by immigrants, a century ago, to cross the river. Visitors can take a 20-minute hike to go down to the base and swim in the pool. The **Nossa Senhora do Caravaggio Sanctuary** is 6 kilometers from Downtown, in Caravaggio. It was built between 1945 and 1963, next to an 1890 temple, today dedicated to votive offerings. At the patron saint festival, in May, over 200,000 faithful visit the site.

★ Flores da Cunha

60 kilometers from Bento Gonçalves, via Caxias do Sul (from there on RS-122).

Of the 460 wineries of Rio Grande do Sul, 172 are located in the city, and answer for over 100 million liters of wine produced yearly. These numbers make Flores da Cunha, with a little over 23,000 inhabitants, the largest wine producer in Brazil. The city is also the second largest garlic and furniture producer in the State, plus having natural treasures. The most important can be seen from the **Gelain Observatory**, in Alfredo Chaves: the 135-meter-high **Bordin Waterfall**, that flows into the Antas River, with a bar, restrooms, tourist center, and trails. It´s also a site for rappelling. In Otávio Rocha, see the **Gruta Waterfall**. The 1914 neo-Gothic

The Antas River seen from Belvedere Sonda ▶

Rappelling at Salto Ventoso, in Farroupilha

style **Matriz Nossa Senhora de Lourdes Church**, Downtown, is worth visiting. The 55-meter **bell-tower** has 5 French bells.

Garibaldi

16 kilometers from Bento Gonçalves on RS-470.

Named after the Italian revolutionary Giuseppe Garibaldi, the city produces 65% of all the champagne in Brazil. Most of the 65 wineries are in the urban area. Start by **Peterlongo**, on Manuel Peterlongo Street, producer of the first Brazilian champagne, in 1915. Two blocks down, on Independência Avenue, stands one of the largest wineries in America, the **Cooperativa Vinícola Garibaldi**. At **Casa Chandon**, sample the champagne approved by French masters. Visit the **Matriz São Pedro Church**, inspired by the French Lourdes Sanctuary, and the **Municipal Museum**, from 1878, displaying immigration items.

Veranópolis

43 kilometers from Bento Gonçalves on RS-470.

Veranópolis is the longevity land. It´s the first in Brazil and third in the world with the highest life expectancy – 78 years, ten more than the national average. It´s attributed to the quality of living of the inhabitants. Good nourishment, exercise, good family relationships, religiousness and contact with nature may also account for the fact. One of the city´s attractions is the **Ernesto Dornelles Bridge**. The violence of the waters of the river prevented the construction of pillars and, in 1952, the first bridge supported by parallel arches was built in the world. On the way to the **Três Monges Park**, on RS-470, is the **Belvedere Espigão**, at the 104 km marker. A little farther, the **São Marcos Chapel**, built in 1901. The park has a jeep-cross and a motor-cross track, a lake and the 112-meter-high **Três Monges Waterfall**, formed by the Retiro River. Formed by the same river, the **Usina Velha Waterfall**, in Vila Azul, has the ruins of the first hydroelectric plant built in the backlands, from 1912.

TIPS

- At the Salto Escondido Cascade, in Nova Roma do Sul, you can swim, practice rappel, and enjoy a beautiful view of the Antas River. Bring a guide along. (Radical Sul 453-6934).
- Farroupilha has the best malls to buy wool clothing in the region.

Caçapava do Sul

Dressed in typical attire, locals parade to celebrate the Farroupilha Revolution

Porto Alegre 264 km
Rio Pardo 170 km
Torres 450 km
Pelotas 200 km
35,000
55
281-1599
turismo.cacapava.net

Situated on the southwestern part of the State, the city is the main access route to the Rio Grande do Sul and Argentine Pampas region. It´s the entrance gate to the huge prairie region where the horizon is never-ending. "Paragem de Cassapava" emerged from a Portuguese military camping built on the site of an old Charrua Indian camp, in the mid-18th century. In Tupi-Guarani, the name means "a clearing in the woods." The Farrapos Revolution marked the history of the city because at that time the Rio Grande do Sul Republican Government was transferred to Caçapava do Sul. From February 1839, when the city of Piratini lost its capital status, to May 1840, the city was the second capital of the Farrapos government.

Copper in the tower of N. S. da Assunção ►

Historic Downtown

Dr. Rubens da Rosa Guedes Plaza is right in the middle of several old and well-preserved buildings. The most important of them all is the **Matriz N. Senhora da Assunção Church**, which began to be built in 1815. Having part of its towers made of copper extracted from local mines, it was declared a Historical Landmark in 1985. On 15 de Novembro

Segredo rock: two twin rocks, 160 meters high and three caves

Street, in front of the square, the majestic architectural design of two buildings deserves attention. Number 84 is the **União Caçapavana Club**, which was founded in 1900, but was transferred to the imposing building only eight years later. And on the corner of Barão de Caçapava Street stands the **Arnaldo Luiz Cassol Cultural Municipal Center**, where the first flag of the Republic was raised, in 1839. The building underwent a renovation in 1935, to commemorate the Farroupilha Revolution Centennial, and currently houses the City library, the Historic Archives and the **Lanceiros do Sul Museum**, that tells the story of the fearsome Farroupilha squadron, formed by the Charrua Indians, the creators of the *boleadeiras* (a kind of instrument to knock down cattle and part of the region´s folklore). Still on 15 de Novembro, at the **City Stall**, you can buy homemade food products, such as sweets, orange wines and the *bergamota* (kind of tangerine). Nearby, at the end of Ulhoa Cintra Street, stands the only military fort in the South, the **D. Pedro II Fort**. During the Farroupilha Revolution, Barão de Caçapava was worried about invasions to the village, and wanted to build a fort. The construction began only in 1848, and dragged until 1856, when it finally stopped. The fort covers an area of 27,000 square meters, in hexagonal shape, with 8- to 10-meter-high by 1-meter-wide rock walls, and it is part of the city now. Passersby are a common sight and boys play soccer in its interior. At two different corners, stand two of the most important historical monuments in Caçapava. The **Casa dos Ministérios**, at 521 Sete de Setembro Street, was where the Farrapos ministers worked, including the owner of the building, José Pinheiro de Ulhoa Cintra. In 1863, the house on the corner of Borges de Medeiros Street was where the man who gave the name to the street and later, in 1898, would become the State President was born. Borges de Medeiros´ house was declared a Historical Landmark in 1991.

Pedra do Segredo

10.2 km from Downtown (5 km on a dirt road) on RS-357, exit to Lavras do Sul. On Esquina do Segredo, make a right.
20 minutes.

It´s called Pedra do Segredo (Secret´s rock) because of the many legends about Jesuit treasures, supposed to be hidden there, somewhere. It´s a conglomerate of ferruginous sandy rocks used for climbing. In fact, Pedra do Segredo is formed by two twin rocks, resembling gorillas´ heads, with their faces glued to each other. It´s 160 meters tall and has three caves in its interior: the **Percival Antunes**, named after its discoverer, is the prettiest, at 90 meters high; the **Caverna da Escuridão (Darkness**

Cave), which has a completely dark 60-meter-long tunnel (it´s necessary to take a lantern) that goes to the other side of the rock; and the **Salão das Estalactites (Stalactites´ Salon)**, the most ample of them all. There´s an information center at the beginning of the trail that goes up the rock, but sometimes there´s nobody there. Climbing to the top is tough and takes four hours, on the average. Don´t go without a guide.

Salso Cascade

8 km from Downtown (3 km on a dirt road), via Estrada da Aviação. 30 minutes.
It´s an over 30-meter-high waterfall, formed by Salso´s stream, amidst hills covered with vegetation. On the upper part, there´s the old hydroelectric´s cement dam. The well that forms in the bottom is excellent for baths.

★ Guaritas

50 km from Downtown on BR-392 and BR-153. At the 506 km marker, turn left on RS-625 (access to Minas do Camapuã). 1 hour and 10 minutes.
These are a series of mountains that alternate with deep valleys and huge rocks, where visitors can admire the work of the rain and wind after thousands of years. After driving for 11 kilometers on RS-625, a dirt road, the rock formations can be seen. About two kilometers farther, stands the **Guaritas Home Owners Association** (9982-5787), where you can ask for information and have a rural lunch (order beforehand). Guaritas was the place chosen by Rio Grande do Sul director Sérgio Silva to shoot several scenes for his movie *Anahy de las Misiones*.

D. Diogo Museum: the story of the conflict ▶

Minas do Camapuã

70 km from Downtown on BR-392 and BR-153. At the 506 km marker, turn left on RS-625 and drive 18 km on a dirt road. 1 hour and a half, 281-1666, Cia. Brasileira do Cobre.
The region of Caçapava do Sul gathers the largest mineral specimen in the State, with several different kinds of rocks, with ages ranging from2 billion to 60 million years old. The copper mines are among the "younger" sedimentary sequences, which gave the city, for a long time, the title of Brazilian Capital of Copper – currently, the city is the Rio Grande do Sul Capital of Limestone. In Minas do Camapuã, a 1,300-hectare town, there was a mine for extracting the metal, discovered in 1865. Currently, besides producing zync, limestone, copper sulfate and ornamental rocks, the place is an ecotourist complex. At the place, among the major activities are water sports, climbing of the **Pedra da Cruz** and hikes.

SURROUNDINGS

Bagé

165 km from Caçapava do Sul. 53.
The name of one of the main cities of the Rio Grande do Sul Pampas has become known outside of the State thanks to a good-humored book by writer Luís Fernando Verissimo, called *O Analista de Bagé* (Bagé´s Analyst). The work satirizes the fame Gaúchos (Rio Grande do Sul inhabitants) have of being rough, and the book has become a successful play. In fact, the local inhabitant was

molded by the battles for the land that marked the region. Even before becoming a city – in 1846 it became independent from Piratini –, Bagé became the home of the **Santa Tecla Spanish Fort**, in 1774. Today, the remains of its foundations can be seen at the **Patrício Corrêa da Câmara Museum**, on Estrada Municipal. The city staged marches of the Farroupilhas and imperial armies and was one of the centers of the movement that gave origin to the 1893 Federalist Revolution. This history is shown in the D. Diogo Museum. On Conde de Porto Alegre Street, the **São Sebastião Cathedral**, finished in 1863, was used as hospital during the Federalist Revolution and its outside walls were full of bullet holes. Other architectural witnesses of the past that should be visited are the **Palacete da Intendência Municipal**, dating from 1900; the neoclassical **Palacete Pedrinho Osório**, where the Cultural Municipal Ministry is located; the **Casa Vermelha**, a sophisticated house dating from the beginning of the 20th century; and the **General Military Quarters** and the **old railroad buildings**. The historical link the city has with horses is present in the 16th English horse farms for pure-breds. Mountain climbers cannot afford to miss the **Serra dos Encantados**, about 75 kilometers from Downtown, in the Palmas district. Those interested should call the Bagé Mountain Climbing Association (☎ 241-2195).

Piratini

100 km from Caçapava do Sul.
⊕ 53.

Piratini, or Piratinim (primitive denomination) means "noisy fish," a name given by the Tupi-Guarani to the river that used to cut through the region. It´s one of the most important historical towns in the State because it was the first capital of the Farroupilha Republic, between 1836 and 1839. A large portion of the Portuguese colonial-style heritage that staged the Farrapos saga is still present. The best way to get in touch with it is to walk along Coronel Manoel Pedroso, General Bento Gonçalves da Silva and Gomes Jardim streets, all lined with old buildings. Start by the **Farroupilha Historical Museum**, dating from 1819, where the Republic of Rio Grande do Sul War Ministry was. The museum was created in 1954 and includes a vast array of items related to the Farrapos War. The house where the Italians Giuseppe Garibaldi and Luigi Rosseti lived, and also where the Farroupilha newspaper *O Povo* was located currently houses the **City Tourism Ministry**. Dating from 1826, the **Palácio da República** Riograndense housed the Farroupilha government. It stands next to the two-story house where the City Council was located and where, during the revolution, the **Ministry of the Treasury** and of the Interior was.

TIPS

• To go to Caçapava do Sul, leaving Porto Alegre, take BR-290 (with toll booths) to the intersection with BR-392. Take this highway.
• The dirt roads leading to the Salto Cascade, Pedra do Segredo, Guaritas and Minas de Camapuã are in very bad condition.
• Bagé is located 393 kilometers from Porto Alegre. The best thing to do is to take BR-290 and BR-153.

◀ The action of erosion in Guaritas

Cambará do Sul

Cambará do Sul is the starting point to go to the Aparados and Serra Geral parks

Porto Alegre: 186 km
Gramado: 116 km
Torres: 80 km
Bento Gonçalves: 188 km
6,843
54
251-1320

The small city of Cambará do Sul used to be a cowboys´ route in the 19th century. It was only in 1864, with the donation of 200 square meters of land for the building of a chapel, that it became an urban conglomerate. The name, Cambará, originated from a tree found in the region and means "rugged leaf" in Tupi-Guarani. The city is a good starting point to visit the Aparados da Serra National Park and the Serra Geral Park (an extension of the first). The area of both parks belongs to the State of Santa Catarina. Despite the fact that they weren´t sites of any event of the Farroupilha time, the Itaimbezinho and Fortaleza canyons were used as setting for the TV miniseries *A Casa das Sete Mulheres* (The House of the Seven Women), based on the Farrapos War in Rio Grande do Sul.

★ Aparados da Serra National Park

18 kilometers from Cambará do Sul on RS-429, 251-1262 or 251-1277. Wednesday to Sunday, from 9 am to 5 pm.

The region was first occupied by Tupi-Guarani Indians, until the arrival of the first European immigrants, and recently has been the site for many cattle ranches. Since 1959, it´s been home to one of the oldest Brazilian parks, with excellent visitation infrastructure. The 102-square-kilometer area isn´t completely in order. The park houses the most famous canyon in the region, the **Itaimbezinho**, which means "sharp stone" in Indian language. Two panoramic trails afford a view of its main attractions. The shortest, the **Vértice Trail**, is a 45-minute trek, and has three observatories, signs explaining about the region and is 1.4 kilometer long, most of it through passageways. If you go along the canyon, the first observatory affords a view of the 300-meter-high **Andorinha Waterfall**, formed by the Perdizes stream. It´s named *andorinha* (swallow) because of a crack in the rocks, behind the water, where swallows live and nest. See the birds coming in and out, all the time.

From the second observatory, the view is of the 500-meter-high **Véu de Noiva Waterfall**. It´s formed by Arroio Preá, and when the waters fall, they help form the Boi River. The third observatory affords a view of the two waterfalls and the beginning of the Itaimbezinho, vortice-shaped.
The 6.3-kilometer **Cotovelo Trail** takes approximately ◔ 2 and a half hours (both ways), is mild and safe, because 4 kilometers are taken on the dirt road that used to cross the park. The remaining journey goes along the canyon. At the Cotovelo Observatory, you´ll see the classic image of Itaimbezinho, with its huge rock walls around the **Boi River**, which runs amid the vegetation. From here, it´s possible to see a large portion of its 5,800 meters. The two waterfalls and a smaller one, called Seu Marçal Waterfall, are right before the eyes. The last trail, the Boi River Trail, is the longest and most difficult, and requires good physical preparation and experienced guides. The route goes through the canyon, and the beginning goes through the city of Praia Grande, in Santa Catarina. The Boi River (Ox River) has this name because of the cattle that oftentimes fell down the canyon, blinded by the fog. The trail

Origin of the canyons

Between 150 and 200 million years ago, an intense seismic and magmatic activity shook the region where the State of Rio Grande do Sul is located today. The successive lava spread originated the Meridional Plateau, where 50% of the Gaúcho territory is located. The present continents date back from that period, when the American continent separated from the African continent. With time, the terrain that was molded by the lava, in what today is the Serra Geral, had abrupt cracks, caused by the violent movement of the tectonic plaques. Steep walls were formed, supported by the magma that came out and cooled instantaneously, opening cracks in the rocks.The several fractures, also caused by erosion, formed what today is considered to be the largest canyon complex in Brazil. In the canyons regions, there are several ecosystems and transition zones between them.

At the Itaimbezinho Canyon, the Andorinhas Waterfall has a 300-meter fall

Foggy woods

Several ecosystems live in harmony in the Aparados da Serra region. The Atlantic Rainforest, with its many pine trees, is present in the lower parts of the canyons, spread in clusters in the upper parts and at the edges of the cliffs, where it´s called *matinha nebular* (foggy woods). The fields are spread in the prairie regions, among peat bogs in the humid sections. Seasons are well marked, with rains from December to March, including thunder and lightning, and intense frosts from June to September. The fog happens all the time, covering or uncovering deep valleys in just seconds. On the cliffs, green areas sprout from the rocks.

Flowers on the walls

ends when the rock canyons reach their maximum height: 720 meters (from the riverbed). Currently, the trail is closed because Ibama, the agency that administers the park, is conducting studies on the environmental impact on the Boi River region. Also part of the park´s area is the 7,000-meter-long **Faxinalzinho Canyon**, on the border of the Serra Geral Park. This canyon is richer in terms of vegetation, but visits are forbidden.

★ Serra Geral National Park

22 kilometers from Cambará do Sul on RS-423, ☎ 251-1262. Daily, from 8 am to 6 pm.

The 17.5-square-kilometer Serra Geral National Park was created in 1992, and is linked to the Aparados National Park on the northeastern and southwestern portions. There´s no entrance gate, and visitation is free of charge. There´s only one house on the road leading to the **Fortaleza Canyon**, one of the most beautiful in the region. It´s the largest of all canyons, having 30 kilometers of edges, if the curves are taken into account, and 7.5 kilometers long. The 900-meter rock walls (from the bottom of the canyon) are similar to fortress walls, and that´s why the canyon was named Fortaleza (fortress). The Fortaleza Observatory, from where you have a panoramic view of the canyon, with the Pedra River flowing in the lower part, stands at 1.8 kilometers upward the mountain in a 50-minute walk, just to get there. If *viração* – the thick fog that covers everything in just seconds – doesn´t show up, it´s possible to see, from up there, part of the Santa Catarina plains and the Gaúcho coast. On the 1.5-kilometer, 50-minute trail to **Segredo Rock**, visitors can enjoy the **Tigre Preto Waterfall**, with three waterfalls that reach 400 meters high. It´s a medium-difficulty trail, and crosses the Segredo creek, a narrow stream but having a very slippery bottom. After the creek comes the waterfall and above it the observatory facing the Segredo Rock, a 5-meter-high rock formation and believed to weigh 30 tons, supported by a very small and thin base, more or less 50 centimeters in diameter. Two other canyons are inside the park, the **Churriado** and the **Malacara**. The first, having a name that reminds of

◀ **At the Fortaleza Canyon, 900-meter walls**

manure, is located 12 kilometers and over 3 hours away from the point that can be reached by car. Next to it is the Malacara, with a height of up to 800 meters. This canyon can be reached from the upper part, on a 8-kilometer hike, during 4 hours, or from the lower part, leaving from Grande Beach in Santa Catarina. The 3-hour trek goes through the canyon, on the Malacara riverbed. As the trails in the park have no signs and the edges have no protection, it´s necessary to take an experienced guide along. Ibama has temporarily closed the trails to the Malacara and the Churriado and some campsites in the park´s area. Get information before going.

Other canyons

The Índios Coroados Canyon is smaller than the others, and can be reached on an easy and short trail. It´s only 15 minutes away from the police post on the border between Santa Catarina and Rio Grande do Sul, on Serra da Faxinal road. It´s located in the lower part of the mountain range. Also located in the lower part, the Molha-Coco canyon has a big attraction: one of the most beautiful local waterfalls, surrounded by the Atlantic Rainforest. Mountain climbers flock to the area, and cross the canyon in its interior. The Molha-Coco (Wet Head) is an allusion to the water that comes from above and wets passersby.

Tigre Preto Waterfall: 400 meters high

Waterfalls

There are many waterfalls near Cambará. On the border with Jaquirana, 25 kilometers from Downtown, is the **Venâncios Waterfall**, formed by the Camisas River. The river has an extra series of crystal-clear waterfalls. The region is locally known as "mini Foz do Iguaçu" because the waterfalls are similar to the ones found in Paraná, except for the fact that they´re smaller. When the rapids of the Camisas River get milder, the 50-meter-long **lajeado das Margaridas** (a dry creek) is formed. It´s located 12 kilometers from Downtown on João Francisco Ritter Street and is perfect for a swim. The area has camping facilities. **Dona Délcia** Waterfall is formed by the Campo Bom creek and is located 6 kilometers from Downtown. The **Lajeado das Camarinhas** is located inside the area of the **Parador Casa da Montanha** (286-2544), an attraction in itself, between the Aparados da Serra Park and Cambará do Sul. Lodging is inside rustic and cozy Canadian thermal tents, with a bathroom, and air

◄ View of the Itaimbezinho Canyon

The Silveira River, on Rodrigues Farm, affords a beautiful view of the town

conditioning. Both the tents and the panoramic restaurant, which can be used by non-guests too, are located on the border of the creek, also a good swimming spot in summer.

SURROUNDINGS

★ São José dos Ausentes

55 kilometers from Cambará do Sul on RS-020.

It´s the highest city, at 1,200 meters, and the coldest region in Rio Grande do Sul. In the winter months, between June and August, it generally snows. In the upper region, the mountain ranges don´t have the valleys, like the other European-settled regions and become vast grassy fields, and acquire the obvious name of upper mountain fields. It´s a common sight that reminds one of the Pampas region, on which locals ride horses, generally *pilchados* (with typical Gaúcho loose pants and boots) and drink their *chimarrão*. The city was given this name, São José dos Ausentes (missing people), because in the 18th century, some farmers abandoned their land and it was necessary to auction them twice, in what was called "trial of the missing people." Just like Cambará, São José dos Ausentes is located by the cliff formed by the Serra Geral Hill, and its main attractions are: the Monte Negro Peak and Canyon. Boasting 1,000-meter walls, the canyon is as beautiful as its neighbors Itaimbezinho and Fortaleza. **The Monte Negro Peak**, 45 kilometers from Downtown, is the highest point in the State, at 1,403 meters. Contrary to what is thought, it´s a 70-meter rocky hill and may be climbed on foot. As the region is

A frozen lake in São José dos Ausentes

located at an altitude of over 1,200 meters, the peak is the highest point. But the view is stunning. The **Rodrigues Waterfall** and the **difference in levels of the Silveira and Divisa** rivers are other attractions, also in nearby areas. 35 kilometers from Downtown, where the Rodrigues Waterfall is located, there´s a succession of over 20-meter-long waterfalls, formed by the Silveira River. A little farther ahead, separated by a narrow strip of land, the Silveira and Divisa rivers run parallel to each other, with an 18-meter difference of level. When it rains a lot, the waters from one river flood and blend in the riverbed of the other, forming rapids. Old farms turned into farm-hotels are a good option to stay, where visitors can experience a day´s life on a farm, eat typical food and ride horses on the fields.

Bom Jesus

92 kilometers from Cambará do Sul on RS-020 and BR-285.

São José dos Ausentes was once part of Bom Jesus and was emancipated in 1992. Bom Jesus was the largest revenue collector post and controlled the imperial government in the São Pedro do Rio Grande do Sul province, in the 18th century. As cowboys went through the region taking cattle to São Paulo, the city was given a post to register and charge taxes from cowboys, in the intersection of the Touros and Pelotas rivers. In addition to a rich history, Bom Jesus has privileged landscapes, with over 80 waterfalls, streams, rivers and a lot of vegetation. Among them, highlights are the **Barragem Waterfall**, 16 kilometers from Downtown, having a dam that is used for swimming in summer and the two **falls of the Cerquinha River**, 34 kilometers from Bom Jesus, one of them 50 meters high; the **Quatro Bocas Waterfall**, with a cave; the **Felizberto cascade**, on the Antas River, 38 kilometers from Bom Jesus, in Governador; the **Fumaça Fall**, on the Pelotas River; the **Água Branca Waterfall**, 12 kilometers from Downtown, and the eight **falls on Touros River**.

TIPS

• The best route from Porto Alegre to

The Pampas flicker in São José dos Ausentes

Cambará do Sul is on RS-020, a paved road.

• Coming from the beaches to Cambará do Sul, it´s better to use the Praia Grande entrance, going up the Faxinal Mountain Range. The view is fantastic, but the road is in bad shape.

• Most of the roads leading to Cambará do Sul, São José dos Ausentes and Bom Jesus and to the national parks are dirt roads. The region is very dangerous for cars when it rains.

• It´s advisable to always hike with experienced guides, because cliffs may appear out of nowhere, behind hills or trees. The constant fog, called *viração* in the region, brings more risks. In addition to making your journey safer, the guides also provide valuable information. Even at the Aparados da Serra National Park, with marked trails, a lot more can be learned from a guide. To hire them, contact the Guide Association in Cambará do Sul (☎251-1320) or in Praia Grande (☎48- 532-1414).

• The best time to visit the canyons is in winter, from June to August, when there isn´t much fog. But you´ll have to bundle up, for the temperatures are low and it can even snow.

• The canyons have attractions also in the summer months, from December to February. Summer is good for swimming in the waterfalls. But the excursions should be taken very early in the morning, so as to avoid the dense fog at the end of the day.

• The Refúgio Ecológico Pedra Afiada Inn, in Praia Grande, is the place that has the best view of the region (☎48- 532-1059). The inn was built at the base of the Malacara canyon, outside of the Serra Geral Park, according to architectural ecological standards, with projects for the sustainable use of energy, treatment of effluents and garbage recycling.

Gramado / Canela

The European style is present at the city´s entrance, preserving the symbols of Christmas

Porto Alegre 115 km
Canela 7 km
Bento Gonçalves 110 km
Torres 320 km
29,372
54
286-1475
gramadosite.com.br

The cities of Gramado and Canela are only 7 kilometers away from each other, and in the 19th century, cowboys passed through the cities taking cattle to the prairies. The shady fields full of soft grass that served as a resting place for travelers named Gramado (grassy field). Canela (cinnamon) owes its name to the large cinnamon tree under which cowboys rested before resuming their trip. Both cities owe to cowboys their tourist vocation. Today, both Gramado and Canela thrive on the tourism industry. Up until 1924, when the railway transportation was inaugurated in Canela – a section of the same line of Gramado –, Canela still belonged to the neighboring city. The German, Italian and Portuguese colonization left marks on both towns.

Hydrangeas: a symbol for all the region ▶

GRAMADO

Downtown

The best of Gramado can be seen on the well-kept streets, with flowery gardens and German architecture. Walking along **Borges de Medeiros** and **Hortênsias** avenues and neighboring streets reveals a refined artwork, delicious chocolate, woolen shirts, leather goods, beautiful colonial-style furniture and good restaurants. Right in the middle of this open-air shopping mall is the **Matriz São Pedro Church**, in front of Major Nicoletti Plaza, and a Tourist Information Center. The church opened in 1952, with a 46-meter tower and a basalt-stone façade. On Hortênsias Avenue is the Lutheran Confession Church, in a hydrangea garden. From 1961, it´s known as **Igreja do Relógio**. Going to Canela,

Tradition on the table

Tables full of food as seen in the mountain region of Rio Grande do Sul reflect the mixture of cultures that helped form it. From the Germans, came the *Café Colonial* (a coffee meal, serving around 50 kinds of cakes, pies, cold cuts, cheeses, jams and breads). There are two versions to explain its origin. The first accounts for the distance of one house to the other and the difficulty in meeting people. So, workers partied with banquets in which the housewife cooked everything she knew. The other version says that in the afternoon, workers had to get their strength back, after a hard day´s work. Italians contributed with the *galeto* (chicken), accompanied of pasta, salad, polenta, cheeses and wine. The traditional *churrasco na vala* (barbecue made in holes on the ground) is also present.

Abundance of food from various countries

there´s the City Hall, a good example of European architecture.

★ Santa Claus´ Village

353 Bela Vista Street 286-3075. Monday to Friday, 1:30 pm to 9 pm; Saturday and Sunday, 10:30 am to 9 pm.

Located in one of the most beautiful places, the **Knorr Park**. Created in 1940 by Oscar Knorr, the park has a 57,000-square-meter garden. He lived there with his family, in a Bavarian-style house, now Santa Claus´ home. It´s said Mr. Knorr started the tradition of hydrangeas, and other residents appreciated the flower. Neighboring cities adopted it, and now the area is known as the Hydrangea region.

★ Black lake

Casa da Juventude Street with 25 de Julho Street, in the district of Planalto.

The dark-water lake is surrounded by hydrangeas and European-style buildings. The artificial lake has cyprus trees brought from the Black Forest, in Germany, in the 1940s. The lake region boasts a walking track, paddleboats and, on weekends, artwork shops.

Minimundo

291 Horácio Cardoso Street 286-4055. Daily, from 1 pm to 5 pm.

This mini-city was idealized 20 years ago by the owners of Hotel Ritta Höppner, Otto and Heino Höppner. There are acryllic pieces, replicas of castles, railways, houses and windmills. The São Francisco de Assis and the Ouro Preto churches, the Gasômetro Plant, from Porto Alegre and the Bariloche airport are also represented.

Hollywood Dream Cars Museum

4,151 Hortênsias Avenue, on the way to Canela, 2 kilometers from Downtown. 286-4515. Daily, 9 am to 6 pm.

Antique car aficionados will be delighted. Created by a family from Blumenau, 20% of the museum´s collection comes from car owners. There are 25 cars and 11 Harley-Davidson motorcycles from the 1940s to the 1960s, from Hollywood movies.

Palácios dos Festivais

709 Borges de Medeiros Avenue 286-1058.

The famous Gramado Film Festival takes place at a beautiful building with

The city strives to have beautiful gardens

"Mobile homes"

The Germans gave origin to a different style in building techniques that made moving much easier, by taking your own house along. The wooden beams are put together and can be disassembled any time. When immigrants moved from one region to another, they simply removed the bricks that were glued with a mixture of mud and manure, took the beams out and rebuilt the houses somewhere else.

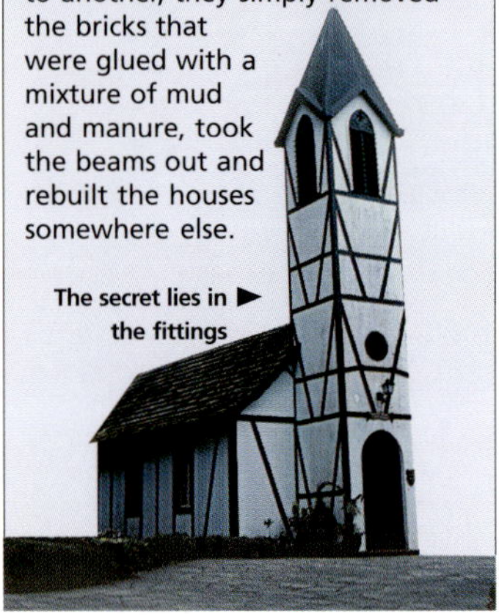

The secret lies in ▶ the fittings

German architecture. The festival gathers 1,200 people. The rest of the year it hosts events and movies.

★ Vale do Quilombo

6 kilometers from Downtown on a dirt road.

Gramado and Canela are located on the upper part of Vale do Quilombo, with observatories. One, 850 meters high, is on Hortênsias Avenue, on the way to Canela. The valley can be seen from the inside, too. There are excursions along its trails, forests and waterfalls. One of them takes visitors to the Sperry family farm, with three cascades, and also to the Quinta dos Conte, with one of the oldest houses in Gramado, with wooden poles on the outside. The four-hour excursion requires reservations in advance, 504-1649. Campofora offers horse rides, 9971-4000.

CANELA

Downtown

The main attraction in town is the Matriz Nossa Senhora de Lourdes

The miniature city impresses visitors because of the details of each replica

◄ Lago Negro: dark waters and cyprus trees

Church, known as Catedral de Pedra (Stone Cathedral), on Felisberto Soares with Borges de Medeiros Street. The 1953 stone church, in English neo-Gothic style, has a carillon with 12 bells and 65-meter-tall towers. Nearby, in front of João Correa Plaza, the old railroad building houses the Tourist Information Center, ☎ 282-2200 and the Casa do Artesão. Oswaldo Aranha Street lights up for Christmas.

★ Caracol Park

At the 7 km marker on RS-466 (Caracol Highway). ☎ 282-3035. 9 kilometers from downtown Canela. Daily, from 8:30 am to 6 pm.

That´s where the city emerged, in the beginning of the 19th century. It was a forest richly adorned with pine trees that attracted lumbering companies. The opening of a celluloid plant and a railway in the 1920s attracted business. Today, it´s the most visited place in the State thanks to the infrastructure of the park and beauty of the forest reserve that houses the 131-meter Caracol waterfall. It has several observatories, and a highlight is the 927-step stairway that leads to the base of the cascade, where visitors can appreciate a beautiful view from bottom to top, A panoramic elevator takes visitors to the 27-meter-high glass platform.

★ Floresta Encantada Park

At the 7.5 km marker on RS-466 (Caracol Road) ☎ 504-1405. 9.5 kilometers from downtown Canela. Daily, from 9 am to 5 pm.

The best view of the Caracol cascade is from the Floresta Encantada Park. A cablecar crossing a distance of 415 meters offers a splendid view of the fall.

★ Ferradura Park

At the 13 km marker on RS-466 (Caracol Road) ☎ 282-4300. 15 kilometers from downtown Canela, 6 on a dirt road.. Daily, from 9 am to 5:30 pm.

An area of 4.1 square kilometers of native forest, with monkeys, coatis, deer, anteaters and squirrels. It has three observatories, one overlooking the horseshoe-shaped Caí River Valley, another the Arroio Caçador region and the third the Arroio Caçador Cascade, in a 420-meter-deep canyon.

Castelinho Caracol

At the 3 km marker on RS-466 (Caracol Road) ☎ 282-2268. 5 kilometers from downtown Canela. Daily, 9 am to 1 pm and 2:20 pm to 5:40 pm.

The first house in Canela built in typical German architecture, between 1913 and 1915, next to Arroio Caracol. It became a museum in 1984, in memory of Geman builder Pedro Franzen, who made the furniture. There´s a tea house that serves irresistible apple pies.

Sequoia Park

1,747 Godofredo Raymundo Street ☎ 282-1373, 2 kilometers from downtown Canela.Daily, from 10 am to 5 pm.

A stone Cathedral in Canela ►

It´s an open-air museum, for it houses one of the largest collections of conifera in the world. Created in 1945 by the German Curt Mentz, it has circa 140 tree species, all identified, in 450 square meters. Trails lead to two water cascades, the 15-meter-high Marmeleiro and the 20-meter-high Mentz cascades. JM Rafting (282-1255) offers rappelling tours. The Sequoias Hotel is located inside the park and is the first ecological hotel in the State.

Other parks

At the entrance to Canela, the 90-square-meter Palácio Park offers trails in the Atlantic Rainforest 282-1287. The Laje de Pedra Park, 2.5 kilometers from Canela, affords a beautiful view of the Quilombo Valley. Sesi Park 282-1311 has a structured entertainment area, with trails and water cascades along 170 square meters. The Pinheiro Grosso Park 278-3035, on Caracol Road, has a giant 700-year-old pine tree: it´s 48 meters tall with a 2.75-meter diameter.

Mrs. Claus´ Village

400 Nações Avenue, ☎ 282-3043.
Monday to Friday, from 11:30 am to 9 pm; Saturday and Sunday, from 10 am to 8 pm.
Santa Claus lives in Gramado and Mrs. Claus lives in Canela, in a wooden house dating from 1916, all decorated with Christmas motifs and antique furniture. It has several toys, a fountain, a carousel, farm animals and several other fun areas.

Caracol Waterfall, a big attraction in Canela

Mundo a Vapor

1,177 Don Luiz Guanella Avenue, exit to Gramado. ☎ 282-1125.
Daily, from 9:15 am to 5 pm; closes on Wednesday.
A theme park on steam trains from the beginning of the 20th century. The façade depicts an accident in which a derailed locomotive breaks through the wall of a train station in Paris, in 1895, and falls onto the street. There are 11 miniature units run on steam that present the work done in a brick factory, an iron factory, a stone quarry, a saw mill and a paper mill.

Anos Dourados Automobile Museum

281 Nações Plaza ☎ 282-9364
Tuesday to Sunday, from 10 am to 6 pm.
There, 36 cars tell the story of the development of the car industry between the 1920s and 1970s. There are also around 200 automobile miniatures in the collection.

SURROUNDINGS

Nova Petrópolis

34 kilometers from Gramado on RS-235.
The city is depicted on 15 de Novembro Avenue, Downtown, in a theme park showing a typical German community that lived between 1870 and 1910. Ten colonial buildings were removed from several places in the city and rebuilt there. There, you´ll see a teacher´s house, a blacksmith´s shop, a dance hall, but the biggest attraction is the chapel, having the tower and chambers built in typical German architecture – the only one in Brazil. The city boasts many natural attractions, but all have a poor infrastructure, such as the Panelão, a rock formation with a waterfall and lake, 18 kilometers from Downtown on a dirt road. Cars are not allowed. Ecoturismo Jaguatirica (☎ 9113-4620) offers rappelling tours, hikes and canoeing. At Ninho das Águias, at 720 meters high, there´s a free-flight ramp,

The Caí River Valley and the shape that gives the name to the Horseshoe Park

used for hang-gliding and paragliding, plus an observatory.

São Francisco de Paula

47 kilometers from Gramado on RS-235 and RS-020.

It´s the highest city among the cities in the Hydrangea region, with altitudes ranging from 900 and 1,083 meters. It was part of the cowboys´route who took cattle to São Paulo and the Prata region, in the 18th century. This created a rural, farm-like culture, still present today. This can be seen in rodeos, dance balls, horse-riding tours and traditional music festivals. Cachoeira Park, 504-1446, has three waterfalls and trails, where visitors can ride horses, camp, go boat-riding, fish and practice extreme sports from the Passo do Inferno iron bridge, dating from 1935, and having a 74-meter opening. The 1,900-meter São Bernardo Lake is the main attraction and is near Downtown. Ronda Cascade, 2 kilometers away, has 5 falls. See the Salto Dam too.

Três Coroas

20 kilometers on RS-115 (toll booth on the 23 km marker)

Três Coroas is bathed by the waters of the Paranhana River and is surrounded by mountains. It´s the last city of the river valley before the mountain range. Because of its location, 700 meters lower, it´s from 6° C to 8° C hotter than the neighboring cities, which has contributed to its main tourist activity, rafting. Five agencies offer rafting, canoeing, hikes and rappelling at the Laranjeiras Municipal Park, 11 kilometers from RS-115. Rafting on the Paranhana River is the most popular activity. Brasil Raft, 286-5444 offers the longer tour. The Chagdud Khadro Buddist Temple 51- 546-1563 is the largest in South America.

TIPS

• Those leaving Porto Alegre towards Gramado have several options: either BR-116 to Nova Petrópolis, with many trucks, and from there RS-235, full of curves, toll booths and slow, but with a beautiful view. Or BR-116 to Novo Hamburgo, and from there RS-239 (with toll booths) to Taquara, at the base

Castelinho do Caracol: German-style

of the mountains, and then RS-115, a section up the mountain with beautiful scenery. Or take BR-116 and RS-239, on RS-020 to Taquara.

• Those who like hydrangeas should visit the region in springtime.

• A small passenger bus and a *dindinho* (kind of streetcar pulled by a truck) go along the main spots in Gramado (one hour and a half). Leaves daily, from the Igreja Matriz (Main Church).

Lagoa do Peixe

Migrating birds find shelter and food in Lagoa do Peixe

Porto Alegre 212 km
Mostardas 4 km
Tavares 12 km
São José do Norte 139 km
51
673-1464
ibama.gov.br

The Lagoa do Peixe National Park is the largest haven for migrating birds in all South America. It´s situated between Laguna dos Patos and the Atlantic Ocean and covers an area of 344 square kilometers, spread among the cities of Tavares (80%), Mostardas (17%) and São José do Norte (3%). These lands are home to the Lagoa do Peixe, a hotel-restaurant, open 24 hours for approximately 40,000 birds that rest and feed on the leftovers. Most of the birds come from the extreme tips of the American continent. The so-called Lagoa do Peixe is a lagoon, because it´s linked with the ocean. The 35-kilometer-long and over 1-kilometer-wide and from 10- to 6-centimeter-deep lagoon is the largest in the park, consisting of a complex of coastal ecosystems including freshwater lagoons, saltwater lakes, beaches, dunes, swamps, sandbank vegetation and even a marine area.

Lagoa do Peixe has salt water, resulting from the proximity to the sea, which, once in a while flows into its waters, bringing thousands of mollusks and algae. The mixture of salt and fresh water, combined with strong gusts of wind and the concentrated nutrients provide food for the birds, and indirectly to several mammals. A large number of those come from the Northern Hemisphere, fleeing from the winter, on long and tiresome journeys. Several shore birds, terns and plovers are good examples of birds that come to the vast waters of lakes and eat continuously to boost energy and save enough for the trip back home. An American shore bird comes in September and leaves in May to nest on New York bridges. But the waters of the lagoon receive birds from South America, like the Chilean and Argentine flamingoes, that fly in flocks. With beautiful plumage, they have become the symbol of the park, the only place in Brazil these birds can be seen all year long.

★ Barra da Lagoa do Peixe

To go to Barra da Lagoa do Peixe, take

the 12-kilometer secondary dirt road, that leaves Mostardas and goes to the beach. From there, it´s another 33 kilometers on the sand. You can also go to Tavares, situated around 30 kilometers after Mostardas. It´s a few more kilometers till you get to the lagoon. Barra da Lagoa do Peixe has the largest concentration of migrating birds in the park and it´s also the deepest part, reaching 2 meters deep. This is where the communication channel between the lagoon and the sea opens up, from June to December. It has a very rich flora and fauna, but fishing is prohibited along a 500-meter stretch to the north and 500 meters to the south. A small fishermen´s community lives on the fishing of shrimp, crabs, manatees, mullets and flounders.

★ Beaches

The 36-kilometer stretch of beaches in the park is called "flamingoes´ trail." It´s located 18 kilometers from the Mostardas Lighthouse (which in fact belongs to Tavares) to Barra da Lagoa do Peixe and, from there to the southernmost point, another 18 kilometers. The lighthouse dates from 1940, and is entirely covered with tiles. It´s at this point that birds, such as shore birds, oyster-catchers and flamingoes can be observed. From June to December the sandbar is open, blocking the passage.

A *Nymphoide indica*, or water white flower

Trilha das Dunas

The Trail of the Dunes is also called Balneário Mostardense Road. It´s about 12 kilometers long and cuts the park through swamp areas, sandbank vegetation and dunes to the beach, out of the limits of the preservation unit.

Trilha das Figueiras

It´s 6 kilometers on a sandy road from Tavares to the Trail of the Fig Trees. From the trail to the sandbar, the one-kilometer section is covered with water during the flood season, making driving in the region impossible.

A yellow-beak swallow

The Brazilian lapwing

The oyster-catcher *(Haenatopus pallatus)*

The black skimmer *(Rynchops niger)*

Azorean influence on the homes of Mostardas

Trilha do Talha-Mar

The Trail of the Talha-Mar is more popularly known as Estrada da Véia Terra (Old Land Road). It´s about 10 kilometers long and links the main road to the beach. Along the way, see the huge moving dunes. From June to August, it may become impossible to pass because of the water.

SURROUNDINGS

Mostardas

6 hours from the park

The small town is calm and does not have a good tourist infrastructure, but it´s the best access route to reach the Lagoa do Peixe National Park. The town had an Azorean origin, and still has traces of its colonization period, such as low houses, narrow streets and other characteristic traits. The Casa da Cultura has a good collection, with period pieces, photographs and a library. Miniatures of sea birds and pure-wool clothing, woven in manual looms, are the main local art. Make sure you buy the famous blankets and ponchos from Mostardas, to keep the strong and dry Minuano wind away in wintertime.

Tavares

6 hours from the park

The highlights of the town are its festivals and cultural manifestations. The Ternos Juninos (June Feast) and the Cavalhadas, both having an Azorean heritage, take place in June. The Shrimp and Onion Exposition is in March. And be sure

Secluded area

The constant action of winds and the coming and going of the ocean waves– resulting from the glacial and interglacial periods – formed the coastal prairie where the Lagoa do Peixe National Park is located. Its first inhabitants date from 7,000 years ago. They survived on mollusks and fishing on Lagoa do Peixe, and the leftovers were accumulated in shellmounds. Numerous evidences of the presence of these inhabitants have been found on the 21 archaeological sites in the park and surroundings. Next came the ceramist peoples, and in the 16th and 17th centuries, the Minuano, Arachanes and Carijós Indians, who almost disappeared completely, with the attacks of the trailblazers. In 1763, the then-village of São Luiz das Mostardas was founded by Azoreans, but the difficulty in getting to the sandy prairie region and the climate contributed to the isolation of the region, which still maintains this characteristic. Exactly because it´s a secluded region, the coastal ecosystems have remained well-preserved. In the 1980s, scientific studies called attention to the innumerable bird species in Lagoa do Peixe, and all this transformed Lagoa do Peixe into a National Park, in 1986. The region is the last one in Rio Grande do Sul, where the coastal marshes predominate, a vegetation with bushes and trees such as the Brazil cherry trees and fig trees.

Well-preserved sandy prairies ►

◄ Flowers on the prairies of Lagoa do Peixe

to visit the Santo Antônio Church, a replica of Azorean churches.

Farol da Solidão

60 km from the park 4 hours

Located on Farol Beach, it was built in 1929 and is 21 meters tall. The roads are in bad condition, but the dunes and the flooded areas along the way are worth the effort.

Laguna dos Patos

12 km from Mostardas and 10 km from Tavares an average of 6 hours

Laguna dos Patos is erroneously called a lake. It´s very large, over 9,000 square kilometers. It has plenty of shrimp and other invertebrates and attracts a large quantity of birds, which feed on those animals. The Barquinho Port, on the banks of the lagoon and 25 kilometers away from Mostardas, can be reached in a 6-hour hike through the woods. Visit the Capão da Marca Lighthouse, one of the oldest, on the banks of the Patos lagoon, where there are remains of an Indian campsite.

TIPS

• If you´re driving, leaving Porto Alegre, take RS-040 to Capivari, on a 90-kilometer paved section. From there, take BR-101 to Mostardas (an extra 120 kilometers on a paved road), where the park´s administration is located. From the headquarters to the park´s limits it´s another 25 kilometers. There are regular bus lines that go from Porto Alegre to Mostardas and from that point on, there are urban lines that take visitors to the coast, through the park.

• Entrance to the park is free and the park is open daily. However, visitors should check the working hours at the headquarters in Mostardas, where there´s also a model park and permanent exhibition of photographs, videos and books.

• You can enter the park through three different ways. But the park doesn´t have an organized infrastructure for tourists, so be careful. Get information before going or hire a guide authorized by Ibama.

• You can ride your bike in the park, but it´s forbidden to camp in the area. There are very rustic lodges in Mostardas or in Tavares.

• The park receives more tourists in summer, from December to March, when the temperatures are more pleasant and the birds from the Southern Hemisphere show up.

• Between June and September, whales can be sighted in the ocean, right in front of the park, on their way to Santa Catarina. In winter, it´s common to see penguins, manatees and sea lions.

• Between September and March, the air is filled with mosquitoes, so don´t forget a repellent.

• São José do Norte is one of the three towns where the park is located, and if you want to visit the city, located at the end of the narrow stretch of sand between the sea and Laguna dos Patos, try another route (see Rio Grande). Don´t take BR-101, known as "hell´s highway" in the 1980s, in the section between Tavares and São José do Norte, because that part of the highway was in terrible shape. Now almost all the highway is paved but there are still some dangerous parts. It´s for those who are driving 4WD vehicles.

Solidão Lighthouse: revealing dunes and swamps

Pelotas

Manor houses of the Charque barons, on Coronel Pedro Osório Plaza

Porto Alegre 250 km
Rio Grande 60 km
Santa Maria 311 km
Bagé 187 km
323,034
53
225-7755 ou 225-3733
pelotas.com.br

Known as the National Capital of Sweets, Pelotas ironically had its economic and cultural heyday in the 19th century, thanks to the salt. More specifically, to the jerked beef industry, which bequeathed an extremely rich architectural heritage to the city. The pioneer was the Portuguese José Pinto Martins, who founded the first jerked beef industry in 1780, on the banks of what today is the Pelotas stream. Pinto Martins produced jerked beef in Ceará, but due to a drought, he came to the South attracted by the abundance of cattle and transportation facilities. The stream flows into the São Gonçalo Channel, and Pelotas is located on its banks, which links Lagoa Mirim to Laguna dos Patos. It was the excessive humidity of the region in summer – the best time to produce jerked beef – that was responsible for the name given the technique used to preserve meat with salt and sun. To prevent meats from rotting when exposed to the sun to dry,

Sweet Heritage

Pelotas owes its tradition in sweets to Portuguese immigrants who came from 1777 on, leaving the colony of Sacramento, given to Spain, and joined the Portuguese who fled Rio Grande in 1763, During the jerked beef cycle, parties were given a sweet taste with Portuguese sweets: pastéis de santa clara, ninhos, camafeus etc. Recipes passed from generation to generation, and others, from Italy or Germany, were incorporated. Pelotas is one of the largest producers of peaches and hosts the largest sweet fair in the country, the Fenadoce.

The city is famous for its bakeries ▶

they were put in tanks with warm water and salt, and there they remained for 24 hours, in a process prior to cooking. In Portuguese, the meats were *encharcadas* (drenched in salt water), and the name *charque* (jerked beef) is derived from that word. The product made the then-Freguesia de São Francisco de Paula the true economic capital of the province. The name Pelotas – the name of the boats made with sticks and leather that crossed the rivers at the time – came only in 1835, when the village became a city, and was nicknamed Princesa do Sul (Princess of the South).

★ Historic Downtown

It´s surprising to see so many historical mansions, bearing a European influence, spread all over the city. There are well over 1,000 buildings that resist the passing of time and abandonment. Some of the most beautiful houses, true representatives of the aristocratic architecture of the 19th and 20th centuries, are in downtown Pelotas, near **Coronel Pedro Osório Plaza**, an attraction in itself, with sculptures by Antônio Caringi and the **As Nereidas** French fountain, imported in 1875 to supply water, and installed where there used to be a whipping post. Still in the square, check out the old mansions of the jerked beef barons, some already restored. Three of them take up a whole block, on Félix da Cunha Street, between Butuí and Lobo da Costa streets. The **houses number 2, 6 and 8** make up the largest preserved neo-Renaissance architectural complex in Latin America. They were built, respectively, in 1830, 1879 and 1878. At 849 Lobo da Costa Street, visit the 1921 neoclassical **Guarani Theater** House, which seats 1,600 people. At number 51, on the same street, see the luxurious **Grande Hotel**, an art-nouveau building, declared Historical heritage, which once had President Getúlio Vargas as guest. On the corner of Lobo da Costa with 15 de Novembro, stands the **City Hall**, and next to it, the **City Library**, both founded in 1881 in eclectic style. It was in the City Hall building that the Pelotas Freedom of the Slaves Declaration was signed, four years earlier than in the rest of Brazil. From this corner, you can see, on 7 de Julho Plaza, the **Public Market**, dating from 1847, bearing a German clock tower that resembles the Eiffel Tower, in Paris. Surrounding the plaza, other highlights are the **7 de Abril Theater House**, dating from

Aldo Locatelli´s frescoes at the cathedral

As Nereidas: a fountain that came from France

1834, with its art-deco façade – a result of a full-scale renovation project in 1916 – and the oldest still in use; and the **Caixeiral Club**, from 1904. On the corner of Floriano Peixoto and Anchieta streets, you´ll see the eclectic building created by traveling salesmen from Pelotas for weekend entertainment. The Carnaval festivities of the city used to take place there too. While still in downtown Pelotas, it´s worth visiting the **São Francisco de Paula Cathedral,** at 15 José Bonifácio Plaza, and the **Redentor Cathedral**, at 472, on 15 de Novembro Street. The first is a Catholic church built between 1813 and 1856, and seats 1,700 people. It arouses considerable attention because of the huge dome and the frescoes by the Italians Aldo Locatelli and Emílio Sessa. The Redentor Cathedral is an Anglican church. That explains its Gothic-Celtic style, resembling English temples. Known as the "Hairy Church" because of the climbing ivy weed that covers its walls and changes colors each season – going from gray to reddish pink, from green to brown – it was founded in 1892, and at the time the New York glass windows and the 27-meter tower were already there. Right in the middle of the Piratinino de Almeida Plaza stands its biggest attraction, a **French water tank**, supported by 45 ornamented wrought-iron columns. It was put together in 1875 and declared Historical Landmark, since it´s the only one of the kind in Latin America. In the middle of the

The baron´s house turned into a museum

reservoir, still in use, there´s a circular stair that takes visitors to an observatory. In front of the square, at number 53, is the building that houses a hospital and takes a whole block, the **Santa Casa de Misericórdia**, built in 1861. In 1921, an annex was built, the Tuberculosis Pavilion, with a suspended bridge linking both buildings.

Baronesa Museum and Park

2.5 km from Downtown, at 1490 Domingos de Almeida Avenue, Areal. ☎ 228-4606. Tue-Sat, 1:30 pm-6 pm; Sunday, from 10 am to 6 pm.
In 1863, the enormous 820-square-meter house, with 22 rooms and an inner patio with a well, combining the neoclassical and colonial styles, belonged to Três Serros´ barons. It became a City Hall property in 1978. The 70-square-meter Baronesa Museum has gardens, lakes, a cave, a small replica of a castle, and a collection of over 1,000 items from the 19th and beginning of the 20th centuries. There´s furniture, fans, porcelain and silver items, clothing and uniforms.

Laranjal beaches

12 km from Downtown. Access via Ferreira Viana and Adolfo Fetter avenues.
The first land on the banks of the Laguna dos Patos to be inhabited in Pelotas. It was in current Laranjal that the Portuguese sought refuge, coming from Rio Grande village, after the

◀ Redentor Cathedral: domineering climbing weed

Spanish invasion, in 1763. Now, the two kilometers of Valverde, Santo Antônio and Prazeres spas are favorites in the summer because of restaurants, bars, sand stalls, trees and benches.

★ Charqueada São João

7.5 km from Downtown. 500 Costa Road, Areal ☎ 228-2425. Visits and boat rides allowed only on prior notice. www.charqueadasaojoao.com.br

A well-preserved place, where beef was sun-dried, and a city´s treasure. It was built in 1810, on the right banks of the Pelotas stream and belonged to the Portuguese Antônio Gonçalves Chaves. Its 33 rooms, all decorated with antiques, have been hosting visitors for three years, guided by the Mazza family, who lives there now. It was built in Portuguese colonial style, and still has remains of the slave quarters, plus a very tall chimney, instruments used for jerking beef and centuries-old fig trees. The boat ride takes you to other seven sites for sun-drying beef, out of 35 that existed in the past. The Charqueada building hosted the French naturalist Auguste Saint-Hilaire, in 1820.

SURROUNDINGS

São Lourenço do Sul

60 km from Pelotas

The Portuguese and the Germans colonized the city in the end of the 18th century, with land donated by Portugal and transformed into agricultural sites. Potato farming is still its main source of income, and in the 19th and part of the 20th centuries it was the largest producer in South America. But what attracts visitors is its strategic location on the banks of the **Laguna dos Patos**. A boat ride in the calm waters of the **São Lourenço River**, that cuts through the city and flows into the Laguna dos Patos, is fascinating. It takes one hour on the largest schooner, the Bucaneiro ☎ 9838-4775, or an hour and a half, with a stop for swimming, with Lancha Capri ☎ 9963-7840. The most important beaches, **Ondinhas, Nereidas and Barrinha**, have clear waters and infrastructure for tourists: hotels, restaurants, boats, tree shades, lifeguards, in 2.5 kilometers. The **Boqueirão Village** is where the spas that originated the city started, and where houses show Portuguese traces.

TIPS

- From Porto Alegre to Pelotas, take BR-116 (three toll booths). From Santa Maria, BR-392 has a toll booth. The entrance to São Lourenço do Sul is at the 462 km marker, on BR-116. From Pelotas to São Lourenço one toll booth.
- Laguna dos Patos in Laranjal is inappropriate for swimming, but good for windsurfing, which can be learned at a local school (☎ 226-3939). Boat rides must be booked (☎ 226-0071).
- In São Lourenço do Sul, information can be obtained at the Casa do Turista 251-5979, www.adetur.com.br
- Besides being a tourist attraction, the Sobrado Farm (☎ 251-2141) has been, since 1994, a farm-hotel, with sports and entertainment activities.

São Lourenço Beach: calm, crystal-clear waters, with good tourist infrastructure

R. Grande

Rio Grande

Aerial view of Rio Grande, the only city in Rio Grande do Sul to have a sea port

Porto Alegre 310 km
Chuí 240 km
Santa Vitória do Palmar 232 km
Piratini 150 km
186,755
53
231-3466
riogrande.rs.gov.br

Rio Grande is the oldest city in the State and is located on the southern margin of the estuary that leads the waters of the Laguna dos Patos to the Atlantic Ocean. When the first Portuguese sailors arrived, in the 16th century, the lagoon channel that cut through the sandy beaches was thought to be a river and it originated the name of the city, Rio Grande (big river) and also the name of the State. They also concluded that those lands, according to the Tordesilhas Treaty, belonged to Spain, and that the present Rio Grande do Sul coastal region was dangerous and straight, with no natural ports, and so gave it up. Thus, the founding of the city happened only in 1737, with Brigadier José da Silva Paes, commander of an expedition that wanted to make sure Portugal got the southern lands, already being disputed with Spain. The exact spot where the Laguna dos Patos waters flow into the Atlantic Ocean was chosen for the installation of a military post. However, in 1763, the village fell into Spanish domain and only 13 years later was definitely conquered by the Portuguese. The strategic position of the city placed it as the only sea port in Rio Grande do Sul, the second largest in Brazil in number of containers and where most of the State´s production leaves.

Historic Downtown

A good walk through Downtown brings the past of Rio Grande back and reveals all the riches brought by its deep-waters international port. **Xavier Ferreira Plaza** is near the old port, and is surrounded by imposing buildings, like the City Hall, the 1894 General Military Quarters and the Rio-Grandense Library, the oldest in Rio Grande do Sul, dating from 1846. Next to the neoclassical library building is the Municipal Public Market, a good place to buy fish. In front of the lake in the square is the magnificent building that housed the Customs in 1879. It was

The Oceanographic Museum is one of the most complete in Latin America

declared a National Historical Landmark and currently houses the **City Museum**. São Francisco de Assis Chapel, dating from 1792, is at one end of the square. It houses the Sacred Museum of Rio Grande, and displays circa 2,500 pieces. Behind the chapel, take Travessa M. Eurico Magalhães to General Bacelar Street, where the oldest church in the State is, the São Pedro

The neo-Gothic style of the Carmo Church

Cathedral, built in 1755 in Portuguese colonial Baroque style. On the same street, see the impressive neo-Gothic style **Nossa Senhora do Carmo Church**, inaugurated in 1938. On huge **Tamandaré Plaza**, between General Netto Street and 24 de Maio Street, amidst sculptures, small lakes with bridges, bird nurseries and monkeys the tomb-monument honoring General Bento Gonçalves, dating from 1909, keeps his mortal remains. In front of one of the sides of the square visitors can still see the beautiful buildings of **Beneficência Portuguesa**, dating from 1859, and the Salvador Anglican Church, built from stone in English neo-Gothic style.

★ Furg Museums

10 Capitão Tenente Heitor Perdigão Street, next to the Yacht Club. 232-9107 and 231-3496

Less than 10 minutes away from Downtown, the Universidade Federal do Rio Grande Foundation keeps three excellent museums that can be visited together. The **Oceanographic Museum** (Tuesday to Sunday, from 9 am to 11 am and from 2 pm to 5:30 pm) displays marine specimen and equipment. It has eight aquariums, a collection of 150,000 specimen and is considered to be the most complete of its kind in Latin America. In an annex is the

The splendor of Taim Ecological Station ▶

Recuperation Center for Sea Animals, to where the animals in dangerous situations are brought. Having the same hours as the Oceanographic Museum, the **Antarctic Museum** is a replica of the Brazilian Station in the icy continent. Photographs and panels tell the story of man in the poles. The **Eco-museum** of Ilha da Pólvora deals with the ecosystem of the region and is located on the estuary island by the same name, 400 meters away from the Oceanographic Museum, from where the boats with visitors leave. It can be visited only from Friday to Sunday, from 2 pm to 5:30 pm.

Balneário do Cassino

18 kilometers from Downtown.

It´s the longest beach in the world – 212 kilometers – and it´s part of the *Guinness Book of Records*. It´s also the oldest resort in the State, dating from 1890 and one of the most popular. In the beginning of the beach there are the **Molhes da Barra**, two arms of rock that jut into the sea. It´s four kilometers into the ocean, which protect the ships when docking at Barra de Rio Grande. At the time of the first explorers, the place became known as Barra Diabólica (Diabolic sand bar) because of the difficulties it presented. The piers, built in 1915, were the largest construction of the Brazilian oceanic engineering and put an end to those problems. At the west pier, functional carts (small sail cars) run on rails that go to the end of the stone arms, in a fun ride. The place is very much used by amateur fishermen.

Marinheiros Island

30 minutes on a boat, leaving from Central de Hortigranjeiros, Capitão Tenente Heitor Perdigão, next to the Oceanographic Museum.

The largest island in the State was settled almost at the same time as the then Rio Grande de São Pedro Village, was supplied water, wood, fruit and vegetables to the Portuguese settlers. It was the first place in Rio Grande do Sul to produce wine. At present, it still produces over half the quantity of vegetables the city needs. Its Portuguese heritage can be seen in the chapels and houses built in colonial style located on the road that surrounds the island. Dunes, lagoons and ecological trails are the natural attractions of this huge piece of land surrounded by the waters of Laguna dos Patos. Cassino Tur ((233-2548) offers guided tours to the island.

SURROUNDINGS

Taim Ecological Station

88 kilometers from Rio Grande on BR-471. It´s located on the narrow strip of land between the Atlantic Ocean and the Lagoa Mirim, in the cities of Rio Grande and Santa Vitória do Palmar.

Of its 338-kilometer territory, 60% is formed by swamps and lagoons, which has given it the nickname of Pantanal dos Pampas. This ecosystem has a rich diversity of life species and an enormous food potential for migrating birds that come mainly from Patagonia. This is a resting place for them, they mate, their babies are born, and then they go away. Taim is home to over 230 bird species, 60 kinds of fish and several herbivorous rodents. Among the animals that roam the region is the black-necked swan –

Cassino Beach is the longest in the world (212 kilometers) and has protection rocks for boats

the only swan in South America. It´s threatened with extinction and that was the main reason the area was created in 1986. Other animals are the tachã (southern screamer), whose sound of the female scream baptized the "Taim," the bittern, the coscoroba swan, the broad-nosed cayman, turtles, the Amazon lungfish and the tamboatá, a fish that can leave water and move along the swamps. The Taim Ecological Station is the State´s largest natural preservation area and is used only for preservation purposes and research. Visits are allowed only with a n Ibama permit ((☎ 503-3151). However, you can observe the Station from BR-471, in the 15 kilometers the highway crosses the reserve.

São José do Norte

30 minutes on a motorboat (☎ 233-5451) or a ferryboat (☎ 231-1099), leaving from the Hydrostation, at the old port.

The small town of São José do Norte, located on the opposite margin (north) of the Laguna dos Patos estuary, has many historical buildings dating from the 19th century. Because of its strategic location, in 1840, it housed one of the bloodiest battles of the Farrapos War. Its resistance to invaders and loyalty to the Empire was the primary reason Emperor D. Pedro II visited the city, in 1845. The Imperadores Solar, where he stayed, and where his late father had also been a guest in 1826, is the main attraction. The Matriz Church is also worth visiting, as well as Mar Grosso Beach, which has a ship stuck in its sands.

Chuí

Located 23 kilometers from Santa Vitória do Palmar and 249 kilometers from Rio Grande, the city is situated on the extreme tip of the country, bordering on Uruguay. It emerged in 1737 and became a village in 1939 and finally a city in 1995. The trading business is all around on Uruguai Avenue, the borderline of Brazil and Uruguay. It´s worth visiting neighboring Chuy (on the Uruguayan side) to shop or even to see the San Miguel Fort and the Santa Tereza Fortress, both built in 1737 by the Portuguese.

TIPS

- To go from Porto Alegre to Rio Grande, take BR-116 to Pelotas and then BR-392, a section with four tollbooths.
- Many preserved historical buildings are located along Marechal Floriano Peixoto Street, Downtown. Such is the case of Paris Hotel (☎ 231-3866), dating from 1826, where Emperor D. Pedro II was a guest, in the 19th century and it´s still a hotel. Also worth visiting is the two-story house all covered in Portuguese tiles, from 1862, and the manor house that currently houses the Municipal Cultural Center.
- Winter on Cassino Beach surprises visitors with a great attraction. It´s a resting place for whales, manatees and sea lions, who come to the Molhes da Barra to rest before they resume their migrating journey.

- The best season to go to Taim is Spring, when the migrating birds come too.

◀ Chuí is the southernmost tip of the country, almost in Uruguay

Santa Maria

Arts and Letters Center, at the Santa Maria Federal University

Porto Alegre: 298 km
Rio Grande: 345 km
Caçapava do Sul: 101 km
Bagé: 338 km
243,392
55
226-6729
www.santamaria.rs.gov.br

The city is the geographical heart of Rio Grande do Sul and is located against the counter-forts of Serra Geral and the prairies that form the so-called central depression. This region concentrates the 17 towns that are home to the most important animal and vegetal fossil records in Brazil, and where the oldest dinosaur fossils in the planet were found (similar to those found in Argentina). These dinosaurs are estimated to have lived between 300 and 130 million yers ago. One of the most important findings of the history of paleontology in Santa Maria occurred in 1936, when bones of an extremely old species, the staurikossaurus pricei, were found. At the time, fossil preservation laws disn´t exist, so they were all taken to the Comparative Zoology Museum, in Harvard, in the United States. The city was founded officially in 1858, and was colonized mainly by Italians and Germans. And Santa Maria was the place to open the first university in a small town in the country, the Santa Maria Federal University.

Vila Belga: built in 1898

Downtown

As all the interesting places to visit are near, you should walk around the city and see them all. Start by the **Diocesana Cathedral**, on Rio Branco Avenue, bearing four panels by Italian

24-Hour street in Santa Maria

artist Aldo Locatelli, depicting the life of Our Lady. The building, dating from 1909, has an eclectic style. There´s a bronze bell, from the old Santa Maria Jesuit Reduction. Really close by, there´s the **24-hour Street**, an all-exclusive pedestrian street, a true open air mall, with bars, shopping stands ann services. The valuable natural heritage of the town is kept at the **Vicente Pallotti Historic and Cultural Museum**, one of the largest of its kind in Brazil. It houses around 40 thousand pieces, and in the paleontology hall, fossils from the Superior Triassic Period, dating back to 200 million years ago. Other rooms house collections on mineralogy, zoology, archaeology, iconography, numismatics, weaponry and filatelia. **Gama d´Eça and Victor Bressani Educational Museum**, on Acampamento Street, also shows many fossils found in the region. Don´t miss the **Belga Village**, the first condo in the State, built in 1898 for the employees of the Compagnie Auxiliaire des Chemins du Fer, who were responsible for buildiong the railroads at the time. The place was declared a Historic Landmark.

SURROUNDINGS

★ Mata

86 km from Santa Maria.

If it weren´t for the stubbornness of a Catholic priest, Mata, "the stone city which once was wood" wouldn´t be known by this slogan. Before the arrival of the new priest, Daniel Cargnin, dozens of trucks left town, full of rocks that were a nuisance to farmers. Hey thought they were cleaning the land, but instead they were sending out an over 200-million-year-old heritage. However, from 1976 on, the priest and amateur paleontologist started a long campaign that turned

Wood turned into stone

Fossilization is a rare and accidental process that takes millions of years. For an animal or plant to become a fossil, it´s necessary that it be covered by earth and water, soon after its death, before it decomposes. Underground, it suffers the action of elements transported by water. In the case of animals, the mineral elements that the water brings are deposited in the pores and bone cavities and crystallize. In the vegetable kingdom, mineral substances, mainly silica, substitute its organic matter, thus preserving the plant structure. The combination of the factors that make this process possible still has another component: vegetables and animals use different types of mineral elements for fossilization. That is, if the place lacks that specific substance, the process won´t happen. This explains why there are many vegetable fossils in Mata and no animal fossils. Santa Maria and São Pedro do Sul, on the other hand, have both, mainly fossilized animals.

Wood dating back to 200 million years

A church on Matriz Plaza preserves wood

Mata into a true open-air museum. In order to preserve one of the main archaeological sites in the country, Father Daniel started to decorate the town with the vegetal fossil reserve, dating from the Triassic Period of the Mesozoic Age. **The Matriz Plaza** was the first in town to have the sidewalk decorated with the petrified wood. Soon, everybody in town wanted to have a petrified tree decorating the wall, the sidewalk or the garden. Today, everywhere you go in the city, there´s a trunk displaying the great wealth present in Mata, a city that bears one of the largest petrified wood reserves in all the world, estimated to be of 7 square kilometers. **Martiniano Eggres da Costa Plaza** boasts a majestic fossilized trunk, approximately 200 million years old, 11 meters long and 1 meter thick, that weighs 15 tons, right in front of the beautiful Lutheran Church. The **Santo Brugali** and **N. Senhora Medianeira** plazas were decorated with the precious fragments too. The **Guido Borgomanero Museum**, on Comércio Street, displays some 2,500 smaller pieces. Besides the petrified wood found in the region, the place displays animal fossils from nearby cities, dating from as far back as 40 and 350 million years. The **Paleobotanical Garden**, on Sertão Street, keeps, on an area of 36 square meters, a group of vegetal fossils as they were found. Four kilometers from Downtown, the Haesbaert family put together the **Fragmentos do Tempo Museum** (Time Fragments Museum), and display their rich collection of antiques, that help tell the story of the German immigration to Mata.

The 146-meter-long iron bridge over the Toropi River

At the 33-meter-high **Boa Esperança Waterfall**, there´s a pool where visitors can swim and a huge wall from where rappel addicts can practice their art. At the same place, five kilometers from Downtown, a **suspension bridge** and a **mini-canyon** enrich the already beautiful setting. In Vila Clara, 14 kilometers from Downtown, be sure to visit the enormous **railroad bridge** over the Toropi River, which is 146 meters in extension and 21 meters high.

TIPS

• To reach Santa Maria, leaving Porto Alegre, the shortest route is via BR-116, through the city of Canoas, and a little farther ahead, via BR-386 (Rodovia da Produção) until you come to the intersection with RS-287 highway. Go ahead until your final destination.

• São Pedro do Sul, 36 kilometers from the city of Santa Maria, is also an archaeological site, but a little less preserved than the others. Dinosaur fossils and fossilized trees can be seen at the Walter Ilha Paleontology and Archaeology Museum (☎ 276-2620) and also at the Piscina and Ermida paleobotanical sites, both with access via BR-287.

• It´s advisable not to take the section of BR-287 between the cities of São Pedro do Sul and Mata. The highway is in bad condition because of the huge potholes on the highway.

• All the excursions in Mata can be arranged with Casa do Turista/ Tourist House (☎ 259-1438).

◄ Paleontobotanical Garden: a fossil site

S. Miguel das Missões

The São Miguel ruins tell part of the Rio Grande do Sul history

Porto Alegre 485 km
Santo Ângelo 58 km
Santa Maria 255 km
São Borja 170 km
7,682
55
3381-1294

The small city of São Miguel das Missões developed around the ruins of the São Miguel Arcanjo Reduction, founded in 1687 by the priests of the Companhia de Jesus. They were composed of seven missionary peoples on lands ferociously disputed by Spain and Portugal, which only in the 18th century became Brazilian. All the Missions had names of saints: São Francisco de Borja, Saint Nicholas, São Luiz Gonzaga, São Lourenço Mártir, São João Batista and Santo Ângelo Custódio. Besides São Miguel Arcanjo, only three still have Jesuitic ruins (read in Surroundings). If you want to visit them, do the Caminho das Missões (Way of the Missions) 3313-3962, www.caminhodasmissoes.com.br), a walking tour inspired by the pilgrimage to Santiago de Compostela, in Spain. It´s perfect for those who want to combine History, mysticism and walking. The guided tour can be taken in 7 days (180 kilometers) or 3 days (78 kilometers), and includes mostly traveling on the old missionary roads leading to Sete Povos. In the surroundings, there are families that host and feed the pilgrims.

★ São Miguel Arcanjo Archaeological Site

São Luiz Street, 3381-1399
Daily, from 9 am to 12 noon and from 2 pm to 6 pm.

It´s the most complete collection in Sete Povos das Missões, with the imposing ruins of the church, which give us an idea of how exceptional the Jesuit-Guarani civilization was. The huge temple was built in 1745 for 6,000 Guarani Indians. The façade is a replica (made with local stones) of the Gesù Church, in Rome. In 1983, the ruins were declared Cultural and Historical Heritage for All Humanity, by UNESCO and, in 1997, it was where the Spanish tenor José Carreras gave a concert. In the former vestry, two computers and an 8-minute video clip tell the story of the old Missions. **The Missões Museum**, a building designed by the architect Lúcio Costa (the one who helped with the Brasília project), displays one of the richest national collections of items used in the Missions. Every night (at 8 pm, paid tickets), the ruins light up for the exciting **Som e Luz** (Sound and Light) show, the only one in Brazil of its kind. With voices of actors Lima Duarte, Fernanda Montenegro and Paulo Gracindo, the Missionary saga, its conquests and misadventures are told in 50 minutes. At the site, you can buy artwork with motifs reminiscent of the Missions.

Santo Ângelo

58 km from São Miguel das Missões on BR-285 and RS-344

There are no vestiges of the youngest Sete Povos Reduction, founded in 1706. But the most populous city in the region and its beautiful **Angelopolitana Cathedral** are worth visiting. The Cathedral was built in 1929, exactly where there used to be a Jesuit church. It´s a replica of the São Miguel Arcanjo Temple, and has a huge image of a dead Christ, painted at the Missions´ time. While in the square, visit a 19th-century house, built with stones of the ruins, that currently houses the **Dr. Olavo Machado City Museum**. It displays archaeological material of the former mission. Be sure to visit the English colonial-style Railroad Station, built in 1921 by the engineer Luís Carlos Prestes. At present, the building houses the **Coluna Prestes Memorial**. The good taste and the quality of the art pieces invite visitors to stop by **Flecha Mágica**, a shop next to the Cathedral.

Other missionary ruins

BR-285; towards São Nicolau; also RS-168 and RS-561.

There´s very little of what was left of the three Missions in the region. In **São Nicolau**, 110 kilometers from São Miguel das Missões, some walls dating from the time of the 1687 Mission still stand, sustained by trees, in the middle of Padre Roque González Plaza. The **São Lourenço Mártir** ruins date from 1690 and are in the same condition. They belong to the city of São Luiz Gonzaga, 20 kilometers from São Miguel. While you´re in town, go Downtown, where the **São Luiz Gonzaga Church** displays ten extremely beautiful and rare missionary sculptures. Located 20 kilometers from São Miguel, in Entre-Ijuís, the **São João Batista** ruins boast a better tourist infrastructure. Founded in 1697 by the talented priest Antônio Sepp, it held choir presentations, orchestras formed by Guarani Indian boys and housed the first sawmill in South America. The **Santuário do Cáaro**, in Caibaté, is a good stopover on the way to São Luiz. A memorial is a reminder of the sacrifice of three Jesuits who were killed by the Indians.

A portico shows the grandiosity of S. Miguel

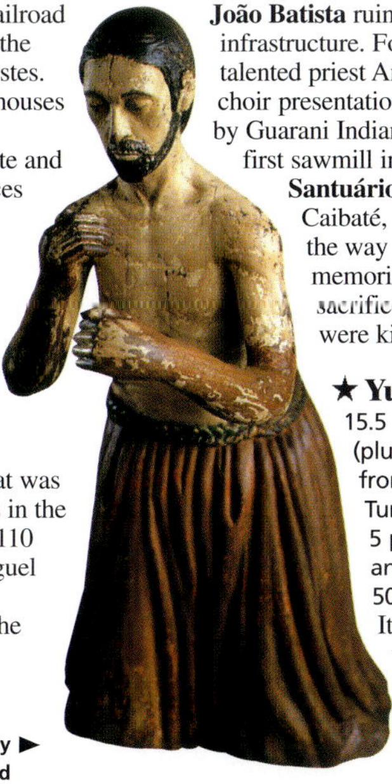

Sculptures are artistically ► high valued

★ Yucumã Falls

15.5 km on a dirt road (plus 500 meters walking) from the entrance to the Turvo State Park 9 am to 5 pm; closes Monday and Tuesday 3744-5050

It´s the longest waterfall on the planet, located in the Turvo State Park, in northwestern Rio Grande do Sul,

Yucumã is 1,800 meters long ►

bordering on Argentina. The Yucumã waterfall isn´t very tall, with an average height of 12 meters, but what impresses visitors is its extension: 1,800 meters. It can be seen only from November to April, in the drought period of the Uruguay River. The Yucumã – meaning roar in Guarani – falls parallel to the borders with a roar. Swimming is dangerous, because of a treacherous 90-meter corridor hidden under the current. About 90% of the park´s 170 square kilometers is covered by the subtropical forest, the last in Brazil. The park was created in 1947 to protect the Yucumã and the local flora and fauna. It´s located in Derrubadas (felling), given this name in the 1930s after an intense exploitation of the native forests. Today, half the city is in the Turvo Park.

TIPS

• Leaving Porto Alegre, the best way to get to São Miguel das Missões is this: take BR-116, via Canoas, and a little farther ahead take BR-386 (Rodovia da Produção) towards Carazinho, where you´ll come across the intersection with BR-285, which goes through the Missions region. From BR-285, take RS-536 to get to São Miguel. The section on BR-386 and BR-285 is long, with several toll booths. The road is not duplicated, but it´s in reasonable condition, and the traffic is mild. Another option is to catch a plane to Santo Ângelo.

• From São Miguel, there are excursions that take visitors to the ruins of the Argentine and Paraguayan Missions, such as **San Ignácio Mini, Trinidad and Jesus del Tavaranglie**, all declared Historical Sites for Humanity by UNESCO. It´s also possible to visit a typical farm in Rio Grande do Sul, to see 150 years of History and Azorean colonial architecture. On **Triunfo Farm**, you can ride horses on the prairies, see a typical chimarrão

gathering and eat typical food. Missões Turismo offer both excursions (☎ 3381-1319, www.missoesturismo.com.br).

• In summer (from December to March), visitation hours at the São Miguel Arcanjo Archaeological Site change and the *Som e Luz* shows are presented later. Check before leaving.

• Drinking *chimarrão* is a friendship ritual for the Gaúchos. Very rarely they drink *chimarrão* without company, so don´t be surprised if the "bitter drink" is offered to you. It´s a gesture of friendship, and the gourd goes from hand to hand – always to the person on your right – and the *bomba* (a kind of metal straw) is the same for everyone. As it is a typical ritual in the South, it may not please all tourists. According to tradition, the liquid has to be drunk until a sound that tells the gourd is empty is heard. And when you´re through drinking it, return the gourd with your left hand; this is the signal.

Remains of the Missions in S. João Batista

Torres

Huge rock walls named the charming city of Torres

Porto Alegre: 197 km
Cambará do Sul: 79 km
Caxias do Sul: 258 km
Florianópolis: 280 km
30,877
51
626-1937
torres.com.br

Without a doubt, Torres is the pearl jam of the Rio Grande do Sul coast. Having as an important characteristic the lack of geographic accidents, the stretch of 618 kilometers of the Rio Grande do Sul coast form a straight line that begins in Chuí and ends in Santa Catarina. The first city, on the northwest border, presents huge basalt "towers" that jut into the ocean and break the monotony of this almost unending straight line. And it was precisely these three huge rock blocks of approximately 140 million years that named the city. Torres (towers) is a calm city, but has a good tourist infrastructure. In the summer, the city receives ten times more its inhabitants, with the arrival of thousands of tourists. During the high season, it´s advisable to leave the car and walk or ride a bike instead. It becomes very difficult to find a parking space near the popular Grande Beach. Before Europeans came to what today is Torres, the region was already a passageway for the Carijó Indians, from Santa Catarina, and the Arachanes, from Rio Grande do Sul, in the trading business. Part of the old trail between the northern and southern beaches that were built at the base of the hill – today Morro do Farol – along the swamps that surrounded the current Violão lagoon, is now Júlio de Castilhos Street, the first in the municipality. It´s also the one bearing 19th-century buildings. The old Indian trails on the northern coast were used also by the Jesuits, trailblazers, military men and cowboys, as happened with the current RS-389, the so-called Estrada do Mar (Sea Highway), one of the oldest known highways in the State. Torres was born out of the need for protecting this strategic location. First came a police checkpoint, later a military lookout, between 1774 and 1776, and soon, in 1809, the São Domingos das Torres Fort and a jail. Seventy years later, the village became a town. Its tourist industry is also very old. It started in 1915, with the opening of the Picoral Spa, a landmark in the Torres tourism industry.

A profusion of lagoons

Violão Lagoon: part of the southern strip

The design of the 618 kilometers of the Rio Grande do Sul shore was achieved thanks to the coming and going of the ocean, for over 200,000 years. These transformations kept vast extensions of the ocean, originating dunes and lagoons. The lagoons comprise 12,908.10 square kilometers, 4.57% of the territory. It´s the largest lagoon complex in South America, with the Patos, Mirim and Mangueira lagoons, plus swamps and smaller lagoons. Of the 61 lagoons and lakes along this line, 40 are on the northern coast, between the sea and the mountains. The coastal prairies and the Rainforest brought tree ducks, alligators, coypuses, and other animals. Most of the lagoons are interconnected by rivers and channels, making navigation possible.

★ Guarita Park

Bom Fim Street, next to Cal Beach, one and a half kilometers from Downtown.

Two of the "towers" (or hills) that give their name to the city are inside the area of the State Park. Right between the Meio and Sul towers is a small tower, Guarita, which named the park created by environmentalist José Lutzenberger, in 1971, with gardens designed by Burle Marx. The three towers, plus Guarita Beach, the tree nursery, lakes, trails and gardens form a beautiful area. Start by climbing the Meio Tower, a long 135-square-kilometer plateau. The climbing is mild. From up there, it´s clear why this tower is called Furnas hill. Among the sea cliffs that form its eastern coast, are the caves formed by the strength of the waters. There are five of them, all with steps and a concrete handrail. Those who don´t want to come down the hill can walk on the mountaintop and enjoy the spectacular view. Then go down through Guarita Beach, the smallest and most beautiful beach in town. Among the three towers, it´s the ideal place to go up the 109 steps of the Sul tower, since it´s not allowed to do so on Guarita. From the top of the Sul hill, enjoy the fantastic view that spreads along the hill and Itapeva Beach, outside of the park, an area soon to be protected with a preservation unit. Having beautiful dunes, this is the largest beach in Torres (6 kilometers), and was given this name because of the hill, which means "flat rock" in Tupi-Guarani.

Guarita Beach is the smallest and most beautiful beach in town

Fun up above: the ballooning festival held in Torres has become a tradition

Beaches

Torres has five beaches along its 23 kilometers of shore, three very close to Downtown. The closest and most popular, Grande Beach, starts right after the Mampituba River mouth. It has a two-kilometer all-exclusive pedestrian street, dunes and calm waters and is the favorite beach for baths and entertainment. It offers the best infrastructure, with several food and art stalls, parking lot, bleaches for concerts and sports activities. It´s the ideal venue for summer soccer, volleyball and surf championships. The next beach, Meio, also called Prainha, is the calmest, located by the Farol hillside. It´s a 600-meter beach, inappropriate for swimming, but the rocky soil gives it an incredible natural beauty. The 800-meter Cal Beach divides the Farol and the Furnas hills and is ideal for surfing. The word Cal (lime) derives from the old ovens for burning shells, to produce mineral lime, common until the 1940s.

The Mampituba River

The "river with many curves," as its Tupi-Guarani name suggests, marks the end (or beginning) of Torres and borders on Santa Catarina. To cross to the other side, Passo de Torres, there´s a huge concrete suspension bridge with steel cables. That´s from where most of the boats leave, for excursions along the river and the coast. The surroundings of the Mampituba River come to life at night, with the best restaurants in town.

Lobos Island

It´s the only sea island in Rio Grande do Sul and the smallest Brazilian ecological preservation area. The area, slightly larger than a soccer field, is a haven for the animals that name the island, Lobos (wolves). Wolves and sea lions are the only ones who can enjoy the basalt rocks, since a 1983 law prohibited fishing and the human presence in a 500-meter distance from the island. From July to November, they can be found there, fleeing from Patagonia in search of a hotter place to mate. Excursion boats that take visitors along the coast pass by Lobos Island, 1.8 kilometers from Grande Beach. The one-hour boat ride is offered all year long, but mostly in summer.

Farol Hill

Also called North Tower, for being the first rock formation to be seen when coming from the north, where the lighthouse is located. The first lighthouse, dating from 1912, was a wooden lighthouse and fell down in 1935. Now, the new lighthouse is 18 meters high and can be seen from a distance of 12 kilometers. Well before the lighthouse was built, the hill housed a police station, a chapel and a fort. It was around it that the city developed, and its rocks, together with mud, shell lime and wood, were responsible for the construction of its colonial houses. The view is worthwhile: you can see all the beaches, the dunes, Lobos Island and the Violão Lagoon. Behind the Farol hill stands the most beautiful local architectural landmark, the Matriz São Domingos Church, which boasts Portuguese images, donated by Emperor Dom Pedro I.

SURROUNDINGS

Capão da Canoa

66 km from Torres via RS-389.

Together with Torres, it´s the city with the best infrastructure for tourists on the northern coast. It has good hotels and restaurants, nightclubs, a shopping mall, movie theaters and the two largest water parks in the State. Both the Acqua Lokos Farm (☎ 625-2992) and the Marina Park (☎ 625-3049) open only in summer. Capão da Canoa has 18 kilometers of open seas, which draws hordes of surfers interested in its high waves. The 11 beaches are linked by a huge and illuminated street, which allows for night baths. When you go, visit the Quadros Lagoon, the largest lagoon on the northern coast, four kilometers from Downtown.

Osório

103 km from Torres via RS-389.

It´s one of the best places to get to know the potential of the lakes on the northern coast and relive the golden age of the region´s lagoons. Between 1870 and 1940, the waters formed an important commercial transportation system between Torres and Osório. The route was deactivated with the construction of roads, and the lagoons were forgotten for a long time. Today there are camping sites and inns on the outskirts, like the Pinguela Park (☎ 628-8080), the Pontal dos Diehl (☎ 9973-6967) and the Maribo Farm (☎ 501-6604). They offer ecological routes, trails in the woods, water sports, boat rides on the Pinguela, Palmital and Malvas lagoons and visits to colonial products manufacturers. Also worth a visit is the Crocodilo Zambezi Zoo (☎ 9692-5104), with crocodiles from the Nile River and a mini-zoo, and the Borússia hill, which from the top of its 400 meters affords a beautiful view of the lagoon, the ocean and the mountains. It´s also the place to go if you´re a free-flight buff. Borússia Waterfall is located 12 kilometers from downtown Osório, with areas for pick-nicks and barbecue.

TIPS

• If you´re going from Porto Alegre towards Torres, you´re lucky: there are good access options. First take BR-290, or Free Way. When you arrive in Osório, there are two options: you can either take BR-101, with heavy traffic but fast lanes, or RS-389, where trucks

Pinguela Lagoon: entertainment in Osório

are prohibited, but with an 80-km speed limit. And the speed limit is well controlled by electronic radars.

• There´s no entrance fee to the Guarita Park, but they ask for a symbolic contribution if you´re driving.

• The place to enjoy one of the best views of the Guarita and Sul towers (reflected on a lake) is from the snack bar. Eat some fish and enjoy the setting.

• The best time to see the wolves and the sea lions is either early in the morning or late in the afternoon.

• Between April and May, Torres becomes the Brazilian capital of ballooning, when the International Balloon Festival is held. Torres has been the venue for the festival for 15 years, and attracts thousands of visitors.

SERVICES

The list of services starts by the capital city of each State and goes on in alphabetical order. After each city, there is a list of services of the highlights in the surroundings too.

PARANÁ

Curitiba

41

TOURIST INFORMATION

• **Tourist Information Center: 24-Hour Street,** between Visconde de Nácar and Visconde do Rio Branco streets, Downtown ☎ 352-8000; **Rodoferroviária,** Presidente Camargo Ave. ☎ 323-4007; **Afonso Pena Airport** (São José dos Pinhais) ☎ 381-1326.

• **Transportation: Rodoferroviária** ☎ 320-3000; **Afonso Pena Airport** (São José dos Pinhais) ☎ 381-1515.

• **Hospital: Clínicas** ☎ 360-1800; **Santa Casa** ☎ 224-5550; **Evangélico** ☎ 322-4141; **Eye Hospital** ☎ 222-4222.

• **Banks: Banco do Brasil** ☎ 263-2400; **Banespa** ☎ 221-8400; **Bank Boston** ☎ 304-1400; **BBV** ☎ 232-1834; **BCN** ☎ 233-9133; **Bradesco** ☎ 264-4346; **Caixa** ☎ 263-1542; **Citibank** ☎ 221-6717; **HSBC** ☎ 362-1818; **Itaú** ☎ 322-4022; **Mercantil do Brasil** ☎ 322-5432; **Nossa Caixa** ☎ 322-2822; **Real** ☎ 322-0105; **Safra** ☎ 322-4342; **Santander** ☎ 234-1020; **Sudameris** ☎ 309-1999; **Unibanco** ☎ 221-1200.

• **Car rental: Avis** ☎ 381-1381; **Yes** ☎ 366-2525; **Hertz** ☎ 269-8000; **Localiza** ☎ 253-0330; **Unidas** ☎ 332-1080.

• **Exchange: Banco do Brasil,** 410 Tiradentes Plaza, 2nd floor ☎ 321-2348.

• **Shopping: Estação Mall,** 2775 Sete de Setembro Ave. ☎ 3025-9000; **Novo Batel Mall,** 517 Cel. Dulcídio St., Batel ☎ 222-4484; **Crystal Plaza Shopping Center,** 731 Comendador Araújo St., Batel ☎ 323-2744; **Shopping Muller,** 127 Cândido de Abreu St., Civic Center ☎ 224-0510; **24-Hour Street.**

• **Internet: 24-Hour Street.**

• **Tourism agency: Serra Verde Express** (train tours and packages in the State); **Rodoferroviária**, 330 Presidente Camargo Ave. ☎ 323-4007, serraverdeexpress.com. br.

LODGING

• **Bourbon & Tower,** 102 Cândido Lopes, Downtown ☎ 322-4001, bourbon.com.br. Tv, air conditioning, minibar, sauna, thermal pool, presidential suite. $$$$

• **De Ville Express,** 73 Amintas de Barros St., Downtown ☎ 322-8558, deville. com.br. Tv, air conditioning, minibar. Next to Guaíra Theater. $$

• **Eduardo VII,** 15 Cândido Leão St., Downtown ☎ 322-6767, hoteleduardovii.com.br. Tv, air conditioning, minibar. A 1954 building, in front of Tiradentes Plaza. $

• **Elo Inn,** 456 Augusto Stellfeld St., ☎ 3025-9400, hoteiselo.com.br. Tv, air conditioning , minibar, pool, sauna. $$$

• **Grand Hotel Rayon,** 1424 Visconde de Nácar St., Downtown ☎ 322-6006, rayon. com.br. Tv, air conditioning, minibar, safe, sauna, thermal pool. $$$$

• **Guaíra Palace,** 537 Rui Barbosa Plaza, Downtown ☎ 232-9911, hotelguaira.com. br. Tv, air conditioning, minibar. Good location. $

• **Lumini,** 1094 Gen. Carneiro St., Downtown ☎ 264-5244, hotellumini. com.br. Tv, minibar. $

• **Mabu Curitiba,** 830 Santos Andrade, Downtown ☎ 219-6000, hoteismabu.com.br. Tv, air conditioning, minibar. $$$

• **Sheraton Four Points,** 4211 Sete de Setembro, Água Verde ☎ 340-4000, fpsc.com.br. Tv, air conditioning, minibar, sauna, thermal pool. Near Shopping Curitiba. $$$$

• **Slaviero Braz,** 67 Luís Xavier Ave., Downtown ☎ 322-2829, hotelslaviero. com.br. Tv, air conditioning, minibar. Near 15 de Novembro St., Landmarked bldg. $$$

RESTAURANTS

• **Alameda Fast Grill,** Shopping Curitiba, 2300 Brigadeiro Franco St., Downtown ☎ 326-1555. Smorgasboard. $$

• **Armazém Italiano**, 4750 Sete de Setembro Ave., Batel ☎ 342-0572. Great food by the kg. Feijoada on Saturdays and fish on Sundays. $$

• **Barolo,** 2487 Silva Jardim Ave., Downtown ☎ 243-3430. Italian, with

30 different sauces. $ $
- **Boulevard,** 539 Vol. da Pátria St., Downtown ☎ 224-8244. Sophisticated dishes. Over 300 wines. $ $ $
- **Cantinho do Eisbein,** 863 Estados Ave., Água Verde ☎ 329-5155. Specialized in teal filled with cabbage, *kassler* (pork ribs) e *eisbein* (pork knee). $ $
- **Divino Mestre,** 25 Raul Carneiro Filho St., Água Verde ☎ 333-1081. Pasta and beef. $ $
- **Estrela da Terra,** 176 Jaime ReisSt., Downtown. ☎ 222-5007. Regional, highlighting barreado. $ $
- **Fabiano Marcolini Ristorante,** 747 Emiliano Perneta St., Downtown ☎ 324-0062. Homemade pasta, highlighting a veal dish. $ $
- **Madalosso,** 5875 Manoel Ribas St., Santa Felicidade ☎ 372-2121. 13 Italian dishes on as-much-as-you-can-eat basis. Across the street, cozy Velho Madalosso. $ $
- **Schwarzwald (Bar do Alemão),** Largo da Ordem, Downtown ☎ 223-2585. Varied. Traditional, highlighting the *Submarine*, beer with steinhäger. $ $
- **Tempero de Minas,** 5026 Manoel Ribas St., Santa Felicidade ☎ 272-1413. Minas Gerais fare. $
- **Yü,** 485 Osório Plaza, Downtown ☎ 232-3500. Japanese food for lunch and à la carte at dinner. $ $

Castro

☏ 42

TOURIST INFORMATION

- **Tourist Information Center:** João José de Farias Plaza ☎ 232-7269.
- **Transportation: Bus Station** ☎ 232-1552.
- **Hospital: Ana Fiorillo** ☎ 232-4208.
- **Banks. Banco do Brasil** ☎ 232-5000. **Bradesco** ☎ 232-5051. **Caixa** ☎ 232-4114. **HSBC** ☎ 232-4344. **Itaú** ☎ 232-4411.

LODGING

- **Central Palace,** 18 Cipriano Marques St., ☎ 232-1516. $
- **Fazenda das 100 Árvores,** PR-151. ☎ 232-4201, 100arvores.com.br. Tv, pool, horse rides. $ $
- **Hotel Buganville,** 99 Manoel Ribas Plaza, ☎ 232-5099. Tv, air conditioning, minibar. The best in town. $ $
- **Pousada Ribeirão das Flores,** Vale do Vargedo ☎ 222-9424. Cabins for 4 people. Horses and jeep tours. $ $

RESTAURANT

- **2 Leões Churrascaria e Buffet,** 321 Rosário St., ☎ 232-2091. Varied. $

SURROUNDINGS

TIBAGI

TOURIST INFORMATION

- **Transportation: Bus station** ☎ 275-1233
- **Hospital: Luiza Borba Carneiro** ☎ 275-1282.
- **Shopping: Tapetes,** 582 Antônio B. de Macedo St.,
- **Tourism agencies: Itayapé** ☎ 275-1766; **Canyon Aventuras** ☎ 275-1357.

LODGING

- **Pousada Figueira,** 84 Leopoldo Mercer Plaza ☎ 275-1194. Tv, fan. Cozy atmosphere. $

RESTAURANT

- **Empório Tibagy,** 70 Leopoldo Mercer Plaza ☎ 275-1133. Varied, highlighting Italian fare. Perfect service and cozy atmosphere. $ $

Foz do Iguaçu

☏ 45

TOURIST INFORMATION

- **Tourist Info. Center:** 260 Getúlio Vargas Plaza, Downtown ☎ 521-1455.
- **Transportation: Bus station** ☎ 522-3633; **Airport** ☎ 521-4276.
- **Hospital: Internacional** ☎ 521-4200.
- **Banks: Banco do Brasil** ☎ 521-2525; **Banespa** ☎ 521-4300; **Bradesco** ☎ 523-2200; **Caixa** ☎ 523-1311; **HSBC** ☎ 523-1166; **Itaú** ☎ 523-1113; **Real** ☎ 523-2112; **Santander** ☎ 523-1224; **Sudameris** ☎ 523-2355; **Unibanco** ☎ 523-1424.
- **Car rental: Avis** ☎ 529-6160; **Localiza** ☎ 529-6300; **Unidas** ☎ 572-5060; **Yes** ☎ 522-2956.
- **Exchange: Banco do Brasil** ☎ 521-2545.
- **Tourism agencies: Cassino Tur** ☎ 572-4434; **Da Mata Ecoaventuras** ☎ 529-6279; **STTC Turismo Ltda** ☎ 529-6464.

LODGING

- **Albergue Paudimar,** 634 Rui Barbosa

St., Downtown ☎ 574-5503, paudimar.com.br. Tv room, kitchen, public bathrooms. $

• **Bourbon & Tower,** Cataratas Rd., Km 2.5 ☎ 523-1313, bourbon.com. br. Tv, air conditioning, minibar, safe, thermal pool, sauna, sports courts, playground. $$$$

• **Cassino Palace,** 381 Rio Branco St., ☎ 523-2300, cassino.com.br. Tv, air conditioning, minibar, safe, pool. $$

• **Florença,** Cataratas Rd., km 13 ☎ 523-4555, hotelflorenca.com. Tv, air conditioning, minibar, insulation, pool, game room, playground. $$

• **Líder Palace,** 3146 Juscelino Kubitschek, Ave. ☎ 522-2121, liderpalace.com.br. Tv, air conditioning, minibar, pool. $$$

• **Mabu Thermas & Resort,** 3175 Cataratas Rd. ☎ 523-4000, hoteismabu.com.br. Tv, air conditioning, minibar, safe, pool, sauna, massage, sports courts, playground. $$$$

• **Rafain Centro,** 984 Marechal Deodoro St., ☎ 523-1213, rafaincentro.com.br. Tv, air conditioning, minibar, safe, insulation, pool, game room. $$$

• **Royal Park,** Cataratas Rd., km 11 ☎ 572-2424, brasil.com/royal. Tv, air conditioning, minibar, insulation, pool. $$$

• **Suíça,** 3580 Felipe Wandsheer Ave., ☎ 525-3232, hotelsuica.com.br. Tv, air conditioning, minibar, insulation, safe, pool. $$$

• **Tropical das Cataratas,** inside the National Park ☎ 521-7000, tropicaliahotel.com.br. Tv, air conditioning, minibar, safe, pool, sports courts, playground. $$$$

RESTAURANTS

• **Antônio Maria,** 1466 Almirante Barroso St. ☎ 574-3388. Varied. $$

• **Búfalo Branco,** 530 Rebouças St., ☎ 523-9744. Barbecue. $$

• **Café Laurent,** 625 Jorge Schimmelpfeng Ave. Varied.

• **Don Bruno Ristorante,** 1713 Alm. Barroso Av. ☎ 574-5969. Italian. $$

• **Galeteria la Mamma,** 1327 Cataratas St. ☎ 574-3272. Italian. $

• **Zaragoza,** 882 Quintino Bocaiúva St., ☎ 574-3084. Fish. $$$

Guaraqueçaba

⊕ 41

TOURIST INFORMATION

• **Tourist Center: Ibama** ☎ 482-1262.

• **Transportation: Buses** ☎ 482-1232.

• **Hospital: Municipal** ☎ 482-1232.

• **Shopping: Casa do Artesanato,** 15 de Novembro St. Fibers, necklaces, violins.

• **Tourist agency: Pousada Chauá,** Ferreira Lopes St. ☎ 482-1265.

LODGING

• **Guarakessaba,** 15 de Novembro St. ☎ 482-1262. Tv, air conditioning, facing the sea. $

• **Pousada Chauá,** Ferreira Lopes St. ☎ 482-1265. Hospitable atmosphere. $

RESTAURANTS

• **Restaurante do Barbosa,** Paula Miranda St. ☎ 482-1248. Fish. $

• **Thaíco,** 144 Luís Ramos Figueira St. ☎ 482-1357. Fish. $

SURROUNDINGS

SUPERAGÜI

LODGING

• **Pousada Bella Ilha,** Barra de Superagüi ☎ 455-1564. $

• **Pousada Sobre as Ondas,** Barra de Superagüi ☎ 9978-4213. $

• **Pousada Superagüi,** Barra de Superagüi ☎ 9978-0821. $

RESTAURANTS

• **Golfinhos,** Barra de Superagüi ☎ 9959-8852. Fish. $

• **Pousada Bella Ilha,** Barra de Superagüi ☎ 455-1564. Fish. $

Ilha do Mel

⊕ 41

TOURIST INFORMATION

• **Tourist information Center:** in Brasília and Encantadas next to the boathouse.

• **Hospital: Posto de Saúde** ☎ 426-9004.

• **Shopping: Trilha do Mel** (beach fashion). On the way to the Lighthouse.

LODGING

• **Long Beach,** Praia Grande, on the Lighthouse trail ☎ 9906-4040, lbeach.cjb.net. Cabins facing the sea. $$$

• **Plâncton,** Lighthouse ☎ 426-8026. Standard and double rooms. At night, live MPB at the inn´s kiosk. $ $

• **Pousada das Meninas,** towards the Lighthouse ☎ 426-8023, pousadadas meninas.com.br. Cozy cabins. $ $ $

• **Pousada Enseada,** Lighthouse ☎ 426-8040, pousadaenseada.com. Tree-lined, near the sea. $ $ $

• **Pousada Praia do Farol,** Nova Brasília ☎ 426-8014, praiadofarol.com.br. Comfortable, breakfast is served on the deck. $ $ $

• **Pousada Treze Luas,** Praia de Fora, Lighthouse ☎ 426-8067, pousa datrezeluas.com. Collective rooms, two cabins and a pleasant kiosk. $ $

• **Pousadinha,** Nova Brasília ☎ 426-8026, pousadinha.com.br. Apts., rooms, cabins. $ $

• **Parque Hotel Ilha do Mel,** Fortaleza, 50-min hike from the Brasília boathouse or 10 min motorboat ☎ 426-8075, parquehotelilhadomel.com.br. With marine service. $ $ $

• **Pousada dos Prazeres,** Fortaleza, 1 h hike from the Brasília boathouse or 10 min. motorboat ☎ 243-9649, pousadadosprazeres.com.br. Confortável. $ $

• **Fim da Trilha,** Encantadas ☎ 426-9017, fimdatrilha.com.br. Excellent Spanish restaurant. $ $

• **Pousada Estrela do Mar,** Encantadas ☎ 426-9013, pousadaestre ladomar.com.br. Comfortable. $ $

RESTAURANTS

• **Restaurante Mar e Sol,** Road to the Lighthouse. TV dinner. $

• **Spagueteria da Pousadinha,** Nova Brasília ☎ 426-8026, pousadinha.com.br. Pasta. $ $

• **Toca do Abutre,** Lighthouse, near the boathouse. Tables on a deck, always crowded. Varied. $ $

Lapa

⊕ 41

TOURIST INFORMATION

• **Transportation: Buses** ☎ 622-1010.

• **Hospital: Hipólito de Araújo** ☎ 622-1144.

• **Banks: Banco do Brasil** ☎ 622-1212; **Bradesco** ☎ 622-1066; **Caixa** ☎ 622-1234; **HSBC** ☎ 622-1313; **Itaú** ☎ 622-1055.

LODGING

• **Estalagem Fazenda Roseira,** PR-267, km 12 ☎ 622-4360. Farm atmosphere and natural pool. $ $ $

• **Salles Pousada,** 547 Eduardo Santos Lima St., ☎ 622-1275. Tv. $ $

RESTAURANT

• **Lipski,** 1855 Manoel Pedro St., ☎ 622-1202. Serves traditional quirera lapeana. $

Morretes

⊕ 41

TOURIST INFORMATION

• **Tourist Information: Casa Rocha Pombo,** Dr. José Pereira Plaza ☎ 462-1024.

• **Transportation: Bus station** ☎ 462-1115.

• **Hospital: Public** ☎ 462-1114.

• **Banks: Banco do Brasil** ☎ 462-1204; **Caixa** ☎ 462-1262; **Itaú** ☎ 462-1383.

• **Shopping: Artes da Terra**, artwork and coffee, Lamenha Lins Plaza.

LODGING

• **Pousada Trilha da Serra.** 64 Luiz Brambilla, Morretes ☎ 462-2391. Tv, pool. Next to Historic Downtown. $

RESTAURANTS

• **Armazém Romanus,** 141 Visc. do Rio Branco St., ☎ 462-1500. Besides barreado serves fish, beef and pasta. $ $

• **Madalozo,** 16 Almirante Frederico de Oliveira St., ☎ 462-1410. Barreado. $

• **Terra Nossa,** 109 XV de Novembro St., ☎ 462-2174. Barreado. $

SURROUNDINGS

Porto de Cima

LODGING

• **Pousada e Restaurante Dona Siroba,** Comendador Macedo Plz. ☎ 462-2006, donasiroba.com.br. Apts., houses, rooms and chalets. Inn house declared historical landmark. Traditional. $ $

• **Pousada Ecocatu,** 1219 Reta do Porto Rd., ☎ 462-1512, netpar.com.br/ecocatu. Chalets w/ fridge, stove. $ $

• **Pousada Ilha do Rio,** Graciosa Rd., Km 7.5 ☎ 462-1400, pousadailhado rio.com.br. Located on an island. Tv, minibar, fan. $ $ $

• **Pousada Itupava,** Prainhas Rd. ☎

462-1925, itupava.com.br. Tv, air conditioning, minibar. Chalets w/ veranda where breakfast is served. Rents floats. $ $

ANTONINA

LODGING
• **Hotel Regency Capela.** Luiz. G. A. Valente St., Downtown ☎ 432-3267.

RESTAURANT
• **Maré Alta**, XV de Novembro St. ☎ 432-1601. Barreado.

Paranaguá

⊕ 41

TOURIST INFORMATION
• **Tourist Center:** Praia St. ☎ 422-6882.
• **Transportation: Buses** ☎ 423-1215; **Trains** ☎ 422-8817.
• **Hospital: Public** ☎ 423-3466.
• **Banks: Banco do Brasil** ☎ 423-1212; **Banespa** ☎ 420-1800; **Bradesco** ☎ 423-1177; **Caixa** ☎ 423-1488; **HSBC** ☎ 423-1544; **Itaú** ☎ 423-1100; **Sudameris** ☎ 423-1145; **Unibanco** ☎ 423-3738.
• **Shopping: Mercado do Artesanato,** Gen. Carneiro St.

HOSPEDAGEM
• **Camboa,** João Estevão, Ponta do Caju St ☎ 423-2121, hotelcamboa.com.br. Tv, air conditioning, safe, minibar, playground, heated pool, sauna, game room. Near Historic Downtown. $ $ $
• **Hotel Serra do Mar,** 588 XV de Novembro St., Historic Downtown ☎ 422-8907. $
• **Pousada Itiberê,** 24 Princesa Isabel St., historic Downtown ☎ 423-2485. Simple rooms, collective restrooms. $
• **San Rafael,** 185 Júlia da Costa St. ☎ 423-2123, sanrafael.com.br. Tv, air conditioning, minibar, safe, pool, game room. $ $

RESTAURANT
• **Casa do Barreado,** 78 José Antônio da Cruz St. ☎ 423-1830. The most traditional barreado in town. $

SURROUNDINGS

Caiobá

TOURIST INFORMATION
• **Tourist Information Center:S. Pedro Plz.** ☎ 453-2121, Ext. 215.
• **Transportation: Buses** ☎ 453-1100; **ferry,** 24-hour service to Guaratuba.
• **Hospital: N. S. dos Navegantes** ☎ 452-2000.

LODGING
• **Pousada do Vovô,** 322 Jaguariaíva St. ☎ 452-1926. $
• **Pousada Luar de Caiobá,** 1028 Bandeirantes St. ☎ 473-3686, luardecaioba.com.br. $

RESTAURANTS
• **Casa do Camarão,** 2010 Atlântica Ave. ☎ 452-2849. Fish. $ $
• **Dona Helena Bandeira,** 272 Andirá St. ☎ 452-1163. Fish. $

Guaratuba

TOURIST INFORMATION
• **Tourist Information Center:** Visc. do Rio Branco Ave. and Alexandre Mafra Plz.
• **Transportation: Buses** ☎ 442-1785; **ferry,** all the time to Caiobá.
• **Banks: Banco do Brasil** ☎ 442-1846; **HSBC** ☎ 442-1495; **Itaú** ☎ 442-2040.
• **Hospital: Municipal** ☎ 472-1171.

LODGING
• **Pousada do Sol,** 20 Curitiba Ave. ☎ 472-3650, villareal.com.br. $
• **Santa Paula,** 650 Visc. do Rio Branco Ave. ☎ 443-1299. $

RESTAURANTS
• **Nhô Quim,** 377 29 de Abril Ave. ☎ 442-1595. Fish. $ $
• **Tia Geni,** 297 29 de Abril Ave. ☎ 442-1488. fish. $ $

Matinhos

TOURIST INFORMATION
• **Sports and Tourism Bureau,** 22 Pastor Elias Abraão St. ☎ 453-2121.
• **City Hall,** 22 Pastor Elias Abrahão St. ☎ 452-8000.
• **Transportation: Viação Graciosa,** www.viação.graciosa.com.br.

LODGING
• **Fragata,** 566 Manuel Ribas St. ☎ 452-1540, fragatahotel.com.br. $
• **Mata Atlântica Park,** Alexandra/Matinhos Rd, Km 12 ☎ 336-8366. $ $

RESTAURANTS

• **Pilequinho,** 196 Paranaguá St. ☎ 453-2882. Fish. $

• **Sakura,** 1304 Paranaguá Ave. ☎ 453-1456. Fish. $ $

Prudentópolis

⊕ 42

TOURIST INFORMATION

• **Transportation: Buses** ☎ 446-1330.

• **Hospital: Santa Casa** ☎ 446-1333.

• **Banks: Banco do Brasil** ☎ 446-1288; **Caixa** ☎ 446-1272; **HSBC** ☎ 446-1144; **Itaú** ☎ 446-1276.

• **Shopping: Casa do Artesanato,** 330 São João Ave.; **Museu do Milênio,** Ucrânia Plaza.

• **Tourism Agency: Mayná Palace Hotel,** 935 Osório Guimarães St., (Passeio Salto Francisco) ☎ 446-2091.

LODGING

• **Hotel Lopes,** 2595 São João Ave. ☎ 446-1476. Excellent breakfast. $

• **Mayná Palace Hotel,** 935 Osório Guimarães St. ☎ 446-2091, hotelmayna.com.br. Tv, fan, tel. Offers a very good map of the waterfalls. $

RESTAURANTS

• **Churrascaria e Pizzaria do Penteado,** Domingos Luiz de Oliveira St., corner São Josafat ☎ 446-1334. Also Ukrainian fare. $ $

• **Pizzaria Casarão,** 348 Cel. José Durski Plz. ☎ 446-2113. $

Vila Velha

PONTA GROSSA

⊕ 42

TOURIST INFORMATION

• **Tourist Information Center:** 930 Visc. de Taunay Ave. ☎ 224-2422.

• **Transportation: Buses** ☎ 222-5511.

• **Hospital: Pronto Socorro Municipal** ☎ 223-8467.

• **Banks: Banco do Brasil** ☎ 225-1144; **BBV** ☎ 225-5933; **BCN** ☎ 224-1977; **Bradesco** ☎ 225-1033; **Caixa** ☎ 225-1311; **HSBC** ☎ 225-1022; **Itaú** ☎ 225-1433; **Real** ☎ 225-1717; **Santander** ☎ 225-2355; **Sudameris** ☎ 225-2727. **Unibanco** ☎ 225-2299.

• **Car Rental: Localiza** ☎ 229-3161.

LODGING

• **Genevieve Palace,** 711 Balduíno Taques St. ☎ 223-7844. Tv, air conditioning, minibar. $ $

• **Vila Velha Palace,** 123 Balduíno Taques St. ☎ 225-2200. Sauna. $ $ $

• **Village,** 615 Visc. de Nacar St. ☎ 225-2521, villagehotel.com.br. Tv, air conditioning. $ $

RESTAURANTS

• **Forno de Pedra,** 89 Leocádio Pereira St. ☎ 224-3038. Varied, highlighting the pizzas. $

• **La Taverne,** 1136 Sete de Setembro St. ☎ 224-3534. Varied. $ $

SANTA CATARINA

Florianópolis

⊕ 48

TOURIST INFORMATION

• **Tourist Information Center: Florianópolis Convention & Visitors Bureau** ☎ 224-4904; **Portal Turístico Secretaria de Turismo** ☎ 244-5822; **Central de Atendimento ao Turista Santur** ☎ 224-1516.

• **Transportation: Hercílio Luz International Airport** ☎ 236-0879, 331-4000.

• **Banks: ABN-Amro Bank** ☎ 248-5677; **HSBC** ☎ 221-9000; **Bradesco** ☎ 224-2233; **Banco do Brasil** ☎ 221-1600; **BCN** ☎ 224-9355; **Caixa** ☎ 222-5915; **Itaú** ☎ 223-1811; **Sudameris Brasil** ☎ 224-8555; **Unibanco** ☎ 224-0366.

• **Exchange: Besc** ☎ 222-2293; **Ilhatur Turismo e Câmbio** ☎ 224-6333; **Ivoran Turismo e Câmbio** ☎ 224-3837.

• **Hospital: Celso Ramos (Servidores)** ☎ 251-7000; **Florianópolis** ☎ 271-1300; **Hospital de Guarnição (Exército)** ☎ 222-3588; **Lara Ribas (Military Police)** ☎ 229-6500; **Regional São José** ☎ 271-9000; **Universitário** ☎ 331-9100.

• **Internet: Cyber Point** (Lagoa da Conceição) ☎ 232-1503; **Cyber Café Livros & Livros** (Downtown) ☎ 222-1244; **Collecta** (Ingleses Beach) ☎ 269-1260.

• **Car Rental: Avis** ☎ 0800 7126-2222; **Axel** ☎ 389-5818; **Localiza** ☎ 0800 992-000; **Locarauto** ☎ 225-9000.

• **Transportation: Rádio Táxi (24h)** ☎ 240-6009; **transportation to the Airport** ☎ 331-4102; **Terminal Rodo-**

viário Rita Maria ☎ 224-2777.

LODGING

• **Albergue da Juventude Canasvieiras,** 100 Dr.João de Oliveira St., Canasvieiras ☎ 266-2036. Collective rooms and bathrooms separated by sex. Also collective kitchen. $

• **Baía Norte Palace Hotel,** 220 Beira-Mar Norte Ave., Downtown ☎ 0800 702-2021, baianorte.com.br. Cable Tv, air conditioning, minibar, safe, pool, restaurant, business center. $ $ $

• **Blue Tree Towers,** 2304 Bocaiúva St., Downtown ☎ 0800 150-500, bluetree.com.br. Cable Tv, air conditioning, minibar, bathtub, safe. $ $ $ $

• **Costão do Santinho Resort & Spa,** 2505Vereador Onildo Lemos Rd., Santinho Beach ☎ 0800-7019000, costao.com.br. Luxury and comfort. The largest resort in the South. $ $ $ $

• **Cris Hotel,** 1 Praia da Joaquina Ave., 1, Lagoa da Conceição ☎ 232-5101. Tv, air conditioning, minibar, tel, parking lot. By Joaquina Beach. $

• **Farol da Ilha,** 163 Bento Gonçalves St., Downtown ☎ 0800 480-099. Tv, air conditioning, minibar, tel, garage. $ $

• **Hotel Costa Norte,** 984 Gaivotas St., Ingleses Beach ☎ 269-1305, hotelcostanorte.com.br. Cable Tv, air conditioning, minibar, tel, safe. Bar and restaurant by the sea. $ $ $

• **Maré de Lua Pousada,** Dead-end street, 50 m past Praia da Armação do Pântano do Sul Church ☎ 237-5068, maredelua.com.br. Tv, fan. Plans ecological tours. Archaeological site. $ $

• **Marea Apart Hotel,** D. João Becker Rd., Ingleses Beach ☎ 269-1087, marea parthotel.com.br, complete kitchen, balcony w/ grill, view of the sea. $ $ $

• **Pousada da Vigia,** 291Cônego Walmor Castro St., Lagoinha, north of island ☎ 284-1789, pousadavigia.com.br. Tv, air conditioning, minibar, pool, Jaccuzzi, sauna. View of the sea. $ $ $

• **Pousada Mar de Dentro,** 1929 Caminho dos Açores St., Santo Antônio de Lisboa ☎ 235-1521. Tv, air conditioning. $ $

• **Residencial Fischer,** 128 Manoel Alves Cabral St., Ingleses Beach ☎ 246-0189, lfischer@zaz.com.br. Stove, fridge, cable Tv, fan. $

• **Samuka Hotel,** Pedro Manoel Fernandes St. corner w/ Rendeiras Ave., Lagoa da Conceição ☎ 232-5024. Tv, air conditioning, minibar, tel. $ $

RESTAURANTS

• **Bar & Restaurante das Antigas,** 7484 Baldicero Filomeno Hwy., Ribeirão da Ilha ☎ 337-5770. French cuisine, highlighting shrimp w/ leek andorange sauce. $ $

• **Barracuda,** 30 Rendeiras Ave., Lagoa da Conceição ☎ 232-5301. Seafood and cod. $ $

• **Bistrô D'Câmpora,** SC-401, Km 10, 10,300, Santo Antônio de Lisboa ☎ 235-1073. Contemporary food. Art Gallery. $ $ $

• **Bologna,** 1380 Madre Maria Villac Ave., Canasvieiras ☎ 266-1458. Meat, pasta, seafood by the kilo. $

• **Bragança Restaurante,** 2304 Bocaiúva St., Downtown ☎ 251-5548. International cuisine, highlighting the *bacalla a'll aragosta*. $ $ $

• **Casa do Chico,** 1620 Rendeiras Ave. ☎ 232-5132. Seafood, highlighting the *Camarão à Casa do Chico*. $ $

• **Ondas Restaurante e Bar,** 1750 D. João Becker Rd., Ingleses ☎ 269-2280. International cuisine. Eat the *ondas grill* (grilled salmon with shrimp). $ $

• **Pier 54,** 405 Forte Santana St., Beira Mar Norte (under Hercílio Luz Bridge) ☎ 225-3138. Seafood. Eat the moqueca and shrimp sequence. $ $

• **Pirão,** 3806 Rubens de Arruda Ramos St., Beira-Mar Norte ☎ 228-7354, pirao.com.br. Seafood and typical island fare. $ $ $

• **Santo Antônio Spaghetteria Café,** 30 Cônego Serpa St., back of Casa Açoriana ☎ 235-2356. Santo Antônio de Lisboa. Spaghetti with seafood. $ $

• **Toca de Jurerê,** 78 Acácio Melo St., Jurerê Beach ☎ 282-1188. Try: moqueca de garoupa, Spanish cod and spaghetti with seafood and champagne sauce. $ $

• **Toca do Urso,** Public Market, Box 10, Conselheiro Mafra St. w/ Largo da Alfândega, Downtown ☎ 224-5452. Seafood. Try the camarão à romana (shrimp with cream cheese and shrimp sauce). $

• **Um Lugar,** 371 Manoel Severino Oliveira St., Lagoa da Conceição ☎ 232-2451. Contemporary cuisine of the island. try the tuna with pumpkin mush. $$$

SURROUNDINGS

Palhoça

LODGING

• **Pousada da Bila,** Geral da Guarda do Embaú St. ☎ 283-1256. Open all year long. $

RESTAURANT

• **Amadeus,** Geral da Guarda do Embaú St. ☎ 283-2222. Seafood. Try *Camarão Amadeus* (cooked, cheese topping, with rice and salad). $

Santo Amaro da Imperatriz

LODGING

• **Águas Mornas Palace Hotel,** Geral de Águas Mornas Rd., Águas Mornas. 10 minutes from Caldas da Imperatriz ☎ 0800 481-309, aguasmornasplacehotel.com.br. Tv, air conditioning, minibar, tel, bar, restaurant, 5 thermal pools, sauna, massage, fitness center, sports courts, game room, fishing lake, playground, horse carts, horses. $$$

• **Resort Plaza Caldas da Imperatriz,** Geral Rd., Km 4 ☎ 281-9000, plazahoteis.com.br. Tv, video, air conditioning, minibar, tel, soft music, marble tubs or Jaccuzzi with thermomineral water, thermal pools, sauna, tennis court, jogging track, Swiss soccer field, bar and nightclub. $$$

Balneário Camboriú

☎ 47

TOURIST INFORMATION

• **Tourist Information Center:** 5041 do Estado Ave. ☎367-4422, sectur bc@nts.com.br. **Disque Turismo** ☎ 1516.

• **Banks: Banco do Brasil** ☎ 367-2122; **Itaú** ☎ 367-3999; **Real** ☎ 367-0257; **Bradesco** ☎ 367-4622; **Caixa** ☎ 367-0677; **HSBC** ☎ 367-5252; **Unibanco** ☎ 367-3622.

• **Exchange: C&B** ☎ 367-2012; **Fly Line** ☎ 366-4935; **Heringer Tur Next** ☎ 367-5488; **Planet Câmbio** ☎ 366-4039.

• **Internet: Internet**, 343 1.500 St., ☎ 363-2204; **JRP Internet**, 1271 Brasil Ave.; **Atlântico Shopping Center** ☎ 363-1392.

• **Car Rental: Automarine** ☎ 366-0330; **Brasil Car** ☎ 360-7518; **Carrera** ☎ 367-1655; **Locacity** ☎ 366-3438; **Locasul** ☎ 367-1077.

LODGING

• **Marambaia Cassino Hotel,** 300 Atlântica Ave., Downtown ☎ 0800-472199, marambaia.com.br. Cable Tv, air conditioning, minibar, tel, climatized pools, restaurant, fitness center, game room. $$

• **Hotel Ilha da Madeira,** 159 Central Ave., Downtown ☎ 367-0016. Tv, air conditioning, minibar, tel. $$

• **Hotel Plaza Camboriu,** 1410 Brasil Ave., Downtown ☎ 367-0700, plazacamboriu.com.br. Cable Tv, air conditioning, minibar, tel, safe, thermal pool, fitness center, game room. $$

• **Hotel Sol,** 3906 Estado Ave., Downtown. ☎ 363-4047. Tv, minibar, fan and parking lot. $

• **Royal Atlantic Hotel,** 32 Central Ave., Downtown ☎ 0800-471413. Cable Tv, air conditioning, minibar, tel, safe, pool, sauna, fitness center, convention center, international restaurant, parking lot. $$$

RESTAURANTS

• **American Pizza,** 3ª Av., 950, corner w/ 1822 St. ☎ 367-5611. Pizzas, pasta and meats. $

• **O Pharol,** 5740 Atlântica Ave. ☎ 367-3800, pharol.com.br. Seafood. Feijoada on Saturdays. $$

• **Pedra da Baleia,** Laranjeiras Beach. ☎ 9905-8507. Try the fruit salad with ice cream served in a pineapple. $

• **Poço das Pedras,** 954 D. Afonso St., Via Gastronômica ☎ 367-2300. Traditional shrimp on skewers. Try the caldeirada and the grilled oyster. $$

• **Quarta Estação,** Laranjeiras Beach ☎ 264-0023. Restaurant and snacks, highlighting the risottos.

• **Vila Velha,** 14 511St., room 6, Downtown ☎ 367-5645. Salads, grills, pasta and vegetarian and macrobiotics options. $

Blumenau

☎ 47

TOURIST INFORMATION

• **Tourist Information Center: Castelinho da Secretaria de Turismo,**

1050 XV de Novembro St., Downtown ☎ 326-6797; **Blumenau Convention & Visitors Bureau Tourist Information Center,** 420 XV de Novembro ☎ 322-6933.
• **Civil Police:** ☎ 326-1001.
• **Military Police:** ☎ 326-1000.
• **Procon:** ☎ 326-6853.
• **Transportation: Navegantes Airport** ☎ 342-1132; **Rádio Táxi** ☎ 197.
• **Exchange: Banco do Brasil** ☎ 321-2300; **Besc** ☎ 331-3500; **Quest Câmbio e Turismo** ☎ 326-5555.
• **Shopping: Casarão dos Cristais,** ☎ 326-3042; **Centro Industrial e Comercial (CIC)** ☎ 323-4006; **Centro Comercial Lojas Hering** ☎ 326-2166; **Cristal Blumenau** ☎ 323-0525; **Shopping Center Neumarkt** ☎ 326-5566; **Feira de Artesanato,** XV de Novembro St., in front of the Cultural Foundation (Sun., 8 am-6 pm).
• **Hospital: Sto Antônio** ☎ 326-3477; **Sta Catarina** ☎ 232-2200; **Sta Isabel** ☎ 321-1000.
• **Car Rentals: Blumenau** ☎ 322-9968; **Localiza** ☎ 322-0843; **Locaville** ☎ 326-4501; **The Best** ☎ 326-3888; **Unidas** ☎ 322-5050.

LODGING

• **Garden Terrace Hotel,** 45 Padre Jacobs St., Downtown ☎ 0800 473-939, tecnopan.com.br/gardenterrace. Cable Tv, air conditioning, minibar, restaurant, parking lot. $ $
• **Grande Hotel Blumenau,** 21 Rio Branco St., Downtown ☎ 0800- 703-8363. Cable Tv, air conditioning, minibar, safe, tel, auditorium, convention center. $ $
• **Hotel Baviera,** 165 Nereu Ramos Ave., Downtown ☎ 326-3122. Tv, air conditioning, minibar, tel, parking lot. $
• **Hotel Geranium Blue Tower,** 323 Uruguai St., Downtown ☎ 326-0333. Jaccuzzi, Tv, air conditioning, minibar, tel. $ $
• **Hotel Glória,** 954 Sete de Setembro St. ☎ 326-1988. Tv, air conditioning, minibar, tel. $
• **Hotel Plaza Blumenau,** 818 Sete de Setembro St., Downtown ☎ 0800 471-213, plazahoteis.com.br. Pool, doghouse, fitness center, parking lot, air conditioning, halls for parties and conventions. $ $ $
• **Viena Park,** 670 Hermann Huscher St. ☎ 326-8888, vienahotel.com.br. Cable Tv air conditioning, minibar, tel, pool, sports courts. Meeting and Internet rooms. $ $ $

RESTAURANTS

• **Cafehaus Glória,** 954 Sete de Setembro St., Downtown (annex to Hotel Glória) ☎ 326-0525. The most traditional colonial coffee lunch in town. $
• **Cervejaria Biergarten,** Hercílio Luz Plz., Downtown ☎ 326-8380. À la carte service. Highlight: the cold cuts. $
• **Dolce Vita Ristorante,** 704 República Argentina St. ☎ 322-2755. Italian fare. $ $
• **Moinho Velho,** 66 Paraguai St., Ponta Aguda ☎ 326-3337. Typical german fare. Traditional. $ $
• **Restaurante Frohsinn,** Gertrud Seirich St., Vorstadt ☎ 322-2137. German cuisine. Panoramic view. $ $ $

SURROUNDINGS

Brusque

LODGING

• **Brusque Palace Hotel,** 5 Manfredo Hoffmann St. ☎ 351-4004, brusque palacehotel.com.br. Tv, air conditioning, minibar, tel. recreation area, restaurant. $ $
• **Gracher Hotel,** 56 Cônsul Carlos Reanux Ave., Downtown ☎ 351-1644. Tv, air conditioning, minibar, tel. $ $
• **Hotel Monthez,** Antônio Heil Hwy., Km 29 ☎ 351-3700. Tv, air conditioning, minibar, tel, Jaccuzi, thermal pool, sauna, restaurant, parking lot. $ $ $

Nova Trento

LODGING

• **Mosteiro Park Hotel,** 1 Ribeirão Bela Vista St., Vígolo ☎ 267-1235, mosteiro parkhotel.com.br. Tv, air conditioning, minibar, tel, restaurant. At the top of a mountain, w/ a view of Madre Paulina Sanctuary. $ $
• **Pousada & Cantina Italiana,** 412 Imigrantes St. ☎ 267-0028, pousada cantinaitaliana.com.br. Tv, air conditioning, minibar. Simple accommodations w/ annex restaurant. $

RESTAURANTS

• **Carlinhos Restaurante,** 55 Hipólito Boiteux St., Downtown ☎ 267-0195, restaurantecarlinhos.unetvale.com.br. Typical Italian fare and grill. Self-service system. $

• **Restaurante e Lanchonete Santuário Madre Paulina,** Madre Paulina St., behind the church ☎ 267-0250. homemade food. $

Pomerode

LODGING

• **Fazenda Mundo Antigo,** 1830 Ribeirão Herdt St. ☎ 387-3143, mundoantigo.com.br. Surrounded by mountains and waterfalls. $ $

• **Hotel Bergblick,** 120 Georg Zeplin St. ☎ 387-0952, bergblick.com.br. Alpine-style hotel. Contemporary international restaurant. $ $

• **Max Pousada,** 257 XV de Novembro St. ☎ 387-3070. $

RESTAURANTS

• **Confeitaria Torten Paradies,** 211 XV de Novembro St. ☎ 387-0950. Serves the colonial coffee lunch: pies, breads, cakes, *apfelstrüdel* and lunch. The most traditional bakery. $

• **Restaurante Fazenda Mundo Antigo,** 1830 Ribeirão Herdt St. ☎ 387-3143. In the menu, boar, roast teal and stuffed chicken. $ $

• **Restaurante Pomerode,** 42 Hermann Weege St. ☎ 387-0406. Homemade German food One of the oldest restaurants in town. $

Garopaba

48

TOURIST INFORMATION

• **Tourist Information Center:** ☎ 254-3106

• **Police:** ☎ 254-3190.

• **Hospital: Posto de Saúde** ☎ 254-3124.

• **Banks: Banco do Brasil** ☎ 254-3211; **Besc** ☎ 254-3171.

• **Ponto de táxi:** ☎ 254-3366.

• **Shopping: Mormaii,** entrance at Silveira Beach ☎ 254-3711.

• **Internet: Cyber Hall,** 1545 Pref. João Orestes de Araújo St., Downtown ☎ 254-4772; **Salvation Army,** 173 Marques Guimarães St., Downtown ☎ 254-4690. Serves energetic soup.

LODGING

• **Canoa Azul,** Geral da Praia da Ferrugem Rd. ☎ 254-0105. Tv, fan, balcony with a hammock. $

• **Lobo Hotel,** 81 Marques Guimarães St., Downtown ☎ 254-3745, hot.lobo@terra.com.br. Tv, fan. Excellent breakfast. $

• **Pousada Ilha Mar,** Geral da Praia da Ferrugem Rd. ☎ 254-0337. minibar. Near the beach. $

RESTAURANTS

• **Baleias Bar,** 280 Pref. João Orestes de Araújo Ave., Downtown ☎ 254-4640. À la carte pizza parlor and seafood. $ $

• **Casarão Café,** São Joaquim St., next to the church, Historical Downtown ☎ 254-4221. Express coffee, pies, wine, drinks. Local artist´s paintings. $

• **Cult Beach House,** Silveira Beach ☎ 9119-2770. Fish, meat and salads with blues, jazz and soul music. $ $

• **Trattoria Cosa Nostra,** 760 Francisco Pacheco de Souza St. ☎ 254-3036. Homemade pasta. $

SURROUNDINGS

Imbituba

LODGING

• **Pousada Ibiraquera Park,** Barra de Ibirapuera (via Ribanceira Rd. or at the 276.5 Km marker on BR-101). ☎ 355-0058. $

RESTAURANT

• **O Jangadeiro,** 10 Quintino Bocaiúva St. (Vila Beach) ☎ 255-0092. Serves fish. $ $

Itajaí

47

TOURIST INFORMATION

• **Tourist Information Center: Fundação Itajaiense de Turismo,** 303 Rodolfo Konder Ave., Marejada ☎ 348-1080; **Tourism Bureau,** 4755 Abraão João Francisco St. ☎ 348-9297.

• **Transportation: Navegantes Airport** ☎ 342-1132; **Taxi Barra do Rio** ☎ 348-0837; **Ponto Ferry Boat** ☎ 348-2104; **Ponto Matriz** ☎ 348-4104.

• **Exchange: Exchange Tur,** 53 Hercílio Luz St., room 1 ☎ 348-5108.

• **Shopping: Itajaí Shopping Center,** 234 Samuel Heusi, Downtown. ☎ 348-4609.

• **Post Office: Agência Central,** 175 Felipe Schmidt St. ☎ 348-3535.

• **Hospital: Hospital Maternidade Marieta Konder Bornhausen,** 1111. Marcos Konder, Downtown ☎ 348-3811; **Hospital Infantil Universitário,** 85 Irineu Bornhausen Plz., Downtown ☎ 348-2722.
• **Car Rental: Carrera** ☎ 0800 704-3330; **Locasul** ☎ 0800 472-211; **Localiza** ☎ 348-2624; **Promenac** ☎ 341-9000.

LODGING
• **Itajaí Tur Hotel,** 133 Alberto Werner St. ☎ 348-4600, itajaitur.com. br. Tv, air conditioning, minibar, tel, parking lot. $ $
• **Reese Mariner Plaza Hotel,** 170. Lauro Müller St., Downtown ☎ 348-4033, marinerplaza.com.br. Tv, air conditioning, minibar, tel, pool, sauna, fitness center, dog and cat hotel, ballroom. $ $ $
• **Sandri Palace Hotel,** 1675 Sete de Setembro St., Fazenda ☎ 348-1855, hotelsandri.com.br. Tv, air conditioning, minibar, tel, pool, playground, parking, fitness center. $ $

RESTAURANT
• **La Basque,** 280 Ministro Victor Konder St., Beira Rio ☎ 344-5027. Pizzas and pasta. $

SURROUNDINGS

Penha

TOURIST INFORMATION
• **Tourist Information Center: City Hall,** 190 Nereu Ramos St., Downtown ☎ 345-3904; **Toca de Informações Turísticas,** 954 São João Ave., (next to Pirão D'Água restaurant) ☎ 398-0852.

LODGING
• **Pedra da Ilha Pousada,** 46 Abraão João Francisco St., Alegre Beach ☎ 345-0542, pedradailha.com.br. Tv, air conditioning, minibar, Jaccuzzi, tel, pools, game room, sauna, parking. Faces the sea. $ $ $
• **Penha Praia Hotel,** 1680 Eugênio Krause St., Armação ☎ 345-9280, penhapraiahotel.com.br. Tv, air conditioning, minibar. $
• **Vila Olaria,** 1631 Inácio F. de Souza St., Armação (600 m from Beto Carrero World) ☎ 345-6824, vilaolaria hotel.com.br. Tv, air conditioning, minibar, tel, pool, parking. $ $

RESTAURANTS
• **Petisqueira Alírio,** 26 Elizabeth Konder Reis St., Trapiche Beach, Armação ☎ 345-5168, petisqueira alirio@terra.com.br. Seafood, meats and chicken. $ $ $
• **Pirão D'Água,** 954 São João Ave., Armação de Itapocorói ☎ 345-6742, pirao@ dagua.com.br. Azorean typical fare. Try *Saudade de Peixe* (fish, mush, shrimp sauce with palmetto and fried bananas). $ $
• **Lilo's Praia,** Elizabeth Konder Reis Ave., in front of Armação boathouse ☎ 345-0034. Seafood, highlighting the *Linguado mar azul* (grilled fish w/ palmetto, potatoes, peach and cherries). $ $
• **Lilo Restaurante,** 579 Antônio Joaquim Tavares St. ☎ 345-5297. Seafood. Over 50 options of dishes. $ $

Piçarras

LODGING
• **Hotel July,** 44 Getúlio Vargas Ave. ☎ 345-0644, hoteljuly.com.br. Tv,air conditioning, minibar, parking, colonial breakfast. $
• **Hotel Turismar,** 60 Antônio Tolentino dos Santos St. ☎ 345-0291. Tv, minibar, tel, parking lot, game room. $

RESTAURANT
• **Pastelaria Blumenau,** 409 Nereu Ramos Ave., Downtown ☎ 347-0563. Pastéis and pizzas. A 20-year tradition. $

Joinville
☏ 47

TOURIST INFORMATION
• **Tourist Information Center: Companhia Municipal de Promoção Turística,** XV de Novembro, Moinhos de Vento ☎ 423-2633, promotur.com.br; **Disque Turismo** ☎ 0800 643-5015.
• **Transportation: Airport** ☎ 467-1000; **Bus station** ☎ 433-2991.
• **Exchange: Banco do Brasil** ☎ 431-2000; **Besc** ☎ 431-4000.
• **Shopping: Shopping Müller** ☎ 451-8000; **Shopping Cidade das Flores** ☎ 433-0758; **Expoville** ☎ 453-2161.
• **Hospital: Municipal São José** ☎ 441-6666; **Hospital e Maternidade Dona Helena** ☎ 451-3333; **Maternidade Darci Vargas** ☎ 433-0499.

• **Car Rentals: Locasul** 422-1514; **Hertz** 433-4141; **Inter** 422-7888; **Localiza** 433-9393.

LODGING

• **Anthurium Parque Hotel,** 226 São José St., Downtown 433-6299, anthurium.com.br. Located in the old Episcopal Palace. Neo-colonial style building surrounded by gardens. $ $

• **Hotel Tannenhof,** 340 Visconde de Taunay St., Downtown 0800 998-011, tannenhof.com.br. Traditional. Alpine-style architecture and decor. $ $

• **Le Village Hotel,** 98 Chuí St., 98 (near the Sambaqui Museum) 433-1559, hoteislevillage.com.br. Parking, minibar, air conditioning, cable Tv. $ $

• **Parthenon Prinz Suíte Hotel,** 525 Otto Boehm St., Downtown 0800 111-790, prinz.com.br. Pool, sauna, international restaurant, fitness center, game room, travel agency, business center. $ $ $

RESTAURANTS

• **Biergarten Chopp & Cozinha,** 1183 Visconde de Taunay St. 423-3790. Serves the Warsteiner beer, number 1 in Germany. $ $

• **Kib's,** 1400 XV de Novembro St., Glória. (annex to the Art Museum) 422-8667. Arabian cuisine. Belly dancing on Thursdays. $

• **Lírica Restaurante,** 1483 Max Colin St. 433-0594. German cuisine. Cozy. $ $ $

• **O Fornão Restaurante e Pizzaria,** 240 Visconde de Taunay St., Downtown. 422-3722. Traditional pasta restaurant. $

• **Queen's Restaurante,** 525 Otto Boehm St., Downtown (annex to Parthenon Prinz Suite Hotel) 422-4201. International cuisine. $ $ $

• **Restaurante Glória,** 2250 XV de Novembro St. 422-2919. Free parking. Food by the kilo. $

SURROUNDINGS

Jaraguá do Sul

LODGING

• **Etalan,** 39 Max Wilhelm St., Downtown. 371-1922, hoteletalan@netuno.com.br. Tv, air conditioning, minibar, tel, parking, restaurant. $ $

• **Itajara Hotel,** 2337 Expedicionário Gumercindo da Silva St. 371-3799, hotelitajara@netuno.com.br. Cable Tv, air conditioning, minibar, tel, Internet. $

• **Parthenon Century,** 239 Epitácio Pessoa St., Downtown 372-5800, century@atriohoteis.com.br. Cable Tv, air conditioning, minibar, Internet, pool, sauna and fitness room. $ $

RESTAURANTS

• **Alegro Restaurante Bar**, 847 Getúlio Vargas St. 371-0757. International cuisine. Reservations needed. $ $

• **Antibes,** 239 Epitácio Pessoa St., Downtown. (annex to the Parthenon Century Hotel) 372-5808. À la carte intern'l cuisine. Highlight: *Marreco do cheff e condessa de antibes*. $ $

• **Pizzaria e Choperia Casarão,** 60 Max Wilhelm St. 275-2332. Pasta and 70 pizza toppings. Try the parmeggiana beef. $

Laguna

48

TOURIST INFORMATION

• **Tourist Information Center: Portal Turístico,** Calistrato Müller Salles, St., Portinho 644-2441.

• **Police Station:** 646-0469.

• **Procon:** 646-0533.

• **Hospital:** 646-0522.

LODGING

• **Atlântico Sul,** 360 Senador Gallotti St., Praia de Mar Grosso 647-1166, atlsul@seanet.com.br. Tv, fan. Inside parking. $

• **Laguna Tourist Hotel,** Gi Beach 0800-7046022, lagunatourist.com.br. The most sophisticated in town. $ $ $

• **Ravena Cassino Hotel,** 700 Rio Grande do Sul St., Mar Grosso Beach 647-0450, ravenacassinohotel.com.br. $ $

RESTAURANTS

• **Restaurante Arrastão,** 629 Senador Gallotti, Mar Grosso Beach 647-0461. Seafood. $ $

• **Restaurante Atlântico Sul,** 360 Senador Gallotti Ave., Mar Grosso Beach, annex to the hotel by the same name 647-0013. Food by the kilo. $

SURROUNDINGS

Araranguá

LODGING

• **Araranguá Tourist Hotel,** 10 Pe. An-

tônio Luís Dias Ave., Downtown ☎ 522-0592. Serves colonial coffee. $
• **Becker Hotel,** 35 Presidente João Goulart Ave., Intersection of BR-101 ☎ 524-0770. Tv, air conditioning, minibar, pool, sauna. $
• **Conventos Park Hotel,** 227 Araranguá Municipal Highway ☎ 526-7111,convparkhotel@aru.matrix.com.br. Parking and pool. $
• **Premier Palace Hotel,** 2154 Sete de Setembro Ave., Downtown ☎ 524-2010. TV, air conditioning, minibar. $

RESTAURANTS
• **Paquetá Grill,** 2492 Getúlio Vargas Ave. ☎ 524-6307. Grills. $ $
• **Recanto,** Intersection to the beaches, 4 km from BR-101 ☎ 524-1003. Varied cuisine. $

Criciúma

LODGING
• **Soratur Palace Hotel,** 405 Marechal Deodoro Ave. (SC-446) ☎ 437-1680. Internet access. $

RESTAURANT
• **Veneza,** 51 Humberto Bortoluzzi Plz., (Nova Veneza), 17 km ☎ 436-1168. Varied menu. $

Porto Belo
☏ 47

TOURIST INFORMATION
• **Tourist Information Center** ☎ 369-5638, turismo pb@uol.com.br; **Casa do Turista** ☎ 369-5030, casadoturista@portobelo.com.br.
• **Banks: Banco do Brasil** ☎ 369-4336; **Besc** ☎ 369-4411.
• **Internet: Posto do Sol Cyber Café,** 525 Gov. Celso Ramos Ave. ☎ 369-4920; **Elite Treinamento,** 2123 Governador Celso Ramos Ave., Downtown ☎ 369-4647.
• **Transportation: Buses** ☎ 369-4092.

LODGING
• **Hotel Baleia Branca,** 100 Nena Trevisan St., cross-street of Governador Celso Ramos Ave. ☎ 369-4011, hotelbaleiabranca.com.br. Tv, air conditioning, tel. $
• **Pousada Enseada das Garoupas,** 1112 Governador Celso Ramos Ave. ☎ 369-4383. Tv, minibar. By the sea. $
• **Pousada Porto Belo,** 400 São Luís St., Downtown ☎ 369-4703, pousadaportobelo@terra.com.br. Breakfast with panoramic view. Parking. $

RESTAURANTS
• **Café do Lado,** 2300 Gov. Celso Ramos Ave. ☎ 369-4099. Highlight: double express coffee w/ vanilla ice cream, chopped ice, cocoa topping. $
• **Ilha de Pirão,** access at 2207 Gov. Celso Ramos Ave., and on Porto Belo Beach ☎ 369-4941. Seafood. $ $
• **Restaurante Alentejo,** 2170 Gov. Celso Ramos Ave., Downtown ☎ 369-4511. Portuguese cuisine, highlighting the *Bacalhau com batatas a murro*. $ $

SURROUNDINGS

Bombinhas

LODGING
• **Marbelo Tourist Hotel,** 882 Leopoldo Zarling Ave., Bombas Beach ☎ 369-1455, marbelo.com.br. Thermal pool, restaurant, parking, game room, fitness and reading room. $ $
• **Pousada do Arvoredo,** 99 Tilápia St., between Bombinhas and Quatro Ilhas ☎ 369-2355, pousadadoarvoredo.com.br. Restaurant w/ panoramic view. $ $
• **Pousada Vila do Farol,** 800 Vereador Manoel José dos Santos Ave. ☎ 393-9000, viladofarol.com.br. Sea view. $ $ $
• **Pousada Villa Paradiso,** 5 Garoupas Ave., 5 ☎ 369-0005, villaparadiso.com.br. Suites w/ Jaccuzzi and open-air bungallows inspired on Bali. $ $ $
• **Vila Boa Vida Apart Hotel,** 1 Grafite St., Mariscal Beach ☎ 393-4009. Pool w/ Jaccuzzi, yoga and shiatsu classes. $

RESTAURANTS
Casa da Lagosta, 987 Vereador Manoel José dos Santos Ave. ☎ 369-2235. Lobster and meat stew. $ $
• **Vila do Engenho Restaurante Típico,** 185 Geral Road ☎ 9979-2073. Working mill. Food prepared on a wood stove. $

Governador Celso Ramos

LODGING
• **Palmas Parque Hotel,** Geral de Pal-

mas Rd. ☎ 262-8044. Farm-hotel. Tv, video, minibar, central heating. $ $
• **Ponta dos Ganchos Resort** ☎ 0800 643-3346, pontadosganchos.com.br. Advanced booking only. Luxury accom–modations w/ sea view. $ $ $ $

RESTAURANT
• **Raízes Bar,** 1404 Rosendo Joaquim Sagas St., Vila de Palmas ☎ 262-8025. Seafood, pizzas, snacks, ice creams. $

São Joaquim
⊕ 49

TOURIST INFORMATION
• **Tourist Information Center: Centro de Informações,** Cezário Amarante Plz., Downtown ☎ 233-2790 e 233-0411.
• **Police Station:** ☎ 233-0057.
• **Banks: Banco do Brasil** ☎ 233-0202; **Bradesco** ☎ 233-0024; **Caixa** ☎ 233-0726; **Besc** ☎ 233-0022.
• **Hospital:** ☎ 233-0011.
• **Transportation: Buses** ☎ 233-0400; **taxi Manoel Pinto** ☎ 233-0122.

LODGING
• **Hotel Minuano,** 230 Urubici St. (in front of the Apple National Park) ☎ 233-0472. Chalets and rooms with Tv. $
• **São Joaquim Park Hotel,** 58 João Ribeiro Plz., Downtown ☎ 233-1444, saojoaquimparkhotel.com.br. Insulation, meeting room, parking. One of the best in town. $ $
• **Snow Valley**, SC-438 Km 10 towards Bom Jardim da Serra ☎ 9983-8586. Rustic cabins with Tv, minibar, heating and balcony. $

RESTAURANT
• **Casa de Pedra,** 360 Cezário Amarante Plz., Downtown ☎ 233-0437. Barbecue, pizza. Sun. lunch, food by the kilo. $
• **Taberna Café,** 188 Pe. João Batista Vieceli St., near the main church ☎ 233-0351. Express coffee, snacks, sweets and pizzas. Thursdays to Sundays. $

SURROUNDINGS

Bom Jardim da Serra

LODGING
• **Pousada Santa Rita,** SC-438 Km 31 ☎ 232-0255. Horseriding, ecological trekking, fishing and typical food. $
• **Rio do Rastro Hotel Fazenda,** SC-438 Km 130, Boca da Serra ☎ 491-2610, riodorastro.com.br. Chalets, fishing lake, cascade, observatory, horseriding. $ $

RESTAURANT
• **Cascata,** SC-438, towards Criciúma (Km 121,3) ☎ 232-0123. Barbecue. $

Lages ⊕ 49

LODGING
• **Grande Hotel Lages,** 23 João de Castro St., Downtown ☎ 222-3522, grande hotellages@matrix.com.br. Cable Tv air conditioning, minibar, tel, restaurant, parking. $ $
• **Hotel Pegorini,** 124 Luiz de Camões, 124 Ave., Coral ☎ 223-1988. Tv, air conditioning, minibar, tel, parking area. $
• **Map Hotel**, 522 Hercílio Luz St., 522, Downtown ☎ 222-0411, maphotel@iscc.com.br. Cable Tv, air conditioning, minibar, tel, notebook facilities, restaurant, parking. $ $

RESTAURANTS
• **Cantina Don Pepe,** 320 Emiliano Ramos St. ☎ 222-4727. Serves pasta and pizzas. $
• **Churrascaria Pegorini,** 124 Luiz de Camões Ave., Coral ☎ 223-1988. $ $
• **Laghos Restaurante,** 23 João de Castro St., Downtown (annex to the Grande Hotel Lages) ☎ 222-3522. Feijoada on Saturdays and food by the kilo on weekdays. $ $

Urubici

LODGING
• **Serra Bela Hospedaria Rural,** Geral Santo Antônio Rd., 4 km from Downtown ☎ 278-5113, serrabela.com.br Rooms and chalets with fireplace, fishing lake, horseriding, ecological trekking. $
• **Urubici Park Hotel,** 2278 Adolfo Konder St., 2.278 ☎ 278-5300, urubiciparkhotel.com.br. Ecological outings. $

Urussanga

LODGING

• **Hotel Contessi,** 30 Giovanni de Pellegrin ☎ 465-3194, hotelcontessi@terra.com.br. Cable TV, air conditioning, minibar, tel., parking. $

Treze Tílias

⊕ 49

TOURIST INFORMATION

• **Tourist Information Center:** 25 Ministro Andreas Thaler Plz., Downtown ☎ 537-0176, trezetilias@trezetilias.sc.gov.br.

LODGING

• **Hotel Áustria,** 8 Tirol St. ☎ 537-0132. Simple and comfortable. $
• **Hotel Tirol,** 111 São Vicente de Paula St. ☎ 537-0125, hoteltirol.com.br. Charming and traditional. $ $
• **Treze Tílias Park Hotel,** 585 Videira St. ☎ 537-0277, ttph.tur.br. Annex to Parque Termas Internacional Vale das Tílias, panoramic view. $ $

RESTAURANTS

• **Kandlerhof,** 80 Videira St. ☎ 537-0276. Austrian typical fare. $ $
• **Restaurante e Pizzaria Edelweiss,** 46 Antônio Carlos Konder Reis St. ☎ 537-0531. Pizzas and typical dishes. $ $

SURROUNDINGS

Fraiburgo

LODGING

• **Hotel Renar,** 150 Beira Lago Ave., 150 ☎ 246-2133. Restaurant, thermal pools. The best in town. $ $

RESTAURANT

• **Tio Bressiani,** Renê Frey ☎ 246-5047. Varied food. Self-service. $

Porto União

LODGING

• **Holz Hotel,** 490 Manoel Ribas St., União da Vitória ☎ 522-2144, netuniao.com.br/holzhotel. Tv, air conditioning, minibar, tel. The most luxurious. $ $
• **Hotel Ópera,** 6 Visconde de Guarapuava St, Downtown ☎ 522-3484. For over 40 years. $
• **San Rafael,** 125 XV de Novembro St., Downtown ☎ 522-4344, twinnet.com.br/sanrafael. Suites with Tv, air conditioning, minibar. Parking. $

RESTAURANTS

• **Cantina San Remo,** 400 Prudente de Morais St., Downtown ☎ 522-3868. Pizzas and pasta, live music at night. $
• **San Rafael,** Prudente de Morais St., corner of XV de Novembro St. ☎ 552-4549. Varied food. $

RIO GRANDE DO SUL

Porto Alegre

⊕ 51

TOURIST INFORMATION

• **Tourist Information Center: SAT**, Parque Farroupilha, shop 12, Bom Fim ☎ 0800 517-686 ou 3333-1873. **Buses** ☎ 3225-0677. **Airport** ☎ 3358-2048. Public Market, Glênio PeresPlz., Downtown; **Gasômetro Plant,** 551 Pres. João Goulart Ave., Downtown. **Shop. Praia de Belas,** 1181 Praia de Belas Ave. **Tourism Bureau (Sapiranga)** ☎ 599-1127. **Tourism Bureau (Rio Pardo)** ☎ 3731-3708.
• **Transportation: Salgado Filho International Airport,** 9010 Severo Dullius, São João (6 km from Downtown) ☎ 3358-2000; **Buses,** Vespasiano Júlio Veppo Plz. ☎ 3210-0101.
• **Police Station: accidents** ☎ 3217-2411 ext. 2281/ 2282; **foreigners** ☎ 3337-2111.
• **Hospital: First Aid** ☎ 3316-9600; **Clínicas** ☎ 3316-8000; **toxicological information** ☎ 3223-6110; **Santa Casa** ☎ 3214-8080; **Pronto Atendimento Bom Fim** ☎ 3228-4000.
• **Banks: Banco do Brasil** ☎ 3221-2226; **Banespa** ☎ 0800 702-3535; **Banrisul** ☎ 3215-1515; **Bradesco** ☎ 3212-5777; **Caixa** ☎ 0800 550-101; **Citibank** ☎ 3220-8619; **Itaú** ☎ 0800 904-828; **Santander** ☎ 3337-1099; **Unibanco** ☎ 3220-7730.
• **Car Rental: Avis** ☎ 3342-0400; **Allocar** ☎ 3337-1717; **Easy Car** ☎ 3311-3754; **Hertz** ☎ 3337-7755; **Localiza** ☎ 3328-6000.
• **Exchange: Aerotur,** 1137 Andradas St., shop B ☎ 3228-8144; **Banco do Brasil,** 185 Uruguai St. ☎ 3214-7777; **Prontur,** 445 Borges de Medeiros Ave. ☎ 3221-6566.
• **Internet**: **Cybercafé,** Praia St., Shopping Subsolo ☎ 3286-4244;

Cyberscope, 333 Mostardeiro St., Moinhos de Vento ☎ 3395-4965.

• **Shopping: Mercado do Bom Fim,** Osvaldo Aranha Ave., shop 24, Parque Farroupilha; **Casa do Artesão,** 144 Júlio de Castilhos Ave.; **Rincão Gaúcho,** 1159 dos Andradas St.; **Shopping Iguatemi,** 1800 João Wallig Ave.; **Praia de Belas Shopping,** 1181 Praia de Belas Ave.; **Moinhos Shopping,** 52 Olavo Barreto Viana St.; **R. da Praia Shopping,** 1001 Andradas St.

• **Tourism agencies: Aliátur**, 96 Salgado Filho Ave., 9th floor ☎ 3224-4566; **Fellini,** 393/301 Alberto Bins Ave. ☎ 3228-6388; **Rota.** 137/506 Tobias da Silva St. ☎ 3346-1776.

LODGING

• **Alfred Porto Alegre,** 105 Sr. dos Passos St., Downtown ☎ 3226-2555. Easy access to all districts. Cable Tv, minibar, tel and air conditioning. $$$

• **Blue Tree Millenium Flat,** 3120 Borges de Medeiros Ave., Belas Beach ☎ 3026-2200. View to the Guaíba. Cable Tv, minibar, tel, air conditioning, microwave, safe and living room $$$

• **Continental Business,** 49 Otávio Rocha Plz., Downtown ☎ 3212-1618. Cable Tv, alarm clock, hair drier, minibar, tel and air conditioning. $$$

• **Continental Porto Alegre,** 77 Vespasiano Julio Veppo Plz., Downtown ☎ 3211-2344, deville.com.br. In front of the Bus Station. Cable Tv, minibar, tel and air conditioning. $$$

• **Deville Porto Alegre Aeroporto,** 1909 Estados Ave., Anchieta ☎ 3373-5000, deville.com.br. Cable Tv, bathtub, minibar, tel, safe and air conditioning. $$$$

• **Garibaldi,** 652 Garibaldi St., Floresta 3224-7333. Near Downtown. Cable Tv, minibar, tel and air conditioning. $$

• **Lancaster,** 477 Eng. Acelino de Carvalho St., Downtown ☎ 3224-4737. Near the beach. Cable Tv, minibar, tel, air conditioning. $$

• **Plaza San Rafael,** 514 Alberto Bins Ave., Downtown. ☎ 3220-7000, plazahoteis.com.br. One of the best in town. Free Internet access. $$$

• **Porto Alegre Ritter,** 55 Vespasiano Júlio Veppo Plz., Downtown. ☎ 3228-4044. In front of the Bus Station. Cable Tv, minibar, tel, Internet and air conditioning. $$$

• **Sheraton Porto Alegre,** 18 Olavo Barreto Viana St., Moinhos de Vento ☎ 3323-6000, sheraton-poa.com.br. It´s new and located next to Shopping Moinhos de Vento. $$$$

RESTAURANTS

• **Atelier das Massas,** 1482 Riachuelo St., Downtown. ☎ 3225-1125. Italian restaurant, belongs to Gaúcho painter Gelson Radaelli. The most varied hors d´oeuvre in town, excellent imported wines and homemade pasta, highlighting the *tortéi.* $$$

• **Barranco,** 1578 Protásio Alves Ave., Petrópolis ☎ 3331-6172. À la carte barbecue. Air conditioning hall and open-air tables, under the trees. Famous for the draft beer the the late closing hour, 2 in the morning. $$

• **Bistrô do Margs,** Alfândega Plz., Downtown ☎ 3286-5705. Located at the Art Museum building. Lunch, happy hour and dinner. $$

• **Calamares,** 58 Mercedes Ave., Floresta ☎ 3346-8055. Authentic Portuguese cuisine, highlighting cod dishes and pastéis-de-santa-clara. $$$

• **Chalé da Praça XV**, XV de Novembro Plz., Downtown ☎ 3225-2667. Traditional meeting place – happy hour. Gaúcho typical fare. $

• **Copacabana,** 2 Garibaldi Plz. Cidade Baixa ☎ 3225-9885. Traditional Italian restaurant. Famous for the roast veal. $$

• **Fogo de Chão,** 5200 Cavalhada Ave., Cavalhada ☎ 3248-3940. Refined, grills whole cuts of beef, in traditional Gaúcho style. Salad buffet. $$

• **Fusilli Ristorante,** 80 Veríssimo de Matos St., Bela Vista ☎ 3335-3784. Italian fare. $$$

• **Galpão Crioulo.** Maurício Sirotsky Sobrinho Park, Downtown ☎ 3226-8194. Continuous barbecue, salad buffet and hot dishes. Typical shows every night and Sunday at lunch. $

• **Gambrinus,** 85 Borges de Medeiros Ave., Public Market, Downtown ☎ 3226-6914. The oldest in town, dating from 1889. Portuguese fare. $$

• **Koh Pee Pee,** 83 Schuller St., Moinhos de Vento ☎ 3333-5150. Thai restaurant, with Thai decor and table–ware. Serves fish and shrimp with exotic sauces. And banana cooked in palm sugar and served with coconut milk. $$$

• **Naval,** XV de Novembro Plz., Public Market, Downtown ☎ 3286-3423. Simple and traditional place, is famous for its potato balls, cod and ice draft beer. In winter, serves mocotó and feijoada. $

• **Na Brasa,** 389 Ramiro Barcelos St., Floresta ☎ 3225-2205. Regarded as the best and most abundant barbecue place in town, with 35 salads on the buffet and 25 meat cuts. $ $

• **Steinhaus,** 415 Paulino Teixeira St., Rio Branco ☎ 3330-8661. Regarded as the best restaurant in Porto Alegre. Highlights: typical German fare, such as the *eisbein* $ $

Bento Gonçalves

54

TOURIST INFORMATION

• **Transportation: Bus station,** 19 Gal. Gomes Carneiro St. ☎ 452-1311.

• **Hospital: Galassi** ☎ 451-1088; **Tacchini (private)** ☎ 451-4333.

• **Police station:** Assis Brasil ☎ 452-3200.

• **Banks: Banco Brasil,** ☎ 451-3666; **Banrisul** ☎ 451-3944; **Bradesco** ☎ 451-1288; **Caixa** ☎ 451-2333; **HSBC** ☎ 451-3499; **Itaú** ☎ 451-8404; **ABN** ☎ 223-0105; **Banco do Brasil** ☎ 212-3077; **Banrisul** ☎ 214-8739; **BCN** ☎ 223-5255; **Bradesco** ☎ 223-3555; **HSBC** ☎ 229-0008; **Itaú** ☎ 202-1486; **Unibanco** ☎ 202-2898.

• **Car Rental: Argeu** ☎ 224-3165; **Interlocadora** ☎ 229-9133; **Localiza** ☎ 223-8777; **Locanorte** ☎ 221-7466; **Tripicar** ☎ 213-1202; **Unidas** ☎ 213-5787; **Vancouver** ☎ 214-1593.

• **Internet: Cyber House,** Shopping Bento ☎ 451-2153.

• **Shopping: Vinícola Aurora, 500**. Olavo Bilac St. ☎ 455-2028; **Artesanato do Vale,** Capela das Almas, Vale dos Vinhedos ☎ 453-1055, ext. 1234; **Paisagem do Tempo e Estrada do Imigrante (artwork)**, 1431 Ludovico Cavinatto St., next to the pavilions of the Grape Festival. **(Carlos Barbosa); Varejo Tramontina** (all industry items), 193 Maurício Cardoso St. ☎ 461-8086; **Casa da Neni** (artwork), 34. Luiza Bocchese St.

• **Tourism Agencies: Rio das Antas,** 197 Enry Hugo Dreher St. ☎ 451-2844; **Giordani,** 581/109 13 de Maio St. ☎ 452-6042; **Radical Sul,** 7 Silva Paes St. ☎ 453-6934; **Esporte Aventura,** 40 Refatti St., room 2 ☎ 451-6118; **Criúva Operadora,** 620 15 de Novembro St., Criúva ☎ 267-8255; **Mad River, 1160** Travessão Gablontz St. ☎ 229-3611; **Sky,** 320/701 Angelina Michelon St. ☎ 222-2863; **Fontana,** 1630, room 8, 25 de Julho Ave. ☎ 292-2600 (Nova Roma do Sul); **Cia de Aventuras,** 733 Júlio de Castilhos St. ☎ 294-1455.

LODGING

• **Albergue Belvedere Sonda,** Travessão Mutzel (Nova Pádua) ☎ 296-1200. 5 km from town, with a view of the Antas River. All meals included. $ $

• **Casa Bucco,** RS-470, km 90.4, Tuiuty ☎ 504-2026, casabucco.com.br. Since 1925, has become an inn too, w/ climatized rooms, minibar, Tv and Jaccuzzi. Highlight: the living room with fireplace and the balcony with a view of the Antas River Valley. $ $

• **Casa Mia,** 71 Niterói St. ☎ 451-1215, pousadacasamia.com.br. Simple inn, but comfortable, w/ option of bathroom in the room or collective. Parking, cable Tv and fan – also air conditioned rooms. $

• **Dall'Onder,** 197 Erny Hugo Dreher St. ☎ 451-3555, dallonder.com.br. The best in the region. Thermal pool, sauna, fitness room, piano bar, shop and receptive tourism. As all hotels in the Serra, offers a hearty breakfast. $ $ $

• **Villa Michelon,** RS-444, km 18.9, Vale dos Vinhedos ☎ 459-1800, villamichelon. com.br. Surrounded by vineyards, houses a vineyard mini-museum, mini-farm, native vegetation, fitness room, indoor pool and ecological trails. $ $ $ $

RESTAURANTS

• **Cantina Cândido Valduga,** Oitavo distrito, Vale dos Vinhedos ☎ 453-3620. Italian fare. $ $

• **Giuseppe Posto Per Mangiare,** RS-470, km 222.5 ☎ 463-8505. À la carte Italian fare. $ $

• **Vinícola Cordelier,** RS-470, km 219, Vale dos Vinhedos ☎ 453-2333. Italian fare and special menus. Wineries restaurants, only if you call beforehand. $ $

SURROUNDINGS

Antonio Prado

TOURIST INFORMATION

• **Shopping: Fetina de Formaio (cheeses)**, 167 Rio Branco Ave. ☎ 461-1966.
• **Tourism Agencies: Living Stone,** 356 Graciema Formalo St. ☎ 211-4175.

LODGING
• **Piemonte,** 634 Valdomiro Bocchese Ave. ☎ 293-1280. Located on the main street in town, where most of the historical buildings are. $
• **Pousada Colonial De Rossi,** Linha Silva Tavares ☎ 293-1771, pousadaderossi.hpg.com.br. Fireplace, minibar and Tv. All meals included. $ $

RESTAURANTS
• **Italiano,** 357 Valdomiro Bocchese Ave, Downtown ☎ 293-1746. The building was the backdrop for the shooting of *O Quatrilho*. Serves lunch daily. Dinner only on Wednesday and Saturday. $
• **Nostra Cantina,** RS-122, km 122 ☎ 293-4057. Italian fare – chicken and pasta. Rustic decor. Fireplace. $

Caxias do Sul

TOURIST INFORMATION
• **Tourist Information Center: Pipa Pórtico,** Nono Mazzo St. ☎ 453-2555, pmtur@italnet.com.br; **SEMTUR** ☎ 207-1090.
• **Transportation: Bus Station,** 1341 Ernesto Alves St. ☎ 228-3000.
• **Airport,** Salgado Filho Ave. ☎ 213-2566.
• **Hospital: Geral** ☎ 229-4444.
• **Banks: Unibanco** ☎ 451-2188.
• **Car Rental: Exclusiva** ☎ 451-2990.
• **Internet: Cyber Café,** Posto Di Trento ☎ 212-0004.
• **Shopping: Boccati (wine, cheese),** 2043 Antonio Ribeiro Mendes St. ☎ 224-1950
• **Tourism Agencies: Companhia Caxiense,** 325/105 Itália Ave. ☎ 214-1223.

LODGING
• **Bela Vista Parque,** 1965 Rio Branco Ave., Ana Rech ☎ 283-1177, databrum.com.br/hotelbelavista. A green area with trails, playground, soccer field. Tv, tel, minibar and Jaccuzzi. $ $
• **Intercity Premium,** 333 Terezinha Pauletti Sanvitto Ave. ☎ 3026-1000, intercityhotel.com.br. Game room and fitness center, pool, multi-sports court and living room with fireplace. $ $ $
• **Samuara Parque,** RS-122, km 69, 250 ☎ 227-2222, samuarahotel.com.br. 7 km from Downtown. Multi-sports courts, thermal pool, grove, ballroom. Tv, air conditioning, tel and minibar. $ $

RESTAURANTS
• **Alvorada,** 200 Os 18 do Forte St. ☎ 222-4637. Chicken w/ several accompaniments. and, of course, the wine of the region. $
• **Cantina Pão e Vinho,** 1757 Ludovico Cavinatto St. ☎ 211-2500. Serves pasta, chicken, polenta, radicci salad and wine. $ $
• **Gaudério,** 1766 Mário de Boni St., Floresta ☎ 225-1466. 4 km from Downtown, at the exit to Bento Gonçalves. Continuous barbecue. $ $

Farroupilha

LODGING
• **Don Francesco,** 88 Dr. Jaime Romeu Rossler St. ☎ 261-1132, hoteldonfrancesco.com.br. Cable Tv, minibar, tel, insulation and a.c. $ $

RESTAURANT
• **Bem-Te-Vi,** Caravaggio, 1º Distrito ☎ 260-5184. Italian fare. $

Flores da Cunha

TOURIST INFORMATION
• **Tourism agency: Tosi Matti,** 10 Camilo Marcantônio Ave. ☎ 293-2021.

LODGING
• **Villa Borghese,** 1031 John Kennedy St. ☎ 292-2355. Parking, fitness room, cable Tv, minibar and insulation. $ $

RESTAURANT
• **Sítio da Lagoa,** Travessão Jacinto, Otávio Rocha ☎ 279-1243. Italian recipes. During the week, make reservations. $

Garibaldi

TOURIST INFORMATION
• **Shopping: Associação dos Artesãos,** 77 Dr. Carlos Barbosa St., next to the Municipal Museum ☎ 462-3483.
• **Tourism agency: Novitá,** 510 B Luis Rogério Casacurta St. ☎ 462-2759.

LODGING

• **Casacurta,** 510 Luis Rogério Casacurta St. ☎ 462-2166, hotelcasacurta.com.br. Architecture inspired by the French castles of the Loire Valley. $ $

• **Mosteiro São José,** 3590 Buarque de Macedo St. ☎ 462-1703. Old monastery, today a hotel, at the top of a hill. One of the best views in town. $

Veranópolis

TOURIST INFORMATION

• **Tourist agency: Spatur,** 610/01 Osvaldo Aranha Ave. ☎ 441-4700. **Shopping: Artesanato Fontana,** RS-470, km 102, 530 ☎ 441-1497.

LODGING

• **Princesa dos Vales,** 1106 Osvaldo Aranha Ave. ☎ 441-1499. Located Downtown, with cable Tv, insulation. $

Caçapava do Sul

⊕ 55

TOURIST INFORMATION

• **Tourist Information Center:** 601 XV de Novembro St. ☎ 281-1599, turisa mo@farrapo.com.br; **Associação Caçapavana de Turismo** ☎ 281-1543.

• **Police Station: Civil** ☎ 281-1861.

• **Transportation: Bus Station,** Gen. Osório St. ☎ 281-1404.

• **Hospital: Dr. Victor Lang** ☎ 281-1296.

• **Banks: Banco do Brasil** ☎ 281-1313; **Banrisul** ☎ 281-2222; **Caixa** ☎ 281-1231.

• **Exchange: Celoim,** 825 Sete de Setembro Ave. ☎ 53-242-8171.

• **Internet:** ☎ 281-3558.

• **Shopping: Quiosque municipal** (food and artwork). Ulhoa Cintra St., on the corner of XV de Novembro St. ☎ 281-3045.

• **Tourism agencies: Giro** ☎ 281-1066; **São João** ☎ 281-1754; **Vá-de-Vam** ☎ 281-3883.

LODGING

• **Cyro Palace,** 171 Pres. Kennedy Ave. ☎ 281-1768. Right at the entrance gate of the city, towards Guaritas and Minas de Camaquã. $

• **Karlton,** 487 XV de Novembro St. ☎ 281-1260. Downtown. Standard and luxury apts., with air conditioning and minibar. Indoor parking. $

• **Novo,** 340 Dr. Alfredo Duarte Ave. ☎ 281-1309. On the way to Pedra do Segredo. $

• **Residencial,** 656 XV de Novembro St. ☎ 281-1671. Outdoor parking, Tv, air conditioning or fan, fireplace. $

RESTAURANTS

• **Art & Café,** 400 XV de Novembro St. ☎ 281-1988. Downtown, both a restaurant and coffee shop. $

• **La Picanha,** 703 XV de Novembro St. ☎ 281-1956. Restaurant and barbecue place. Open for lunch and dinner. $

• **Pães e Cia,** XV de Novembro St. ☎ 281-3740. Snack bar and pizza parlor. Several pizza toppings. $

• **Urbanus.** XV de Novembro St. ☎ 281-1657. A blend of Italian and Gaúcho cuisine, with beef, lasagnas and pizzas. $ $

SURROUNDINGS

Bagé

TOURIST INFORMATION

• **Tourist Information Center:** 998 Gen. Osório St. ☎ 53-242-7122.

• **Bank: Unibanco** ☎ 53-240-5430.

• **Exchange: Alpes,** 727 Sete de Setembro Ave. ☎ 53-242-8419.

LODGING

• **Obinotel,** 901 Sete de Setembro Ave. ☎ 53-242-8211. Historic building. minibar, tel, Tv and insulation. $ $

RESTAURANT

• **Arlindo,** 1965 Gen. Osório St. ☎ 241-1616. In the pampa region, be sure to eat a typical barbecue. Try the continuous barbecue. $

Piratini

TOURIST INFORMATION

• **Tourist Information Center:** 150 20 de Setembro St. ☎ 53-257-1479.

• **Bank: Banco do Brasil** ☎ 53-257-1122.

Cambará do Sul

⊕ 54

TOURIST INFORMATION

• **Tourist Information Center:** 39 Adail Valim St. ☎ 251-1320.

• **Transportation: Bus Station,**700 Dona Úrsula St. ☎ 251-1347.

• **Police Station:** 84 Niconiro Pereira St. ☎ 251-1303.
• **Tourist guides: Associação de Condutores** ☎ 251-1320; **Associação Praiagrandense** (Grande Beach) ☎ 532-1414.
• **Hospital: São José** ☎ 251-1167.
• **Banks: Banrisul** ☎ 251-1154.

LODGING
• **Parador Casa da Montanha,** on the road to the Aparados da Serra National Park. ☎ 286-5544, hotelcasadamontanha.com.br. Thermal tents, bathroom, hothouse, fan, by the Camarinhas River. Restaurant serving typical food. Breakfast, lunch, dinner included. $$$
• **Paradouro da Fortaleza,** Estrada da Fortaleza ☎ 504-5183. Wooden rustic chalets facing a lake, 13 km from Downtown. No electricity, but w/ hot showers. Living room w/ fireplace. $
• **Recanto dos Amigos,** Estrada Lajeado das Margaridas ☎ 9832-1615. Farm-inn, 3.5 km from Downtown on a dirt road. With a lake and a waterfall. $

RESTAURANTS
• **Bom Paladar,** 97 Antônio Raupp St. ☎ 251-1280. Food by the kilo. $
• **Galpão Costaneira,** Dona Úrsula St., Downtown ☎ 251-1005. The typical crioulo wooden warehouse serves rural fare and grilled meats. Live music on weekends. $
• **Mata Bicho,** 28 de Dezembro St., Downtown ☎ 251-1203. Packed sweets and snacks for the trails. $

SURROUNDINGS

Bom Jesus

TOURIST INFORMATION
• **Tourist Information Center: Tourism Bureau** ☎ 237-1585.
• **Tourism agencies: Canyon.** ☎ 251-1027, canyonturismo.cjb.net. **Camélia** ☎ 237-1413.

S. José dos Ausentes

TOURIST INFORMATION
• **Tourist Information Center: Reservations** ☎ 234-1100.
• **Tourism Guides: Condutores de ecoturismo** ☎ 234-1072.

LODGING
• **Potreirinhos,** access via Lajeadinho Rd. and Faxinal Preto, 33 km from Downtown ☎ 9977-3482. It´s the closest farm to the steps of the Silveira and Divisa rivers, 5 minutes from Cachoeirão dos Rodrigues. Collective bathrooms. $
• **São José da Silveira,** district of Silveira, 22 km from Downtown ☎ 9972-4035. A 19th-century farm, it houses an antique museum, w/ family items. Horses, fishing rivers and rooms w/ bathrooms. $

Gramado

⊕ 54

TOURIST INFORMATION
• **Tourist Information Center:** 1674 Borges de Medeiros Ave. ☎ 286-1418; Major Nicoletti Plz. ☎ 286-1475.
• **Police Station: Military** ☎ 286-1261; **Civil** ☎ 286-2300.
• **Transportation: Bus Station,** 2100 Borges de Medeiros Ave. ☎ 286-1302.
• **Hospital: São Miguel** ☎ 286-4594; **Health Center** ☎ 286-1236.
• **Banks: Banco do Brasil** ☎ 286-2724; **Banrisul** ☎ 286-1379; **Bradesco** ☎ 286-1955; **Caixa** ☎ 286-1816; **HSBC** ☎ 286-1705; **Itaú** ☎ 286-2158; **Santander** ☎ 286-1308; **Sicredi** ☎ 295-1100.
• **Car Rental: Gramado** ☎ 286-3344; **Eurocar** ☎ 286-3986; **Localiza** ☎ 286-6000.
• **Internet**: **Cafeteria Bello Gusto,** 2193 Borges de Medeiros Ave. ☎ 286-2293.
• **Shopping: Associação dos Artesãos** ☎ 286-2836; **Cor & Tom,** 2040 Hortênsias Ave.; **Belas Artes,** 3165 Borges de Medeiros Ave.; **Lanterna,** 31 São Pedro St.; **Angorá,** 2759 Borges de Medeiros Ave.; **Lucirene,** 463 Dom Pedro I Ave.; **Planalto,** 2918 Borges de Medeiros Ave.; **Lugano,** 374 São Marcos St.; **Caracol,** 2808 Borges de Medeiros Ave.; **Gramado,** 1050 Borges de Medeiros Ave.
• **Tourism agencies: Bella Tur** ☎ 286-2087; **Brasil Raft** ☎ 286-5444; **Campo Fora** ☎ 9971-4000; **Montes Verdes** ☎ 286-2225; **Serra** ☎ 286-2049.

LODGING
• **Casa da Montanha,** 3166 Borges de Medeiros Ave. ☎ 286-2544,

hotelcasadamontanha.com.br. Central, w/ bavarian-style architecture. Decor resembles English hotels. $$$$

• **Cravo e Canela,** 144 Ten. Manuel Corrêa St. 282-282-1120, pousada cravoecanela.com.br. Bavarian style. Tv, free minibar, tel and heating, sauna, thermal pool w/ Jaccuzzi, bar. $$$

• **Continental Serra,** 220 José Pedro Piva St. 282-4444, hoteisconti nental. com.br. Inside a large green area, jogging track, courts and thermal pool, Tv, minibar, tel and air conditioning. $$$

• **Estalagem St. Hubertus,** 974 Carriere St. 286-1273, sthubertus.com.br. View of the Lago Negro, the only State hotel part of Roteiros de Charme. $$$

• **Laghetto,** 1700 Borges de Medeiros Ave. 286-2666, laghetto.com.br. Next to the Joaquina Rita Bier River. Tv, tel, minibar, sound and insulation. $$$

• **La Hacienda,** Estr. Várzea Grande, 9 km from Downtown on RS-115 286-8186, lahacienda.com.br. Cabins w/ fireplace, Jaccuzzi, trails, lake and horses. $$$$

• **Laje de Pedra,** Pres. Kennedy Ave. 282-4300, lajedepedra.com.br. A huge hotel inside a park. Sauna, thermal pool, spa, theater, shops, courts and game room. $$$

• **Hotel das Hortênsias,** 83 Bela Vista St. 286-1057, hoteldashortensias. com.br. Alpine-style decor, near the Knorr Park, where Santa Claus Village is located. $$$

• **Pousada das Sequóias,** 1747 Godofredo Raymundo St. 282-1373. Dirst ecological hotel in the State. Cabins w/ Tv and heating, inside the Sequóias Park, housing one of the largest collections of conifera in the world. $

• **Quinta dos Marques,** 200 Gravataí St. 282-9813, quintadosmarques. com.br. Tv, minibar, heating and fire–place and bathtub optionals. $$$

• **Rita Höppner,** 305 Pedro Candiago St. 286-1334, rittahoppner.com.br. resembles a dollhouse. Suites with thermal pool. Free access to Mini-Mundo. $$$

• **Serra Azul,** 152 Garibaldi St. 286-1082, serraazul.com.br. Downtown, used for conventions. The rooms have a minibar, insulation, sound, cable Tv and tel. $$$

• **Serrano,** 1480 Hortênsias Ave. 286-1332, hotelserrano.com.br. A huge green area. $$$

• **Vovó Carolina,** 3129 Borges de Medeiros Ave. 286-2433, vovocarolina.com.br. Central, near shops and main restaurants. Tv, minibar, insulation, tel, fan and parking. $

RESTAURANTS

• **Bela Vista,** 3500 Hortênsias Ave. 286-1608. It´s one of the most traditional colonial coffee lunches in town, on the way to Canela. $$

• **Gasthof Edelweiss,** 1119 Carriére St. 286-1861. One of the first to serve fondue in town. German cuisine. $$$

• **La Caceria,** 3166 Borges de Medeiros Ave. 286-2544. Specializes in hunt meat. $$$

• **Le Chalet,** 1297 Hortênsias Ave. 286-5460. Alpine-style building, with various options of fondue and raclette – typical Swiss dishes. $$

• **Nonno Mio,** 2070 Borges de Medeiros Ave., Downtown 286-1252. Traditional galeterie in town. $$

• **Scur,** 151 Oswaldo Aranha Ave. 282-3688. Buffet lunch. At night, pizzas. $

Canela

54

TOURIST INFORMATION

• **Tourist Information Center:** João Corrêa Plz. 282-2200; **Tourism Bureau** 282-1287.

• **Police Station: Military** 282-1209; **Civil** 282-1212.

• **Transportation:** R. Ernesto Urbani 282-1375.

• **Hospital: Central** 282-3363. **Caridade** (private) 282-4344.

• **Banks: Banco do Brasil** 282-1702; **Banrisul** 282-4282; **Caixa** 282-4255; **Santander** 282-2132.

• **Shopping: Casa do Artesão,** João Corrêa Plz.; **Casa dos Bonecos,** 266 Oswaldo Aranha St. and 3915 Caracol Rd., 3.915; **Marlyz,** 209 Oswaldo Aranha St.; **Irma,** 236 Oswaldo Aranha St.

• **Tourism agencies: Brocker** 282-2668; **JM Rafting** 282-1255.

RESTAURANTS

• **Al Pesto,** 109 Helmut Schmidt St.

☎ 282-1211. The tradition of Italian pasta is present in this restaurant 2 km from Downtown. In winter, the fireplace is lighted. $ $
• **Pasteleiro,** 252 Oswaldo Aranha Ave. ☎ 282-6440. Famous among the young crowd, w/ a huge variety of *pastéis* and sweets, all named after movies. $

ARREDORES

Nova Petrópolis

TOURIST INFORMATION
• **Tourism agencies: Condor Reisen** ☎ 281-2200; **Ecoturismo Jaguatirica** ☎ 9113-4620.

LODGING
• **Pousada da Neve,** 523 Munique St., ☎ 281-1354, pousadadaneve.com.br. On the road to Gramado. Reading and game rooms, living room w/ fireplace, library, playground. $ $

RESTAURANTS
• **Colina Verde,** BR-116, km 185.5 ☎ 281-1388. The success is in the blend of German, Italian and Gaúcho cuisines. Located at the top of the Morro da Vila Olinda, it has tables with a view of a valley. $
• **Opa's Kaffeehaus,** 96 João Leão St., ☎ 281-1273. The most famous colonial coffee lunch in the region. The small wooden house has 45 salt and sweet options. $

S. Francisco de Paula

LODGING
• **Parque da Cachoeira,** RS-476, Km 10 ☎ 504-1446, parqueda cachoeira. com.br. Apartments, camping area and wooden cabins. Parabolic Tv and fireplace. Amid the dense green area of the park, waterfalls, rivers, trails.Fish-and-pay system, pool. $
• **Pomar Cisne Branco,** Roça Nova Rd. ☎ 244-1204, pomarcisnebranco. com.br. The inn, w/ two buildings, came after an apple orchard. Serves the authentic *churrasco na vala.* $ $

Três Coroas

TOURIST INFORMATION
• **Tourism agency: Extreme 4** ☎ 51-546-1427.

Lagoa do Peixe

MOSTARDAS
⊕ 51

TOURIST INFORMATION
• **Tourist Information Center:** 141 Padre Simão Ave. ☎ 673-1177.
• **Police Station:** 1031 Júlio de Castilhos St. ☎ 673-1144.
• **Transportation: Buses,** 259 15 de Novembro St.☎ 673-1255.
• **Hospital: S. Luiz de Mostardas,** 864. Alm. Tamandaré St. ☎ 673-1411.
• **Banks: Banco do Brasil** ☎ 673-1211; **Banrisul** ☎ 673-1100.
• **Shopping:** 1020 Bento Gonçalves St. ☎ 673-1316; 756 Dr. Jorge Futuro Ave. ☎ 9694-4009.
• **Tourism agencies:** Garça, 847 Alm. Tamandaré St.☎ 673-1463.

LODGING
• **Estrela do Mar,** Balneário Mostardense ☎ 673-1500. Tv and tel, bar and restaurant. $
• **Fazenda Capororoca,** RS-101, km 86 ☎ 9959-1630. It´s a camping, w/ electricity, water, bathrooms, kiosks, fishing and soccer field. $
• **Lagoa da Reserva,** RS-101, km 98 ☎ 9973-7146. Rural property, w/ camping area: electricity, water, bathrooms. Accepts trailers and motorhomes. $
• **Mostardense,** 799 Bento Gonçalves St. ☎ 673-1368. Tv. $
• **Municipal,** 761. Independente Ave. ☎ 673-1500. Restaurant, Tv, tel. $
• **Scheffer,** 1191 Alm. Tamandaré Ave. ☎ 673-1277. 8 apartments and 4 rooms with Tv. $

RESTAURANTS
• **Alternativa,** Pedro Simão Ave.Varied cuisine. $
• **Edmundo's,** 908 Bento Gonçalves St. ☎ 673-1553. Fish and meat. $
• **Ponto de Encontro,** 867 Emílio Ferreira de Lemos St ☎ 673-1314. Serves varied food. $
• **Recanto,** 941 Luis Araújo St. ☎ 673-1527. Serves pizza. $
• **São Francisco,** 11 de Abril St. ☎ 673-1460. Varied cuisine. $

SURROUNDINGS

Tavares

TOURIST INFORMATION
• **Touris Information Center: Eco-**

tourist information, 11 de Abril St.
- **Transportation:** Edgard Pereira Velho St. ☎ 674-1175.
- **Hospital: First Aid,** Alfredo Lisboa St. ☎ 674-1221.
- **Banks: Banrisul** ☎ 674-1166.

LODGING
- **Paiva,** 674 11 de Abril St. ☎ 674-1329. Tv. $

RESTAURANTS
- **Arco Iris,** Edgar Pereira Velho St. ☎ 674-1305. Varied meals. $
- **Colares,** 232 11 de Abril Ave. ☎ 674-1132. Varied food. $

Pelotas
☎ 53

TOURIST INFORMATION
- **Tourist Information Center:** 1274 Lobo da Costa St. ☎ 225-7755; **Infraero,** Zeferino Costa Ave. ☎ 223-1227.
- **Police Station:** 900 Prof. Araújo St. ☎ 225-6083.
- **Transportation: Bus Station,** 4605 Pres. João Goulart Ave. ☎ 284-6700.
- **Hospital: Santa Casa** ☎ 284-4700.
- **Banks: Banco do Brasil** ☎ 2271311; **Caixa** ☎ 225-0092; **Sudameris** ☎ 227-2005; **Unibanco** ☎ 284-7530.
- **Internet: Interativo Bar,** 48 Senador Mendoña St. ☎ 227-7800.
- **Shopping: Otto,** 304 Sete de Setembro St. ☎ 225-5436; **Doçaria Pelotense,** 7 de Setembro with 15 de Novembro ☎ 222-2534; **Berola,** 3721 Bento Gonçalves Ave. ☎ 229-2121.
- **Tourist Guides: Grupo Pelotense de Guias** ☎ 227-6371.

LODGING
- **Curi Palace,** 1279 Gen. Netto St. ☎ 227-7377, curipalacehotel.com.br. In Downtown. Air conditioning and fridge. Travel agency at the hotel. $ $
- **Estoril,** 718 Gen. Osório St. ☎ 225-2411. Downtown, has a direct access to Mamma Pizza. $ $
- **Manta,** 1131.Gen. Netto St ☎ 225-2411, hoteismanta.com.br. Pool and bar, "London-pub" style. $ $

RESTAURANTS
- **Churrascaria Lobão,** 3460 Bento Gonçalves Ave. ☎ 225 6197. Continuous barbecue, salad buffet. $
- **Cruz de Malta,** 143 Júlio de Castilhos Plz. ☎ 222-6835. Good à la carte barbecue restaurant. $ $
- **El Paisano,** 1093 Mal. Deodoro St. ☎ 227-1507. Barbecue restaurant, Uruguayan style, prepares the meat in front of the customers. $
- **Vila do Conde,** 1321 Andrade Neves St.☎ 222-4612. Portuguese fare, highlighting the cod. $ $ $

SURROUNDINGS

S. Lourenço do Sul

TOURIST INFORMATION
- **Tourist Information Center: Casa do Turista,** BR 116, km 462 ☎ 251-5979.
- **Tourism agencies: Turismo Gaúcho** ☎ 251-3117, turismogaucho.com.br.

RESTAURANT
- **Tropicáli's,** 81 Getúlio Vargas St. ☎ 215-3212.Fish and meats à la carte or buffet. $

Rio Grande
☎ 53

TOURIST INFORMATION
- **Tourist Information Center :** Buarque de Macedo St. ☎ 231-3466; **Posto do Cassino,** Rio Grande Ave. ☎ 236-1357.
- **Police Station:** Onório Bicalho Porto Ave.º ☎ 232-3119.
- **Transportation: Buses,** 737 Vice Almirante Abreu Ave. ☎ 232-8444; **Boats,** Silveira Martins Plz. ☎ 233-5451; **Airport,** Uruguai St., 10 km along the road to Cassino Beach ☎ 230-1316.
- **Hospital:** Santa Casa, 325 Gen. Osório Ave. ☎ 231-1588.
- **Banks: Banco do Brasil** ☎ 233-7500; **Banrisul,** ☎ 231-1344; **Caixa,** ☎ 231-1340. **Sudameris** ☎ 231-1055.
- **Car Rental: Unidas** ☎ 231-6649; **Guanabara** ☎ 231-1144.
- **Exchange: Cambisul,** 286 Gen. Bacelar St. ☎ 231-2855.
- **Shopping:** 5 Mal. Floriano St., 1st floor ☎ 232-6372.
- **Tourism agencies: Cassinotur** ☎ 233-2548.

LODGING
- **Atlântico,** 55 Duque de Caxias St. ☎ 231-3833. Air conditioning, minibar, Tv and tel. Downtown. $ $
- **Paris,** 112 Mal. Floriano St. ☎ 231-

3866. 1826 historical building, colonial style. Reasonable price. $

• **Porto Rei Residence,** 468 Cons. Teixeira Jr. St. Cidade Nova. ☎ 231-3722. Air conditioning, minibar, tel and TV. $ $

• **Villa Moura Rio Grande,** 165 Gen. Netto St. ☎ 231-3933. Executive hotel Internet and convention center. Cable Tv, air conditioning and minibar. $ $

RESTAURANTS

• **Marco's,** 400 Silva Paes Ave. ☎ 232-4447. Specializes in fish. $ $

• **Maxi Beef,** 1A João Oliveira Ave. RS-734 to Cassino ☎ 235-1423. 12 km from Downtown, serves barbecue. $

SURROUNDINGS

S. José do Norte

TOURIST INFORMATION

• **Tourist Information Center:** Mal. Deodoro St. ☎ 238-1535.

• **Bank: Banco do Brasil,** ☎ 238-1389.

Santa Maria

⊕ 55

TOURIST INFORMATION

• **Tourist Information Center:** at the Bus Station, room 13; **Tourism Bureau** ☎ 221-5971.

• **Police Station: Civil** ☎ 221-2809; **foreigners** ☎ 222-8066.

• **Transportation: Bus Station,** 1450. Pedro Pereira St. ☎ 222-4747; **Airport,**. Rubens Martins Berta St. ☎ 226-1155.

• **Hospital: First Aid** ☎ 221-2714; **Dr. Astrogildo Cesar de Azevedo** (private) ☎ 222-4444.

• **Banks: Banco do Brasil** ☎ 220-7500; **Banrisul** ☎ 222-7683; **Bradesco** ☎ 222-3333; **Itaú** ☎ 222-7711.

• **Car Rental: Localiza** ☎ 222-9444.

• **Exchange: Planalto** ☎ 222-7733; **Antunes** ☎ 212-2439; **Banco do Brasil** ☎ 222-7171.

• **Shopping: Coqueiro,** RS-287 to Candelária, in Arroio Grande, 20 km ☎ 227-5151; **Big Shopping,** 1483. Fernando Ferrari Ave. **Elegância Shopping,** 1167 Dr. Bozzano St.; **Santa Maria Shopping,** 1263 Dr. Bozzano St.

• **Tourism agencies: Guides** ☎ 222-3210.

LODGING

• **Itaimbé Palace,** 2741 Venâncio Aires Ave. ☎ 222-1144. Downtown, pool and air-conditioned rooms, minibar, tel and Tv. $ $ $

• **Morotin,** 1629 Ângelo Uglioni St. ☎ 222-4453. Standard and luxury apts.and suites. Downtown, 200 m from. Dr. Bozzano St., the 24-hour street and two malls. $ $

• **Park Hotel Morotin,** RS-287 to Candelária, km 6.2, Camobi ☎ 226-5500.5 km from Downtown, in a green area. Pool, game room, fitness center, multi-sports courts. lake. $ $ $

RESTAURANTS

• **August,** 1354 Floriano Peixoto St. ☎ 222-0212. The food is varied, the chicken is the main attraction, served on a stick, cut into pieces and accompanied by polenta and salad. $

• **Bovinu's,** 1596 Venâncio Aires St. ☎ 221-1790. Downtown. Varied food. $

• **Coyote,** 1522 Ângelo Uglione St. ☎ 225-3430. Downtown, serves varied food. $ $

• **La Sorella,** 275 Vitélio Zago St. (via RS-287) ☎ 224-1205. 35 km from Santa Maria, serves typical Italian fare. Make reservations beforehand. $

• **Maccherone,** 28 Prof. Braga St. ☎ 225-4320. Italian cuisine. Closes on Sundays. $ $

• **Vera Cruz,** 1600 N. Sra. Medianeira St. ☎ 222-0606. Serves varied food and the traditional poultry dishes, seasoned with rosemary and bacon. $

SURROUNDINGS

Mata

TOURIST INFORMATION

• **Tourist Information Center: Guido Borgomanero Museum** ☎ 259-1272.

• **Bank: Banco do Brasil** ☎ 259-1224.

• **Tourism agencies: Casa do Turista** ☎ 259-1438.

LODGING

• **Paleon,** 295 Matriz St. ☎ 259-1165. Next to the Matriz Church, simple accomodations, TV, fan or air conditioning. $ $

RESTAURANT

• **Restaurante do Hotel Paleon,** 295 Matriz St. ☎ 259-1165. Homemade cooking, abundant, varied. Very low price. $

S. Miguel das Missões

55

TOURIST INFORMATION

• **Tourist Information Center:** 1345. São Luiz St., Downtown 3381-1294, saomiguel.turismo@sol.psi.br.
• **Transportation: Bus Station,** Antunes Ribas Ave. 3381-1226.
• **Hospital: São Miguel Arcanjo** 3381-1331.
• **Banks: Banco do Brasil** 3381-1242; **Banrisul** 3381-1322.
• **Police Station**: São João St. 3381-1190.
• **Shopping: Avamba'e,** Borges do Canto Ave.; **Herter Escultor,** 202 Sepé Tiarajú St. 3381-1429; **Flecha Mágica,** Pinheiro Machado Plz.
• **Tourism agencies: Missões Turismo** 3381-1319, missoesturismo.com.br.

LODGING

• **Pousada das Missões,** 601 São Nicolau St. 3381-1202, rotamissoes.com.br/pousada. Low-priced, 200 m from the ruins.Also has collective rooms for youth hostel members. $
• **Wilson Park Hotel,** São Miguel St. 0800 510-2909, wilsonparkhotel.com.br. The best in town. $ $

RESTAURANTS

• **O Casarão,** 1.244 Borges do Canto Ave. 3381-1203. Serves barbecue and pizza. $
• **O Guarani,** 1.926. Borges do Canto Ave. 3381-1060. Very ample. Serves meals and sandwiches. $ $

SURROUNDINGS

Santo Ângelo

TOURIST INFORMATOIN

• **Tourism agencies: Caminho das Missões** 3312-9632, caminhodasmissoes.com.br.

LODGING

• **Maerkli,** 1.000 Brasil Ave. 3313-2127 / 3313-2607, Downtown. Luxury, semi-luxury and standard rooms. $ $

RESTAURANT

• **Schatzi's,** 431 3 de Outubro St. 3312-2255. Buffet for lunch and à la carte for dinner. The cakes and chocolates are famous. $

Torres

51

TOURIST INFORMATION

• **Tourist Information Center: Casa do Turista,** 315 Rio Branco Ave. 626-1937.
• **Police Station: Civil** 664-1282.
• **Transportation: Bus Station,** 524 José Bonifácio Ave. 664-1787.
• **Hospital: N. Sra. dos Navegantes** 664-1100; **Health Center** 664-2397.
• **Banks: Banco do Brasil** 664-1711; **Banrisul** 664-1522; **Bradesco** 664-1877; **Caixa** 664-1169; **Santander** 664-1922. **Itaú** 625-1015; **Bradesco** 663-1715.
• **Shopping: Top Torres Shopping,** Julio de Castilhos St., Downtown; **Comercial de Rose**, 235 José Bonifácio St.
• **Tourism agencies: Catour** 626-3598; **Blue Beach** 664-3096.

LODGING

• **De Rose Praia,** 895 Beira-Mar Ave. 664-3003. Pool, game room and fireplace. Panoramic restaurant with international cuisine. $ $ $
• **Dunas Flat**, 275 Borges de Medeiros St. 626-2460. Divides the space in the building with a commercial center, with stores, restaurants and a movie theater. Apartments with kitchen, Tv, tel, air conditioning and balcony. View of the sea. $ $ $
• **Dunas Praia,** 48 Mal. Deodoro St. 664-1011. In front of Grande Beach. Game room, pool. $ $ $
• **Guarita,** 711 Barão do Rio Branco Ave. 664-1822. At the entrance gate of the city. Simple accommodations, with Tv, fan and bathroom. A hearty breakfast and free parking. $
• **Pousada Brisa do Mar,** 51 Borges de Medeiros St. 664-2019. Downtown, near Grande Beach. Air conditioning, minibar and Tv. $
• **Pousada da Prainha,** 138 Alferes Ferreira Porto St. 626-2454. On the access street to Farol Hill, in a colonial-style mansion. $ $

RESTAURANTS

• **Anzol,** 265 Cristóvão Colombo St. 664-2427. By the Mampituba River, near Molhes da Barra. Fish. $

• **Parque da Guarita,** Inside the Guarita Park, via Bom Fim St. ☎ 664-1056. The house specializes in fish. $ $
• **Cantinho do Pescador,** 210 Cristóvão Colombo Ave. ☎ 664-3036. Near Molhes da Barra, on the avenue on the banks of the Mampituba River. Rich variety of fish. $
• **Maria José Grill,** 123 Silva Jardim Ave. ☎ 626-1856. Serves, according to tradition, the favorite dish of the Gaúcho, *churrasco*. $
• **Beira Rio,** 20 Cristóvão Colombo Ave. ☎ 664-3091. Located on the banks of the Mampituba River. Fish. $ $

SURROUNDINGS

Capão da Canoa

TOURIST INFORMATION

• **Tourist Information Center:** 1881 Paraguassu Ave. ☎ 625-2112.
• **Bank: Banco do Brasil** ☎ 625-1822.

LODGING

• **Araçá,** 333 Dois St., Araçá ☎ 625-1433. By the sea. Sauna, heated pool, game room. $ $ $
• **Capão da Canoa Mar.** 2.101 Guaraci St. ☎ 665-3122. Pool, game room, minibar, tel and Tv. $ $ $

RESTAURANTS

• **Taberna Don Cicillo,** 1.826 Guaraci St. ☎ 625-2404. Serves varied dishes. $
• **Kostelão,** Estr. do Mar (RS-389), km 35 ☎ 625-1298. Continuous barbecue. $
• **Bela Vista,** Estr. do Mar (RS-389), km 49 ☎ 622-1555. Colonial coffee lunch. $

Osório

TOURIST INFORMATION

• **Tourist Information Center:** 1.251 Jorge Dariva Ave. ☎ 663-3300.
• **Bank: Banco do Brasil** ☎ 663-3524.
• **Shopping: Maribo Country** RS-389, at the 11 Km marker.

RESTAURANTS

• **Da Montanha,** Antenas Rd. (Borússia Hill), 4 km ☎ 9948-0520. Chicken. $

TO KNOW MORE

ALEXANDRE, Fernando. **Dicionário da Ilha**. Florianópolis: Cobracoralina, 1994.
ANDRADE, Manuel Correia. **Paisagens e problemas do Brasil**. São Paulo: Editora Brasiliense, 1968.
CALDEIRA, J. **Viagem pela História do Brasil**. São Paulo: Companhia das Letras, 2001.
DALTO, Renato. **Missões Jesuítico-Guaranis**. São Leopoldo: Unisinos, 1999.
DIEGUES JR., M. **Regiões culturais do Brasil**. Rio de Janeiro: Centro Brasileiro de Pesquisas Educacionais, 1960.
FERNANDES, C. **Viagem Gastronômica Através do Brasil**. São Paulo: Senac, Estúdio Sonia Robatto, 2001.
FERREIRA, Sérgio Luiz. **Histórias Quase Todas Verdadeiras**. Florianópolis: Ed. Das Águas, 1998.
FISCHER, Luís Augusto. **Dicionário de Porto-Alegrês**. Porto Alegre: Artes e Ofícios, 1999.
FREIRE, R. Freire's. **Brasil Praias**. São Paulo: Mandarin, 2001.
KOCH, Z. & CORRÊA, M.C. Araucária. **A floresta do Brasil meridional**. Curitiba: Olhar Brasileiro, 2002.
LESSA, Barbosa. **Rio Grande do Sul, Prazer em Conhecê-lo**. Porto Alegre: AGE, 2002, 4ª edição.
LEÓN, Zênia de. Pelotas, **Casarões Contam Sua História**. São Lourenço do Sul: Holfstätter, 1998, 2ª edição.
MARCHI, L. et alli. Fandango. **Homem, terra, música e cordas**. Curitiba: Olaria, 2002.
RIBEIRO, D. O Povo Brasileiro. **A Formação e o sentido do Brasil**. São Paulo: Companhia das Letras, 1995
ROSS, Jurandyr L. Sanches (org). **Geografia do Brasil**. São Paulo: Edusp, 2001, 4ª edição.
SACHET, Celestino. **Santa Catarina: 100 Anos de História**. Florianópolis: Século Catarinense, 1997 e 1998
WACHOWICZ, Ruy. **História do Paraná**. Curitiba: Imprensa Oficial do Paraná, 2000.

Updates
We recommend users to always check schedules, prices and other useful information. To keep updated and get further information, visit our site: www.horizontegeografico.com.br. Send us suggestions through letter, fax or e-mail:horizonte@horizontegeografico.com.br

Fauna

AMPHIBIANS

► Treefrog

(Hyla minuta)

It climbs trees when it is frightened. This is why it has suckers or adhesive disks on its feet. The *Hyla minuta* survives well in urban environments, provided there are plenty of trees and places in which to lay the eggs, such as leaves of trees and bushes growing over ponds. It eats insects, spiders and worms. It is common in eastern towns in Paraná and Rio Grande do Sul.

Interesting feature:

- Brazil has more than 200 species of treefrogs in the Hylidae family alone.

▲ Toad

(Bufo ictericus)

It is common in the Atlantic Forest, in the South and Southeast of Brazil.

It lives on fallen leaves in the middle of the forest, but can also be found in urban areas. The female can be up to 9 cm in length, while the male is approximately 15 cm, although it can be as long as 22.5 cm.

Interesting feature:

- The skin is poisonous, but it is unable to project or inject it. This poison is only harmful when it comes into contact with mucous membranes or wounds.

BIRDS

► Blue-and-Yellow Macaw

(Ara ararauna)

This macaw nests in rocky escarpments, cliff faces or holes in the trunks of tall trees. It is found in hyperseasonal savannas, *cerrado* woodlands, woods and the edges of forests in different parts of Brazil, as well as Central America, Bolivia and Paraguay. It lays from 2 to 4 eggs, which have an incubation period of 28 days. It lives on seeds, fruit, young stalks and plant roots.

Interesting features:

- Blue-and-yellow macaws mate for life.
- When trying to capture these birds, hunters frequently need to chop the trees down most of the times, this means killing their nestling.

◄ **Capybaras on the prairies of Lagoa do Peixe**

Neotropic Cormorant

(Phalacrocorax brasilianus)

An aquatic bird, the neotropic cormorant dives for fish and can remain underwater for a considerable period of time, coming up a good distance away, showing only its neck. The Neotropic cormorant is a relative of the pelican, but unlike it, this bird is black and smaller.

Interesting feature:

- The Neotropic cormorant nests in large rookeries together with herons and other river-dwelling birds. It undergoes certain changes during the incubation period, acquiring two plumes on its head and a few white feathers around its brow and the nape of its neck.

Black-necked swan

(Cygnus melanocoryphus)

It lives in lakes, marshes, swamps and other fresh or salt-water areas. It is found throughout Brazil but is regularly seen in flocks in Banhado do Taim in Rio Grande do Sul, and the mangrove swamps of Santa Catarina. It can vary from 102 to 124 cm in size and weigh from 3.5 to 6.7 kg. The young swan has grayish bills and feet. Later, the base of its bills and feet turns red. The female is smaller than the male and has a yellowish stripe near the eyes.

The black-necked swan feeds on aquatic plants, seeds and other plants, small insects and mollusks.

Interesting feature:

- Of the seven known species, this is the only one that lives in South America.

Magnificent Frigatebird

(Fregata magnificens)

It fishes close to the coast and near boats, snatching up leftovers from commercial fishing. It is among the lightest-boned of all birds in relation to its weight and is very flexible. It does not land on water as it becomes waterlogged quickly. It sleeps perched on branches and nests on coastal islands. The female has a white belly and long, forked-tail feathers.

Interesting features:

- Males are black, with red necks during the mating season.
- Fishermen sometimes playfully throw small fish to watch them catch the fish in mid-air.

► Great Egret

(Casmerodius albus)

The great egret has a yellow bill and long black legs. When it flies, it holds its neck back and its legs out straight, often making a low sound. It can be seen in swamps and estuaries, where it reproduces, lays eggs and completes part of its growth cycle, whether alone (when fishing), or in large flocks (especially during the mating season). It walks slowly in the shallow parts of lakes or stands almost immobile waiting for prey. It nests in bushes from July to December. Its wingspan can be up to 40 cm. It is up to 88 cm in length. It can be found from North America to the Magellan strait.

Interesting feature:

- It lives on aquatic insects and larvae, crabs, mollusks, amphibians (including toads), and reptiles. It sometimes eats snakes and wild guinea pigs.

► Azure Jay

(Cyanocorax caeruleus)

It is associated with pine trees because it may "plant" the seeds while carrying the pinecones during flight. It is rather solitary and rarely lands on the ground. It is predatory, since it eats the eggs and nestling of smaller birds. Within Brazil, it can be found from São Paulo to Rio Grande do Sul, always in regions of mild weather. It can be as large as 39 cm and have a robust appearance. Its head feathers are upright and it has dark eyes. The male and the female have the same color feathers.

Interesting features:

- The azure jay became the official bird emblem of Paraná.
- It is a disseminator of pine seeds in the pine groves in the South.

► White-Faced Whistling-Duck

(Dendrocygna viduata)

It lives in large flocks on lakes, marshes and rivers. It is found almost all over South America. However, sport hunting, which was legal until 1991, almost eliminated the species from the South of Brazil. This duck prefers the twilight. It likes rice, seeds and leaves, but also eats grubs, insect larvae and crustaceans. When it becomes an adult its face turns white, creating a kind of "mask."

Interesting features:

- Males sometimes help hatch eggs.
- They weigh from 500 to 800 g.
- They lay 4 to 13 eggs and the hatching period may last 26 to 28 days.

► Sanderling

(Calidris alba)

The sanderling is common on beaches in the South of Brazil, especially during the migration period from April to May, when it follows the changing seasons or migrates for mating reasons. It has a trim body, with long legs and talons.

Interesting feature:

- It does not have webbed feet, and has three front toes and one back one.

► Red-browed, Red-topped or Red-crowned Amazon Parrot

(Amazona rhodocorytha)

This parrot mates for life. If one dies, the other never mates again. They can be seen flying over seaside towns in Paranaguá Bay in Paraná, in the morning and afternoon. It is currently in danger of disappearing from forests. Hunters poach the baby birds, destroying nests and knocking down trees, although hunting and selling this bird is forbidden by law. In the wild, a parrot can live to 35 years of age.

Interesting feature:

- There are 11 catalogued Brazilian species of parrots, which can imitate the human voice very well.

◄ Vinaceous Parrot

(Amazona vinacea)

The vinaceous parrot lives in forests and pine groves in the countryside in the south of Rio Grande do Sul, the west of Paraguay and northeastern Argentina. It looks for holes in tree trunks (hollows) and splits in decomposing trucks. It moves slowly, which helps it to go unnoticed in forests. It feeds on fruits and seeds. It can live until 30 years of age.

Interesting feature:

- Its breast and part of its neck are purplish.
- It flies in flocks.

▲ Brazilian Teal

(Amazonetta brasiliensis)

It has blood-red feet and two white marks on its wings (visible in flight). The male of the species has a red bill, while the female has a bluish bill. It has two types of plumage, one during the mating season (more eye-catching) and another for the rest of the year (called eclipse plumage). It lays its eggs in nests built in tufts of grass in flooded areas.

Interesting features:

- Teal couples care for their nests together, protecting them from predators and from other couples that are looking for a place to mate.
- Whenever a predator approaches a nest, the female gets away making sounds and flapping like a wounded bird to draw attention.

► Red-Winged Tinamou

(Rhynchotus rufescens)

It walks on the ground, where it builds its nests and lays its eggs, which are generally 6 to 9 cm long and violet-brown. Shortly thereafter, the female chirps insistently to call the male to sit on the eggs. It lives in fields, pastures and *cerrado* woodlands. It is common in the Aparados da Serra region. It has previously been abundant in large areas, although it is now disappearing due to hunting and the use of insecticides. Its meat is considered very tasty.

Interesting features:

- Males are bigger and heavier than females, and their head is larger.
- During their first year, they live on insects. However, with time they begin living only on vegetables.

► Red-Breasted Toucan

(Ramphastos dicolorus)

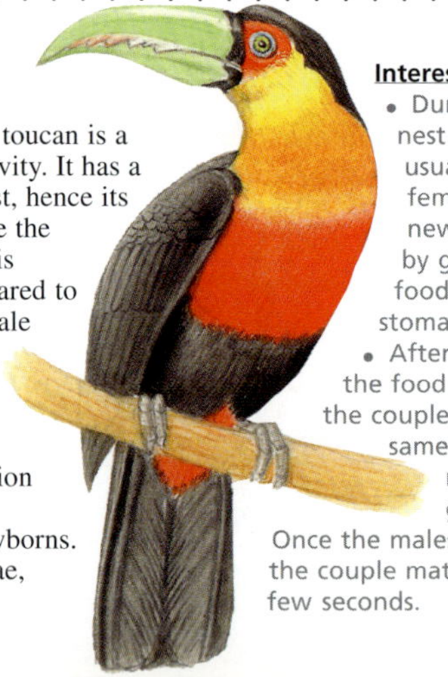

Today the red-breasted toucan is a rare bird living in captivity. It has a green bill and red breast, hence its name. This species, like the channel-billed toucan, is considered small compared to other toucans. The female lays 2 to 4 eggs, which hatch after 18 days of incubation. It spends most of the time in the nest during the incubation period, while the male generally feeds the newborns. It feeds the young larvae, insects and soft fruits.

Interesting features:

- During mating and nest building, males usually offer food to females: either a newly picked fruit or by gushing back the food they have in their stomachs.
- After females accept the food the males offer, the couple stands on the same perch some meters from the ground.

Once the males are accepted, the couple mates and this lasts few seconds.

MAMMALS

► Brazilian Tapir

(Tapirus terrestris)
It is the largest Brazilian mammal and can reach up to 2 meters in length and weigh up to 250 kg. Its fur is short and soft. Its mane has long and dark hair that goes from the forehead to the shoulder. The paws have three toes each. It has excellent smelling and hearing. It eats fruit, leaves, stalks, shoots, grass, aquatic plants and the bark of trees. It hides in the forest during the day, coming out to eat at night. It bathes frequently in mud and fresh water to rid itself of parasites. As it is silent, it is rarely seen.

Interesting feature:
- The tapir is only accompanied by other individual of its species during the mating season and when its offspring are suckling.

▲ Southern Right Whale

(Eubalaena australis)
This mammal can grow up to 18 m in length and weigh as much as 40 tons. It is very docile and usually swims near the shore,which is why it has been frequently hunted in the past. It is different from other whale species as its body is completely black, with the exception of a white mark on its stomach and yellowy-white “warts” on its head. The “warts” differ from one whale to another, enabling them to be identified. In its immense mouth, it has numerous baleen plates (more than 600 in the upper jaw) instead of teeth.

Interesting feature:
- It spends the summer in the Antarctic, where it feeds on small crustaceans.

► Brown Howler Monkey

(Alouatta fusca)
This is one of the three species of primates found in Rio Grande do Sul. It lives in the region around the city of Porto Alegre, but is now endangered due to hunting and particularly the destruction of its habitat – native forests. It eats fruit, tender leaves, shoots and small insects when it can catch them. It normally lives in groups and has one baby per year. It weighs from 5 to 10 kg.

Interesting features:
- Its cranial hyoid is well developed and acts as a sound box. It makes high-pitched sounds that can be heard from as far as 5 km.
- Its forefinger is separated from its middle finger, which makes it easier to travel from branch to branch.

Crab-Eating Fox

(Cerdocyon thous)

Known in the region of Aparados da Serra and Serra Geral as "*guaxaim,*" crab-eating foxes can be seen along roadsides, where they look for the remains of animals which have been run over and are often run over themselves for this reason. They are only seen in pairs during the mating season. They feed on small birds, fruits, insects, river crabs, eggs and small rodents. They weigh from 5 to 8 kg, and are approximately 65 cm in length. They have furry tails about 30 cm long and long muzzles (they are mistaken for European foxes). They live in forests, *cerrado* woodlands and fields, as well as areas of human activity.

Interesting feature:

- The crab-eating fox is also known as a "*furão*" in Portuguese.

Capybara

(Hydrochoerus hydrochoeris)

From head to body, they have 75 to 100 cm. They may weigh 27 to 79 kg. Capybaras live in herds and have nocturnal habits in flooded regions in the South of Brazil, especially around the Iguaçu National Park. Herds always follow the same paths, walking single-filed, each with its head over the hindquarters of the one in front. They sit like dogs and move slowly on the ground. For this reason, never wander far from rivers or lakes, where they live side by side with cattle, horses or even alligators (dangerous to their young). They have always been hunted for their meat, skin and oil.

Interesting features:

- Ancient indigenous tribes kept capybaras as pets.
- Their name (*capivara*) means "grass eater" in the native language Tupi-Guarani.
- The gestation period is from 149 to 156 days and it has four to six offspring. The offspring weigh 1.5 kg and are nursed for 16 weeks.

White-Eared Opossum

(Didelphis albiventris)

It is a marsupial about the size of a cat. It has a solid body, thick neck, long pointy muzzle, short limbs and a prehensile tail. It is a nocturnal animal and, in spite of its slow movements, climbs trees easily, using its tail to grab branches. It feeds on wild fruits, eggs and baby birds. It has 18 incisors, while other mammals have a maximum of 12.

Interesting features:

- The teats are located inside the female's pouch and feed from 10 to 18 newly-born offspring, which are little more than 1 cm in length.
- When it is followed, it plays dead or excretes a foul-smelling liquid produced by its axillary glands.

▼ South American Sea Lion

(Otaria byronia)

The only colony of this species in Brazil lives on the coast of the state of Rio Grande do Sul on Lobos Island, which was made an ecological reserve in 1982. The males can reach up to 3 m in length and weigh 300 kg, while females can grow up to 2 m long and weigh as much as 160 kg. Their limbs are flat and adapted for swimming. However, the hind limbs may turn to look to the front, like the limbs of a land mammal, which enables them to walk. Males are darker and stockier, with a prominent "mane" of long fur, which begins to develop when they are five years of age. They feed on mollusks, octopuses, squid and crustaceans.

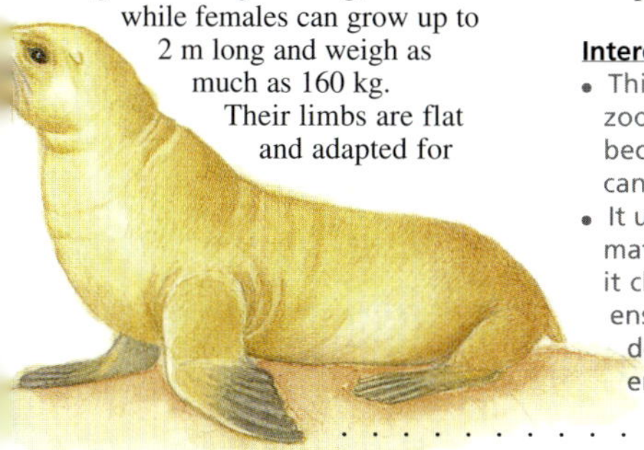

Interesting features:

- This species is very popular at zoos, aquatic parks, and circuses because it is very easy to tame and can be taught drills and acrobatics.
- It usually leaves the sea for the mating season when it changes its fur. This fact ensures its mating, since it does not depend on occasional encounters in the sea.

► Black-Faced Lion Tamarin

(Leontopithecus caissara)

Black-faced lion tamarins were discovered in 1990. Until today they have only been observed on Superagüi Island, and their population is estimated at around 300 to 400 individuals. They live in families or small groups and spend the night in hollow trees, which may be an ecological restriction for the species. They have diurnal habits and sleep all through the night, in old nests or hollow trees, recommencing their activities right after sunrise, when they begin looking for food. They are a bit smaller than a squirrel and have a mane all around their head. They use their claws to dig for food, roots, and insects.

Interesting feature:

- There are four types of lion tamarins in the Atlantic Forest, all of which are endangered since their natural habitat is being destroyed and they are captured to be later sold.

► Eastern Cougar or Puma

(Felis concolor)

It is found in North America as well as in South America. Adults, a bit smaller than leopards, have a uniformly colored fur that, depending on their habitat, may be rusty or grayish yellow. It is a solitary predator and can be up to 75 cm tall, 1.20 m long, with a tail of 60 cm. An adult male can weigh up to 50 kg. They have a small, round head, slender body, thick neck, large eyes and long whiskers.

Interesting features:

- The eastern cougar has five toes on its front paws and four on its hind paws.
- Cubs feed on their mother's milk during twelve weeks or longer, but they start eating meat when they are one and a half months old.

▲ Coatimundi

(Nasua nasua)

They are 41 to 67 cm tall, with a 32 to 69 cm long tail. They have a long snout and their tail has dark rings. They weigh about 11 kg. Coatimundis are social animals, living in large groups in protected areas in the South of Brazil, such as the Vila Velha State Park. They are mostly active during the day. Although they are carnivorous, they can live on fruit alone when there is an abundant supply. They use their long flexible muzzles to investigate holes and cracks when searching for food. Their young remain in their nests until they are two to three weeks old. They are solitary animals, but can be found in groups.

Interesting features:

- They are hunted on account of the meat, even by using dogs trained to catch them
- Females separate from their groups to build their homes on trees.

► White-Lipped Peccary

(Tayassu pecari)

This is the largest wild pig species in Brazil, measuring from 40 to 50 cm, though it can reach up to 1 m long from head to tail. It lives in large herds of 50 to 100 individuals and is more active at night. The white-lipped peccary eats everything, although it prefers fruit, seeds and roots.

Interesting features:

- It has a gland on its back to release a fluid that it rubs on tree trunks. This fluid has a very strong smell.
- It grates its teeth to scare predators away and to warn the other members in its group about danger.

▲ La Plata Dolphin

(Pontoporia blainvillei)

La Plata dolphins are less than 2 m in length and weigh an average of 50 kg. They are common in the South of Rio Grande do Sul, not far from the coast. In addition to inhabiting the River Plate estuary, there are reports of these dolphins in the Lagoa dos Patos estuary in Rio Grande do Sul. They are easily identified by their small size, long nose and ochre-brown coloring that is lighter around the stomach. They are found alone or in groups of up to 5 individuals. They are slow cetaceans, normally not going faster than 10 km per hour. They feed on mollusks, squid, octopuses, prawns and fish.

Interesting feature:

- This is an endangered species, as the dolphins die in fishing nets.

▲ Collared Anteater

(Tamandua tetradactyla)

The anteater, also known as the southern tamandua, lives in forests. Its head and body can be from 47 to 77 cm long, the same length of its tail. Just like any other anteater, it feeds on insects, especially termites. It is a solitary animal and only pairs during the mating season. Its fur is short and thick, and it can be varied in color. It gives birth to a single baby, which the female carries on its back. Its sense of smell helps it locate insects. It uses its long tongue covered in sticky saliva to capture them.

Interesting features:

- A part of its stomach, like chicken gizzards, grinds its food.
- When irritated, the anteater stands on its hind legs and defends itself with the claws on its front paws.

FISH

▲ Bluefish

(Pomatomus saltator)

The bluefish is found in the three oceans, in tropical and mild areas. It lives near the shore and in the open sea. It can also be found in bays and estuaries, though it prefers troubled waters. Its body is dark, with its side and back of a greenish blue, and a dark tail fin. The rest of the fins is light colored and has a dark stain on the basis of the pectoral fin. It may reach up to 1 m in length and weigh up to 12 kg.

Interesting features:

- It is a voracious predator of sardines and shellfish.
- It is very hard to catch since it is very fast and does not surrender easily. That is why very long fishing lines are needed.

► Lambari

(Astianax spp.)

It is a small fish with sharp, serrated teeth. It survives well in almost all rivers, lakes and dams. The largest species are called two-spot tetra (*Astyanax bimaculatus*).

Interesting feature:

- They are known among fishermen for their ability to quickly steal bait.

► Mullet

(Mugil platanus)

The mullet is born in freshwater, spends some time in salt waters, and then leaves to the sea. It lives near rocky shores, sandy beaches and swamps, where it feeds mainly on algae. On very sunny days, the mullet is easily found in the shadows of swamp trees. Mullet fishing is an important activity in the South of Brazil, especially in Santa Catarina.

Interesting feature:

- In the southern coast, mullets form large shoals at the end of winter, when they get ready to lay their eggs. At this time they provide their highly appreciated eggs, which are breaded and fried or cooked in broth in most restaurants.

► Wolf Fish

(Hoplias malabaricus)

This is the most well-known fish in South America, and is very popular in sport fishing in the South. It is found in almost all waters, although it prefers still waters of average depth. It is a voracious predator and stays on the lookout for smaller fish, toads and insects.

Interesting feature:

- Although it has many bones, it is considered very tasty.

MOLLUSKS

► Mussel

(Mytilus)

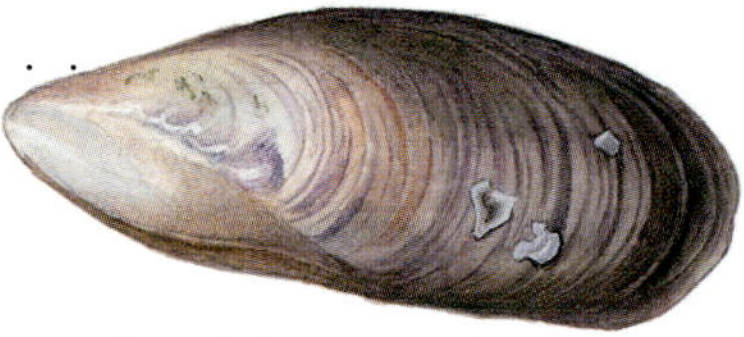

The Azorean colonization of Santa Catarina was responsible for introducing the mussel into local cuisine. The "seeds," or young mussels, are extracted from rocky regions, but can also be cultivated on long ropes tied to rafts anchored in protected areas. Females can lay 20 million eggs. The larvae feed themselves in the water for approximately 21 days, and reach the first stage of maturity after 5 to 8 months.

Interesting feature:

- Mussels attach themselves to walls and can grow up to 8 cm long.

▲ Oyster

(Ostrea edulis)

Oysters live in the sea and are widely consumed. The valves of oysters have different sizes and are not perfectly juxtaposed. The two valves are united by a ligament, which is a kind of hinge joint. When they are young, oysters have feet that allow them to move around, in addition to two adductor muscles to close their shells. As they develop, they lose their feet and one of the adductor muscles. They feed on organic matter dissolved in water and microscopic creatures that are a part of the marine plankton.

Interesting feature:

- There are three species of oysters: swamp oysters, rock oysters, and sea bottom oysters. The latter are the largest ones but they are not as tasty as rock oysters.

REPTILES

► Rattlesnake

(Crotalus durissus)
It is up to 1.80 long. This is the only snake whose tail ends in a small bell consisting of 8 to 20 horny rings which, when shaken, produce a rattling sound. It produces a deadly poison that affects the nervous system, making it difficult for victims to move and breathe.

Interesting features:

- It is slow and usually stays curled up basking in the sun for hours. Whenever man or large animals come near, it shakes its rattle.
- An antidote serum is made especially to treat rattlesnake bites.

▲ Pit Viper

(Bothrops jararaca)
The pit viper is venomous. It is, on average, 1.20 m long and is well camouflaged, making it difficult to spot. Adult vipers feed on small rodents.

Interesting features:

- The pit viper is the most common species in Brazil and can reach 1.60 m in length.
- The pit viper's young have light or yellow tips on their tails. They use this tip to attract small frogs and toads, as well as small lizards on which they feed.
- It is viviparous, that is, it does not lay eggs but gives birth to their offspring, which generally occurs in the beginning of the rainy season.

▼ Black and White Tegus

(Tupinambis merianae)
It is one of the most common lizards in Brazil. It is found in almost all the Brazilian and South American ecosystems. It can reach up to 1.4 m in length. It has black, light gray and white stripes, its abdomen is whitish with black cross-wise stripes. The black and white tegus can be very aggressive, and must be handled carefully to avoid bites.

It is oviparous, and lays approximately 30 eggs, which are incubated for a period of 90 days. It has a long, pointy head, strong jaws with many small sharp teeth, a long, forked pink tongue and a long rounded tail. Its offspring are a greenish color, which fades as they grow.

Interesting features:

- It is found in all of the southern states of Brazil, especially in reserves.
- When threatened it can stay very still in an attempt to camouflage itself or run noisily away.

FLORA

► Açoita-cavalo*

(Luehea divaricata)

Also known in Portuguese as the *pau-de-canga* or *ibatingui*, this tree can grow up to 25 m high and 60 cm in diameter. It is found from the south of the state of Bahia down to the alluvial forests in the southern state of Rio Grande do Sul. It is widely used in the manufacturing of curved furniture, trims, the butts of guns and shoe heels as its wood is extremely flexible. It grows quickly and is appropriate for mixed reforestation of degraded conservation areas.

Interesting feature:

- This tree's uniform crown and discrete flowers in November and December make it ideal for landscaping in general.

◄ Angico-rosa*

(Parapiptadenia rigida)

It grows exclusively in the forests along the basins of the Parana and Uruguay rivers and their tributaries up to altitudes of 800 m. It is very common in the three southernmost states of Brazil, where it can also be found in pine forests. The angico-rosa can grow up to 30 m high and 110 cm in diameter, and its wood is very heavy, durable and resistant. Its bark is rich in tannin.

Interesting feature:

- The flowers of the angico-rosa produce honey.

► Strawberry Guava

(Psidium cattleianum)

It grows best in pluvial areas of the Atlantic Forest, and is found from the states of Bahia to Rio Grande do Sul. It has red or yellow fruits, popular among both humans and birds. Its trunk is smooth and it grows no more than 6 m high and 25 cm in diameter. The wood of this tree is heavy, flexible and durable.

Interesting features:

- This tree is common in domestic orchards.
- It flowers from June to December.
- Its fruit may be picked from the end of September until March.

◄ Laelia purpurata, the flower is the symbol of Santa Catarina

► Araticum-cagão*

(Annona cacans)

It grows in forests at altitudes higher than 300 m in the states of Minas Gerais and Rio de Janeiro and as far south as Rio Grande do Sul. It can grow up to 16 m high and 70 cm in diameter. Its wood is light and easy to work with, but not very resistant or durable. It is used to make toys and veneers. It in an ornamental tree, were it not for its enormous fruits which could hurt someone when they fall.

Interesting feature:

- The fruit of this tree is used as a laxative when ingested in large quantities.

► Parana Pine

(Araucaria angustifolia)

It is common in the state of Paraná, though also present from the states of Minas Gerais and Rio de Janeiro to Rio Grande do Sul. It can grow up to 50 m high and 180 cm in diameter. The wood of this tree is light and not very durable when exposed to the elements, and is used in toys, matchsticks, broom handles and frames. Its fruit, the pine seed, is always served at *festas juninas* or June celebrations in the South of the country. Birds also feed on pine seeds, and the Azure Jay is one of the tree's main disseminators, as it buries the seeds in the ground to eat later. The tree is widely used in urban landscaping.

Interesting feature:

- There is great interest for the parana pine in the South of Brazil for its wood and in the production of cellulose pulp.

*No common name in English

◄ Brazilian Pepper-Tree

(Achinus terebinthifolius)

Also known as the christmasberry tree, it grows no more than 10 m high and 60 cm in diameter. It can be found from the states of Pernambuco to Mato Grosso do Sul and Rio Grande do Sul. Its wood is soft, but resistant and very durable, and for this reason is used in stakes and supports and as firewood. It is appropriate for planting along narrow streets and its wood is suitable for lampposts.

Interesting feature:

- Some people are allergic to its leaves. Its flowers produce honey.

► Bacupari*

(Garcinia gardneriana)

This tree grows from the Amazon all the way down to the state of Rio Grande do Sul, and has a variety of common names in Portuguese, such as *remelento*, *bacuri-miúdo* and *mangostão-amarelo*. It can grow up to 7 m high and 25 cm in diameter. Its wood is light and is used in tool handles. Its fruit is tasty, although not very fleshy.

Interesting feature:

- The Bacupari produces more fruit outside of forests.It handles direct sunlight well in open areas and produces fruit from an early stage in its development.

◄ Pindo, Jelly or Wine Palm

(Butia capitata)

It is found along the coast of southern Brazil. It can grow up to 6 m high and 30 cm in diameter. Its heavy, hard and very fibrous wood is used in rural buildings. Its fruit is widely consumed, whether as nuts or as liqueurs, wines and oils. Its leaves are used in hats, baskets and ropes, and as filling in mattresses and upholstery.

Interesting feature:

- It grows in homogeneous groups in the highlands of Santa Catarina.

◄ Cambuim*

(Myrciaria tenella)

It grows mainly in wet or swampy soil along the banks of rivers and in land depressions in pine forests, around the edges of forests and in isolated clumps of trees. Its wood is compact, flexible and resistant.It grows no more than 6 m high and 30 cm in diameter. Its fruit, which ripens between January and March, attract birds.

Interesting feature:

- This tree's annual production of viable seeds is large, as birds adore its fruits.

► Kereti Silverballi

(Ocotea puberula)

It grows in almost all types of forest and is found from the states of Rio de Janeiro, Minas Gerais and Mato Grosso do Sul down to Rio Grande do Sul. It can grow up to 25 m high and 60 cm in diameter. Its wood is light and soft, and is used to make simple furniture and boxes. It has an abundance of fruit, which birds love, and is thus suitable for the mixed reforestation of degraded conservation areas.

Interesting feature:

- This tree has a large annual production of viable seeds, which are dispersed by birds.

► Canela sassafrás*

(Ocotea odorifera)

Also known in Portuguese as *casca-cheirosa* and *louro-cheiroso*, this tree can grow up to 25 m high and 70 cm in diameter. It is found from the south of the state of Bahia to Rio Grande do Sul in pluvial areas of the Atlantic Forest. It is common in pine forests in the states of Paraná, Santa Catarina and Rio Grande do Sul. Its wood is soft, but not very resistant to rot, and is used for decorative lining, packaging and frames. It is suitable for urban landscaping.

Interesting features:

- It is very leafy and provides excellent shade.
- In high altitude environments, it grows no more than 10 m high and has a very rounded crown.

*No common name in English

◄ Canjerana*

(Cabralea canjerana)

It can be found in the states of Minas Gerais, Mato Grosso do Sul and even Rio Grande do Sul. This tree grows well in wet clayey soils on slopes, reaching 30 m in height and 120 cm in diameter. Its wood is easy to work with, very resistant to insects and damp, and is popular among sculptors. Its fruits attract birds, especially from August to November.

Interesting features:

- It flowers more than once a year.
- It is better suited to the wet clayey soils of slopes.

► Caroba*

(Jacaranda micrantha)

It grows from the states of Minas Gerais to Rio Grande do Sul, in the forests of the upper Uruguay and the basin of the Parana River. Its wood is light, easy to work with, but not very resistant to moisture. It is used in musical instruments and for other cabinetmaking and carpentry purposes. It flowers considerably from October to December.

Interesting features:

- It grows quickly in wet, fertile soils.
- It produces a large quantity of viable seeds annually.

◄ Roupala

(Roupala brasiliensis)

It is known as *carvalho-brasileiro* in Paraná, *canjica* in São Paulo, *tucajé* in Rio de Janeiro and *pau-de-concha* in Bahia. It flowers at different times throughout the year. It survives well in the pluvial forest of the Atlantic plains and slopes, and can grow up to 25 m high and 70 cm in diameter. Its wood is similar to that of the European oak: it is hard and heavy.

Interesting feature:

- Its wood is very durable when immersed in salt water, and popular in the shipbuilding industry.

Catiguá*

(Trichilia claussenii)

Also known as the *quebra-machado* ("axe breaker"), the *Trichilia claussenii* grows from the states of Minas Gerais and Mato Grosso do Sul to Rio Grande do Sul. It can grow up to 12 m high and its hollow trunk can reach 30 cm in diameter. It flowers from August to October and its fruits are well liked by birds. Its wood is used for light cabinetmaking work.

Interesting feature:

- It produces a large quantity of viable seeds annually, which are disseminated by birds.

Caxeta*

(Simarouba amara)

It can grow up to 20 m high and 80 cm in diameter. Its wood splits easily and is prone to insect attacks. It is used to make toys and reels.

Interesting features:

- The wood of this tree is not resistant to moisture.
- It grows slowly when planted in open fields.

Cedro-rosa*

(Cedrela fissilis)

It is found all over Brazil, especially from the state of Rio Grande do Sul to Minas Gerais. It can grow up to 35 m high and 90 cm in diameter. Its wood is light, soft to cut and durable in dry environments. It rots when buried or submerged in water. It is used to make chipboard, door and window frames and furniture, and is employed in civil construction. It is common in parks and gardens, and in the heterogeneous reforestation of degraded areas.

Interesting feature:

- It should never be planted in homogeneous groups as it is prone to attack by borers.

*No common name in English

◄ Cerejeira-do-mato*

(Eugenia involucrata)

It is found from the state of Minas Gerais to Rio Grande do Sul. It is an ornamental tree, and can grow up to 8 m high (or 15 m in the forest) and 40 cm in diameter. It is suitable for planting along narrow streets. It produces delicious fruit from October to December and is eaten on its own as well as being used to make sweets, jams and liqueurs.

Interesting feature:

- It flowers from September to November.

► Yerba Mate

(Ilex paraguariensis)

It is common in the pine forests of Brazil's three southernmost states. It can grow up to 8 m high and 40 cm in diameter. Its wood is light, soft and not very durable, which limits its uses to box making and firewood. Its fruit is eaten by birds from January to March. Its leaves are used to make *mate* – the most popular tea in the country, which is exported all over the world.

Interesting feature:

- Its seeds are disseminated by birds, which feed on its fruit. The *Ilex paraguariensis* is an ornamental tree.

► Fig

(Ficus enormis)

It grows up to 20 m high and 180 cm in diameter. It has an enormous crown of thick leaves and is found mainly in the north of the state of Paraná. Its wood is soft, but not very resistant, which limits its uses to the insides of doors, light box-making and decorative panels. It is used for planting in rural areas and its fruit attracts bats and other animals in December and January.

Interesting features:

- Its trunk is knotted with thick roots.
- Its thick leaves provide excellent shade.

◄ Guabiroba*

(Campomanesia xanthocarpa)

It is found in Minas Gerais, São Paulo, Mato Grosso do Sul and even Rio Grande do Sul, in almost all plant compositions. It can grow up to 20 m high and 50 cm in diameter. Its wood is hard, compact and very durable, and is used to make musical instruments, tool handles and as firewood. Its fruits are high in vitamins and are eaten naturally and used to make liqueurs.

Interesting feature:

- This tree is suitable for landscaping in general sue to its dense, pyramid-shaped crown which is attractive to the eye.

► Guapuruvu*

(Schizolobium parahyba)

It is found in the state of Bahia, where it is known as *pau-de-vintém*, down to the state of Santa Catarina, and has an assortment of other common names. It can grow up to 30 m high and 80 cm in diameter. Its wood is light and soft, but is not very resistant.

Interesting features:

- It is unique to the Atlantic Forest.
- Its long branches are not resistant to the action of the wind. For this reason it should not be planted in areas where there is a lot of human activity.

► Helicônia*

(Heliconia brasiliensis)

It is a medium-sized bush. It can grow up 2 m high and thrives in hot, humid areas. It likes plenty of light. It may be grown indoors, and has bright red flowers.

Interesting feature:

- It does not like direct sunlight on its leaves. It flowers in the winter.

*No common name in English

Imbuya

(Ocotea porosa)

It grows in pine forests and is found in the three southernmost states of Brazil. It is also known as *embuia* in Portuguese and can grow up to 20 m high and 150 cm in diameter. Its wood is hard, varied in color and very durable. It is used in civil construction and luxury cabinetmaking. Its fruit is devoured by birds and its beauty makes it popular in landscaping projects.

Interesting feature:

- The town of Imbuia in Santa Catarina was named after this fruit.

Ipê-amarelo*

(Tabebuia alba)

It is very common in the states of Paraná, Rio Grande do Sul and Santa Catarina. It can grow up to 30 m high and 60 cm in diameter. Its wood is heavy, hard and very durable, even in unfavorable conditions. It is used in outdoor constructions for this reason. It is very beautiful and is popular in landscaping in the South of Brazil.

Interesting features:

- This tree is covered in large yellow flowers from July to September, when it loses practically all of its leaves.
- Its new leaves are renowned for their silvery color.

► Jabuticabeira*

(Plinia trunciflora)

It is found throughout most of Brazil. It thrives in pluvial areas of the Atlantic Forest and in high subforests. It can grow up to 15 m high and 45 cm in diameter. Its wood is used in civil construction and to make furniture. The *jaboticaba* fruit is used to make jams, sweets, liqueurs and even spirits. It can also be eaten as a fruit.

Interesting feature:

- Its flowers and fruits are attached to the stem. It flowers twice a year.

◄ Orchid

(Laélia Purpurata)

Considered one of the most beautiful Brazilian orchids, the *Laélia Purpurata* officially became the flower emblem of the state of Santa Catarina in December 1983. It was found growing abundantly in 1847 along the coast of the then province of Santa Catarina. It was exported to Belgium and England from the 1920s to the 1940s. It was also found from the states of São Paulo to Rio Grande do Sul.

Interesting feature:

- It flowers in November.

► Pinheiro-bravo*

(Podocarpus lambertii)

It grows in the states of Minas Gerais, Rio de Janeiro and down to Rio Grande do Sul in forests at high altitudes and pine forests. It can grow up to 14 m high and 60 cm in diameter. Its wood is not very resistant. It easily rots and is prone to termite attacks. Its fruit attracts a variety of bird species from February to May. It is suitable for use in the heterogeneous reforestation of degraded conservation areas.

Interesting feature:

- This tree is a good source of wood for pencils, pop-sticks and other articles of the genre.

*No common name in English

Red Brazil Cherry

(Eugenia uniflora)

It grows from Minas Gerais to Rio Grande do Sul, in the forest of the high plains and in the Parana River basin. It can grow up to 12 m high and 50 cm in diameter. From October to January, the tree is laden with fruit, called *pitangas*, which may be eaten as fruit or made into juices.

Interesting feature:

- Although it is an ornamental tree, it is not popular because of the mess made by its fruit when it falls, staining the ground red.

Sapopema*

(Sloanea monosperma)

It grows on hilltops and well-drained slopes, and is found from the states of Minas Gerais and Rio de Janeiro down to Rio Grande do Sul. It can grow up to 20 m high and 50 cm in diameter. Its wood is hard and is used to make beams, lathes, supports and tool handles.

Interesting feature:

- As this tree is very leafy, this tree is recommended for places which require shade.

◄ Tarumã*

(Vitex megapotamica)

It grows in pine forests from the states of Minas Gerais and Mato Grosso do Sul to Rio Grande do Sul. It can grow up to 20 m high and 60 cm in diameter. Its wood is hard and resistant even outdoors and for this reason it is used in exposed and hydraulic constructions. Its fruit is popular among monkeys and birds from January to March. It is suitable for urban planting and also mixed planting in degraded conservation areas, especially near rivers and dams.

Interesting feature:

- Its flowers produce honey. It grows no more than 12 m high when planted in isolation. It grows both in dry, rocky soil and in wet areas in gallery forests.

► Earpod Tree

(Enterolobium contortisiliquum)

It is most common is the forest of the Parana River basin, but it is also found in the states of Pará, Maranhão and Piauí, and as far down as Mato Grosso do Sul and Rio Grande do Sul. It can grow up to 35 m high and 160 cm in diameter. Its wood is light and soft to cut, and is used to make boats and canoes. As it grows quickly it is suitable for use in mixed reforestation of degraded conservation areas.

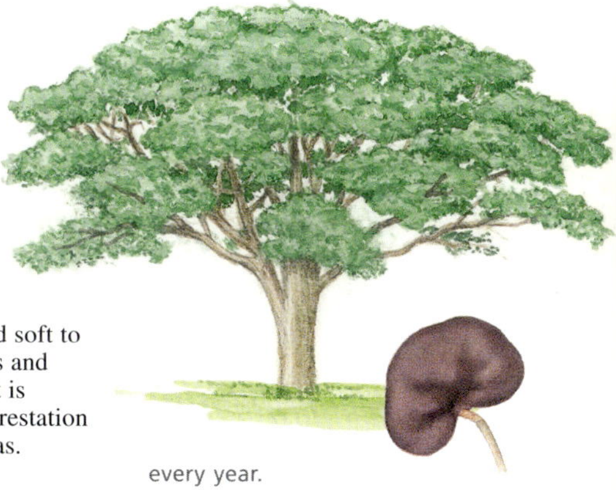

Interesting feature:

- It does not produce seeds every year. Its leafy crown provides excellent shade.

◄ Ombu

(Phytolacca dioica)

It is found in the states of Rio de Janeiro, Minas Gerais and Mato Grosso do Sul and down to Rio Grande do Sul. It can grow up to 25 m high and its trunk can be 160 cm in diameter. Its wood is light and very porous and is rarely used as it rots easily. Its fruit attracts birds from January to February.

Interesting feature:

- It is considered an indication of good land.

*No common name in English

CREDITS

T: top - **Tl:** top-left - **C:** center - **Cl:** center-left - **Cr:** center-right - **B:** bottom - **Bl:** bottom-left - **Br:** bottom-right

Legends of the opening photos
1T: Peter Milko/HG (Iguaçu, PR) – 1Cl: Renato Grimm (Fortaleza Canyon, RS) – 1Cr: Dado Galdieri/Fototeca (Corais Island, SC) – 1Bl: Iolita Cunha (Urussanga, SC) – 1Br: Iolita Cunha (Beto Carrero World, SC) – 6-7: Victor Andrade (Canela, RS) – 9: Christian Knepper (colonial coffee lunch, RS)

Legends of the final photos
298-299: Renato Grimm (Lagoa do Peixe, RS) – 303: Zig Koch (Marumbi, PR)

Cover
Zig Koch – Pine tree (PR): Verônica Dantas – Blumenau (SC): Peter Milko – Itaimbezinho - Aparados da Serra (RS)

Inside Cover
Zig Koch – Pine tree (PR): Peter Milko/HG – Cataratas do Iguaçu (PR): Zig Koch – Marumbi (PR): Christiane Ceneviva – Praia de Bombinhas (SC): Paulo Flores – Baleia-Franca (SC): Cacá Riva – Blumenau (SC): Renato Grimm – Cambará do Sul (RS): Renato Grimm – Missões (RS): Zig Koch – Lagoa do Peixe (RS)

Counter-cover
Renato Grimm – Rafting (RS): Renato Grimm – Bell (RS): Heitor Reali – Farol de Santa Marta (SC): Iolita Cunha – Grupo folclórico (SC): João Correia Filho – Prudentópolis (PR): Zig Koch – Jardim Botânico (PR): Zigh Koch – Lagoa do Peixe (RS)

Discovering the South
12-13: Zig Koch –14T: Peter Milko/HG – 14B: Eduardo Tavares – 15T: Zig Koch – 15B: Zig Koch – 17T: Renato Grimm – 17B: Eduardo Tavares – 18-19T: Zig Koch – 18B: Peter Milko/HG – 19B: Eduardo Tavares – 20B: Enrico Marone/Pulsar – 21T: Victor Andrade

Ecological Scenery
22-23: Peter Milko/HG – 24T: Delfim Martins/Pulsar – 25B: Peter Milko/HG – 26T: Zig Koch – 26B: Zig Koch – 27T: Zig Koch – 27B: Zig Koch – 28T: Marcos Amend – 28-29B: Zig Koch – 29T: Zig Koch – 30T: Zig Koch – 31T: Zig Koch – 31B: Zig Koch – 32T: Zig Koch – 32B: Zig Koch – 33T: Zig Koch – 33B: Zig Koch – 34T: Renato Grimm – 34-35B: Zig Koch – 35T: Renato Grimm

The Man in the South
36-37: Renato Grimm – 38T: Verônica Dantas – 38B: Zig Koch – 40T: Renato Grimm – 41B: Mauro Goulart – 42B: Eduardo Tavares – 44T: Egberto Nogueira/Peixes – 45B: Pinacoteca Municipal de São Paulo/Reminiscências – 46B: Instituto Histórico e Geográfico Brasileiro/Reminiscências – 47T: Iconographia – 47B: Arquivo Histórico do Exército/Reminiscências – 48T: Iolita Cunha – 48B: Iolita Cunha – 49T: Zig Koch – 49B: Renato Grimm – 50B: Renato Grimm – 51T: Zig Koch – 51B: Zig Koch

Paraná
54-55: Zig Koch – 58T: Zig Koch – 59B: Nani Góis/Paraná Turismo – 62T: Zig Koch – 63T: Zig Koch – 63B: Zig Koch – 64B: Christian Knepper – 65T: Reprodução – 66/67T: Nelson Kon – 67B: Zig Koch – 68T: Zig Koch – 68B: Zig Koch – 69T: Zig Koch – 70T: Zig Koch – 70B: Fabrício Brasiliense – 71T: Zig Koch – 72T: Nani Góis/Paraná Turismo – 73Cr: Zig Koch – 74T: Leonardo Papini/HG – 75B: Zig Koch – 76/77: Zig Koch – 78B: Peter Milko/HG – 79T: Zig Koch – 79B: Leonardo Papini/HG – 80T: Zig Koch – 80/81B: Zig Koch – 81T: Zig Koch – 82T: Zig Koch – 82B: Zig Koch – 83T: Acervo Fundação O Boticário – 83B: Acervo Fundação O Boticário – 84T: Zig Koch – 84B: Peter Milko/HG – 85C: Zig Koch – 86/87: Leonardo Papini – 88/89T: Zig Koch – 88B: Leonardo Papini – 90T: Zig Koch – 90B: Divulgação – 91T: Zig Koch – 91B: Zig Koch – 92C: Monalisa Lins/AE – 93T: Zig Koch – 93B: Celso Junior/AE – 94T: Fabrício Brasiliense – 95T: Zig Koch – 95B: Fabrício Brasiliense – 96T: Zig Koch – 96B: Peter Milko/HG – 97T: João Correia Filho – 98T: Zig Koch – 98/99B: Peter Milko/HG – 99T: Olaria/Zig Koch – 100T: Zig Koch – 100B: Peter Milko/HG – 102T: João Correia Filho – 102B: João Correia Filho – 103T: Zig Koch – 104: João Correia Filho – 105B: João Correia Filho – 106T: Zig Koch – 106B: Christiane Ceneviva – 107B: Christiane Ceneviva – 108B: Zig Koch – 109: Zig Koch

Santa Catarina
110/111: Christiane Ceneviva – 114T: Christian Knepper – 114B: Christian Knepper – 116T: Christian Knepper – 116B: Eduardo Tavares – 117B: Eduardo Tavares – 117B: Juca Martins/Pulsar – 118T: Christiane Ceneviva – 119T: Christian Knepper – 119B: David Santos Júnior – 120/121: Christian Knepper – 122T: Christian Knepper – 122B: Christian Knepper – 123T: David Santos Júnior – 123B: Christian Knepper – 124/125T: Iolita Cunha – 124B: Rogério Monteiro – 125B: Eduardo Tavares – 126T: Zig Koch – 126/127B: Iolita Cunha – 128T: Caca Riva – 128B: Verônica Dantas – 129B: Iolita Cunha – 130T: Caca Riva – 130B: Caca Riva – 131T: Iolita Cunha – 131B: Caca Riva – 132Cl: Iolita Cunha – 132/133B: Iolita Cunha – 134T: Iolita Cunha – 134B: Iolita Cunha – 135T: Edson Sato/Pulsar – 135B: Iolita Cunha – 136T: Leonardo Papini – 136B: Caca Riva – 137T: Henrique Raizler/Photomundi – 138B: Leonardo Papini – 139T: Caca Riva – 139B: Caca Riva – 140T: Iolita Cunha – 141T: Iolita Cunha – 141B: Eduardo Tavares – 142T: Iolita Cunha – 142B: Iolita Cunha – 143T: Iolita Cunha – 145: Juca Martins/Pulsar – 146T: Iolita Cunha – 147B: Iolita Cunha – 148T: Iolita Cunha – 148B: Eduardo Tavares – 149T: Iolita Cunha – 149Cr: Iolita Cunha – 150T: Iolita Cunha – 150B: Iolita Cunha – 151C: Iolita Cunha – 152T: Iolita Cunha – 153T: Reprodução – 153B: Iolita Cunha – 154T: Iolita Cunha – 154B: Egberto Nogueira/Peixes – 155T: Egberto Nogueira/Peixes – 156T: Enrico Marone/Pulsar – 156B: Monica Canejo – 157Cr: Iolita Cunha – 158/159: Monica Canejo – 160/161T: Monica Canejo – 160B: Verônica Dantas – 161B: Monica Canejo – 162T: Iolita Cunha – 163T: Iolita Cunha – 163B: Verônica Dantas – 164/165: Roberto Scola/ARBS – 166B: Iolita Cunha – 167T: Verônica Dantas – 167Cr: Iolita Cunha – 168T: Iolita Cunha – 168B: Iolita Cunha – 169T: Iolita Cunha – 169B: Verônica Dantas – 170/171B: Verônica Dantas – 170T: Iolita Cunha.

Rio Grande do Sul
172/173: Renato Grimm – 176T: Renato Grimm – 178T: Renato Grimm – 178B: Renato Grimm – 179T: Renato Grimm – 179B: Delfim Martins/Pulsar – 180Bl: ARBS/AE – 180Br: Paulo Pinto/AE – 181T: Renato Grimm – 181B: Renato Grimm – 182B: Renato Grimm – 183T: Renato Grimm – 183B: Renato Grimm – 184/185: Renato Grimm – 186C: Renato Grimm – 187T: Renato Grimm – 187B: Eduardo Tavares – 188T: Renato Grimm – 188B: Rosângela Rezende – 189T: Renato Grimm – 189B: Renato Grimm – 190T: Delfim Martins/Pulsar – 190B: Renato Grimm – 191T: Renato Grimm – 191B: Rosângela Rezende – 192T: Renato Grimm – 193B: Renato Grimm – 194B: Renato Grimm – 195T: Renato Grimm – 195B: Renato Grimm – 196T: Renato Grimm – 196B: Renato Grimm – 197T: Renato Grimm – 198B: Renato Grimm – 199T: ARBS – 200T: Renato Grimm – 201B: Renato Grimm – 202/203: Rosângela Rezende – 204T: Renato Grimm – 204/205B: Victor Andrade – 205T: Renato Grimm – 206T: Renato Grim – 206B: Renato Grimm – 207T: Renato Grimm – 208T: Daniel Augusto Jr./Pulsar – 208B: Victor Andrade – 209T: Eduardo Tavares – 209B: Mauricio Simonetti/Pulsar – 210Tl: Rosângela Rezende – 210B: Victor Andrade – 210/211T: Roberto Cosulich/Fototeca – 211B: Victor Andrade – 212B: Victor Andrade – 213T: Rosângela Rezende – 213Cr: Victor Andrade – 214T: Renato Grimm – 215T: Zig Koch – 215Cl: Renato Grimm – 215Cr: Renato Grimm – 215Bl: Zig Koch – 215Br: Renato Grimm – 216/217: Renato Grimm – 218T: Heitor Reali – 218B: Zig Koch – 219C: Heitor Reali – 220T: Renato Grimm – 220B: Renato Grimm – 221T: Renato Grimm – 221B: Renato Grimm – 222T: Renato Grimm – 222B: Henrique Raizler/Photomundi – 223B: Henrique Raizler/Photomundi – 224T: Renato Grimm – 225T: Renato Grimm – 225B: Renato Grimm – 226/227: Renato Grimm – 228B: Henrique Raizler/Photomundi – 229T: Renato Grimm – 230T: Henrique Raizler/Photomundi – 230B: Henrique Raizler/Photomundi – 231T: Henrique Raizler/Photomundi – 231B: Renato Grimm – 232T: Renato Grimm – 232/233B: Renato Grimm – 233T: Rosângela Rezende – 234T: Mauricio Simonetti/Pulsar – 235T: Peter Milko/HG – 235B: Peter Milko/HG – 236/237B: Eduardo Tavares – 237T: Renato Grimm – 238T: Henrique Raizler/Photomundi – 239T: Renato Grimm – 239B: Renato Grimm – 240T: Renato Grimm – 241Cr: Renato Grimm.

Fauna and Flora
270/271: Renato Grimm – 284/285: J. Roberto Ciolini/Arts&Photos

Index

Cities

Paraná

Santa Catarina

Rio Grande do Sul

ACKNOWLEDGEMENTS

Antônio Albani, Laerte Domingos e Marlene Montebeller – Zoobotânico Brusque (SC)
Cícero Rohr – Master Comunicação, Curitiba (PR)
Décio Favretto – Tourism Bureau Rio das Antas, Bento Gonçalves (RS)
Eduardo Veras – Zero Hora newspaper (RS)
Ernesto da Silva Neto – Portal Turístico, Laguna (SC)
Guadalupe Vivekananda – Superagüi National Park (PR)
Ibraim Segalla – Itupava Inn, Morretes (PR)
Jean Pierre Perrot e Ana Aveline – Ecotourism Caá-etê (RS)
José Aurélio Cauit – Salto Morato (PR)
Liane Ingberman – O Boticário Foundation (PR)
Luís Francisco Doege – Pegorini Hotel, Lages (SC)
Luiz Everton Fischer – Fischer Inn, Ingleses Beach (SC)
Márcia Alflen – Promotur, Joinville (SC)
Márcia Ferronato e Nestor de Carli – Hotel, Restaurant, Bar Union in the Grape and Wine Region (RS)
Marco Aurélio de Souza – Porto União (SC)
Reginaldo Cândido – Sol Hotel, Balneário Camboriú (SC)
Rubem e Ieda Schreiber – Residencial Hotel, Caçapava do Sul (RS)
Sandra Klahr e Andressa Oppitz – Canela Tourist Information Center (RS)
Sérgio Luiz Sabel – Blumenau Tourism Bureau (SC)
Stella Paiva – Porto Alegre Convention & Visitors Bureau (RS)
Tarcísio Michelon – Dall Onder Hotel, Bento Gonçalves (RS)
Vânia Antunes, Timotheo Machado, Dóris Bethge and Cristine Dilly – Porto Alegre Tourism (RS)
Vivien Vanessa Volkmann – Pomerode Tourism Bureau (SC)
Yvonne Solheid e Zelinda do Rosário – Curitiba Tourism Bureau (PR)

Dados Internacionais para Catalogação na Publicação (CIP)
do Departamento Nacional do Livro

P554 Philips Guides: The South: Brazil 2003. – Rio de Janeiro: Horizonte Geográfico, 2003.
305 pp; 11,5 x 21,5 cm.

ISBN: 85-88031-14-0

1. Brasil, Sul – Descrições e viagens – Guias.

CDD: 918.16

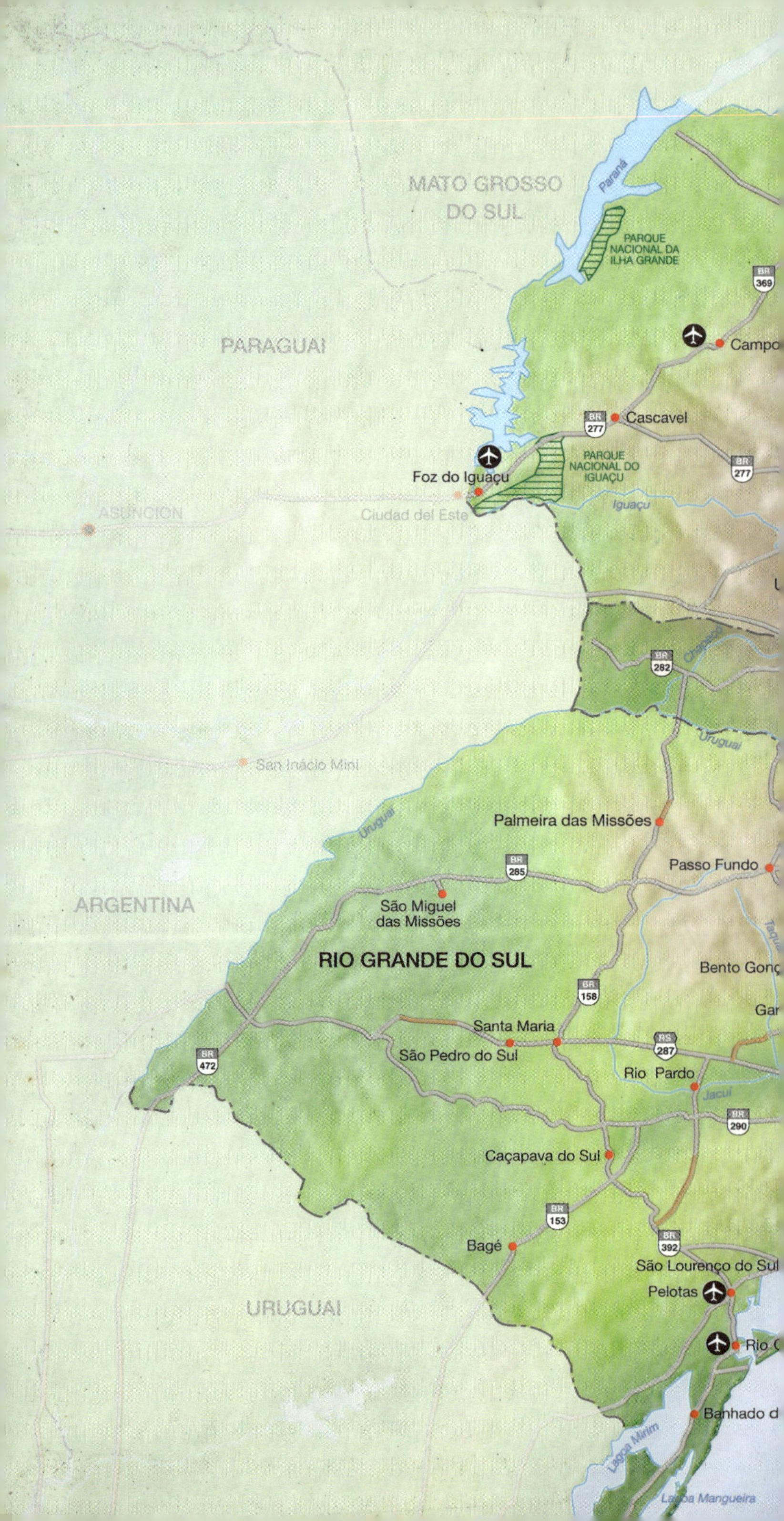

MATO GROSSO
DO SUL
Paraná
PARQUE
NACIONAL DA
ILHA GRANDE
BR 369
PARAGUAI
Campo
Cascavel
BR 277
PARQUE
NACIONAL DO
IGUAÇU
BR 277
Foz do Iguaçu
ASUNCION
Ciudad del Este
Iguaçu
Chapecó
BR 282
Uruguai
San Inácio Mini
Uruguai
Palmeira das Missões
BR 285
Passo Fundo
ARGENTINA
São Miguel
das Missões
RIO GRANDE DO SUL
Bento Gonç
BR 158
Gar
Santa Maria
RS 287
São Pedro do Sul
BR 472
Rio Pardo
Jacuí
BR 290
Caçapava do Sul
BR 153
Bagé
BR 392
São Lourenço do Sul
Pelotas
URUGUAI
Rio G
Banhado d
Lagoa Mirim
Lagoa Mangueira